Yearning for the Living God

Reflections from the Life of

F. Enzio Busche

Edited and Compiled by Tracie A. Lamb

Salt Lake City, Utah

Names in select chapters have been changed to protect privacy.

All images come from F. Enzio Busche's private collection.

Visit us at DeseretBook.com

Library of Congress Cataloging-in-Publication Data

Busche, F. Enzio.
Yearning for the living God : reflections from the life of F. Enzio Busche / compiled by Tracie A. Lamb.
p. cm.
Includes index.
ISBN 978-1-57008-984-8 (hardcover : alk. paper)
1. Busche, F. Enzio. 2. Mormon converts—Germany—Biography. I. Lamb, Tracie A. II. Title.

BX8695.B865A3 2004
289.3'092—dc22 2003027595

Printed in the United States of America
Edwards Brothers Inc., Ann Arbor, MI

10 9 8

My soul thirsteth for God, for the living God:
when shall I come and appear before God?

Psalm 42:2

Contents

Introduction 1

1 Early Learning in War and Pain 5

2 A Terrible Time to Grow Up 20

3 Father 35

4 Illness and Awakening 50

5 Conversion 59

6 Baptism 77

7 Early Membership 96

8 The Chapel Miracle 114

9 Raising a Family 132

10 Making a Living 154

11 Quiet Heroes 166

12 Communion with God 192

13 The Sacred Temple 206

14 Saints of the World 230

15 Gentle Greetings from the Other Side . . . 259

A Final Word 274

Appendix: Christianity and the Hope of the Future 279

A Note from the Editor and Compiler . . . 293

Index 297

INTRODUCTION

I WAS BORN IN GERMANY IN 1930, just three years before Hitler became the elected chancellor of the Reichstag in Berlin. When World War II began, I was a child protected by the love of my parents. I was the only son, with one older and two younger sisters—and one more to come a year later. The shock of the war and its terrible consequences for all people, not only those in Europe, created in me a sharp awareness of the need for understanding. Questions such as Who is man? Is there a God? What is the purpose of our mortal experience? What happens after death? were questions that, while unanswered, generated in me a mood of self-defeating melancholy.

I finally came to a state of awakening when, in my search of various religions and philosophies, I was approached by two young men who presented themselves as missionaries of The Church of Jesus Christ of Latter-day Saints. Being somewhat skeptical and possessing a strong commitment to never again fall victim to nice-sounding words and utopian ideas, I spent the better part of two years investigating and studying. When I began learning how to pray and started understanding that real praying means to communicate with the Living God, I suddenly awakened, as if I was coming out of a deep sleep. I recognized that God had, over and over again, tried to touch me in many ways earlier in my life. I began to understand that agency is what brings true dignity to the life of a human being. I learned that because of agency, we are responsible for what we do with our lives; also, without help and constant influence from divine sources, we would never be able to find purpose, success, or lasting joy. I could see that there was no other purpose in life than to develop in our souls the presence of divine love through which alone we will be able to build a true society of righteousness and peace—a society that we are in need of preparing for because that is the place which every human being throughout the history of mankind has dreamed. I understood completely that worldly or religious societies can succeed only when the Lord Himself and the Father of all truth stands at the helm. The knowledge of this Father of truth and His Only Begotten Son in the flesh does not come by our intellectual reasoning; but as we learn to educate ourselves to become humble and to accept Jesus Christ and His inspired servants as our only guides, this world will finally begin to blossom. The wounds of mankind will become healed and the Master's vision—peace on earth—will be fulfilled.

My wife, Jutta, and I were baptized in The Church of Jesus Christ of Latter-day Saints two and one-half years into our marriage. The Church was, at the time, in the infant stages of existence in places other than the western part of the United States.

Shortly after we joined The Church of Jesus Christ of Latter-day Saints, we learned about the customary practice for church members to serve according to their capabilities, to answer the needs of the congregations—called wards when they are fully organized and branches when they are in the infant stages—as heads of congregations (called bishops or branch presidents), youth leaders, teachers, and so on.

My wife and I were, soon after our baptism, called to serve in various capacities. Giving service brought a growing joy with enduring dimensions. I learned very soon that when we serve the Lord with all our hearts and learn to be so close to His voice that we are never without hearing, He will help us to master all the battles of our lives so that we finally will be so filled with His love that we will overcome all fear.

After nearly twenty years of service in my hometown of Dortmund, I was suddenly and unexpectedly called to serve as a General Authority in the Church's First Quorum of the Seventy. Members of this quorum are responsible for the development of faith and the other fruits of the Spirit in the sons and daughters of Heavenly Father in all the areas of the world. As I traveled through many congregations in the world and saw how rapidly some were growing, I began to understand my tremendous responsibility to listen, to teach, to understand, to love, and to serve. It was not difficult for me to see the goodness, or the potential for goodness, in all of the children of our Heavenly Father. I realized that only through the love of God and the righteous service of humble leaders who have a knowledge of this God, can the world overcome the consequences of mediocre, or even cruel, leadership of lifeless ideas and traditions. I was seventy years old when I received, as is customary in the Church, the status of "emeritus" General Authority, and my official duties with the Church were completed. My enthusiasm for building the kingdom of God, however, has not slowed down. The following book, written by me, with the assistance of Tracie A. Lamb, should be considered as my testimony of the love that God has for all of His children.

1

Early Learning in War and Pain

When I was about ten years old, in the beginning years of World War II, the first air attacks began on my hometown of Dortmund. My father arranged for my mother, sisters, and me to move to Bad Kissingen in Northern Bavaria, where my mother and sisters stayed for the duration of the war. We were in a kind of sanitarium run by Catholic nuns.

We lived in very humble circumstances in two small rooms, but we were protected from the air raids and lived in relative peace. The main rooms of the sanitarium, where people gathered to eat, were available to us. The only real inconvenience was sharing the bathroom with six other families.

This environment was very strange to me, coming from a protected suburb in a large town in the northwestern part of the country. The scent of incense and holy water permeated the air. Our bedroom was directly above the room used by the nuns for their services, so, often in the late evening, I could hear the organ and their singing.

Because we were Protestant, we did not go to their services, but I felt reverence and respect for their religious motives and in some way admired their way of life.

While we were there, I had an experience I have never forgotten—one that had a deep effect upon my life. One night as I was laying in my bed thinking about something I had heard on the news, I was confronted with the word *eternity.* As I lay there, I tried to explain *eternity* to myself, but I could not. I began to add up years, but there was no end as I added a thousand years and ten thousand, a million, and finally billions until it became mind-boggling. I could not begin to comprehend how long eternity was because I could not find names for the numbers I was adding. I could continue doubling and redoubling the numbers as often as I wanted, but there could be no end.

I was overcome by an indescribable feeling of helplessness. I felt like a grain of sand on an ocean beach without anything or anyone to anchor me. It was a devastating feeling, and I could not sleep because I felt so empty, lonely, and desperately in need. As the light of the next day entered my room, I began to cry.

My desperation reached the point where I could hardly stand the thought of living any longer. Then, suddenly, something happened to me. A feeling of warmth and comfort replaced my despair and words came to my mind: "Don't be afraid. You are my child. Have trust in Me." My fear left, and I was comforted. For the first time in my life I felt that there was some unseen power or person who obviously watched over me, loved me, and was concerned about me.

There was little religious influence in my childhood. We lived the life typical of the German people of the time who called themselves *gottgläubig,* meaning they believed in God but left open who that god was and what his message was. There was no prayer besides something small for children to say, something cute and sweet but with no real substance. The Bible was not a part of our home. It was thought of only for its historical value.

The philosophers of the Enlightenment had significantly more influence in our lives than did religion. For instance, the greatest influence on people at that time was Johann Wolfgang von Goethe, the great poet who had set his mind to many ideas and who was honest in his thinking and his questions. He, like others of the Enlightenment, detected the falseness and the criminal acts of stupidity and cruelty done in the name of Jesus Christ by many churches. Therefore, these "enlightened" men rejected churches and the notion of any organized religion. This was the mood of my mother and father, as well as large parts of the general population of Germany, as far as I could see, regarding religion.

In fact, something that Goethe wrote had a profound effect on me later, when I was seventeen or eighteen years old. I learned that two years before Goethe's death, when he was about eighty years old, he made a statement that the times in his life when he was so happy that he wanted the moment to stay had lasted only a few seconds. I remember being shocked by that statement because I had always harbored the hope that one day I would receive lasting joy that would penetrate my whole being to the point that every minute of life would be enjoyable.

I recalled one of Goethe's plays, where Faust, the main character, makes a request to feel joy to such a dimension that he can say, *"Augenblick, du bist so schön! Verweile!"* ("Moment—stay! You are so wonderful!") Yet, just the opposite comes to him. He cannot find joy, and in the end he sees that it is when he learns to work hard and overcome challenges that joy can come to him.

When I learned of the feelings expressed by Goethe, who literally had achieved everything in this life that a person can achieve—in academics, in reputation, in opportunities to travel, in wealth, in love and admiration from myriad people—it brought a feeling of discouragement into my life. I repeatedly asked myself, "What chance do I have to be filled with joy when even Goethe did not have that opportunity?" Not until I became embraced by the light of Christ as a member of His Church did I learn the truth—that as children of a loving Heavenly Father, all human beings might have joy. As explained in the Book of Mormon, "Adam fell that men might be; and men are, that they might have joy" (2 Nephi 2:25). Early in my Church membership, this truth penetrated my soul, and I came to realize that true joy comes only through developing the reality of closeness with the living God.

Of course, because I was born just three years before Hitler came to power, his regime had a tremendous impact on my life. For one thing, I was a member of the Hitler Youth, just like everyone else my age. I always smile when I read things today from people who do not know better and who write that German boys were forced to become a member of the Hitler Youth. At birth, we were enrolled. That was a part of the system. When we turned ten years old, we were not asked, we just became members of that organization. To us, however, it did not seem like being forced. Every boy or girl wanted to be a member. There was tremendous enthusiasm built into the idealistic vision and dream world of youth. As a nine-year-old, I could not wait to become ten because then I could put on the uniform. As Hitler Youth, we became part of something bigger—even to become saviors of the decadent world, we were taught. We were educated to believe that we were going to bring fulfillment of the dreams of mankind, that we would bring righteousness, honesty, and dignity to mankind.

When I was fourteen years old, in 1945, I was drafted into the

Enzio at age 14, just before being drafted as a German soldier.

German army. I had left boarding school to join my mother and sisters in Bavaria. Just after arriving there, I was put into a group of about thirty boys, and we received our marching orders. My first reaction, as a naive kid, was to feel honored. I was becoming a part of this big endeavor and felt like an adult. We got ration cards. We got cigarettes. I was proud of myself. And then, of course, the reality sunk in. The coming days, weeks, and months were a shock of indescribable dimension.

I was issued a gun and told where to go and from whom to take my orders. It was an act, this late in the war, of total desperation on the part of the government bureaucracy that was still functioning. We were recruited merely because we were there. We got fresh, new guns straight from the factory, but I never took a single shot the whole time. We had no transportation. We were given a little pony and a little horse-drawn cart and put all our ammunition, guns, and backpacks on that thing. At first we marched in the daytime, but the planes were everywhere. So instead, we walked and walked at nighttime. In daytime we hid.

There were times when we could not look out the window without seeing an enemy plane. It was mind-boggling. The planes shot at everything that moved—in fields, on the streets, everything. We could all sense that the war was going to end in disaster. Our leader was probably seventeen years old—just a kid. But to me, a fourteen-year-old, he seemed like an adult. We did not fight. In reality, we were fleeing the war, walking away from enemy lines. We could always hear gunfire, but we never fought.

The emotional stress I went through at the time was unbelievable. I did not know where my father was. I did not know what had happened to my mother and sisters. I was alone. We could not bathe. We had no hygiene kits. We did not know what to eat. We had to beg or steal from farmers. We slept in haystacks or similar places.

At that point, we still believed in the government but began to have many questions. Then I saw something that deeply affected me. After a few weeks of walking, we finally gave up our endeavors. People everywhere were running and hiding, trying to survive until the end of the war. We were in a village where the grandmother of one of the boys in our group lived. He had escaped and left our group. I had not realized he was gone until I heard a boy screaming in utmost desperation. Later I learned that the boy had been captured by the Gestapo and hanged on a tree in front of his grandmother's house for desertion.

With this event, the whole tragedy of the war—and the realization that it literally affected my own existence—sunk in. I had always had a tremendous love of freedom. The smallest intimation of force, of making me do something someone else wanted me to do, had the opposite effect on me. I had always had the romantic idea that serving my country was a matter of honor and chivalry. The reality I faced changed that very quickly.

We went as far as the Czech border, where we could retreat no further. The boy in charge said, "We won't go any further. We'll dig a hole here, throw our weapons in, and bury them. We'll get rid of our uniforms and try to find civilian clothing. I want you to be on your own and try to go home." And so we did. We went in small groups, usually two by two. I was with a boy about a year older than I, but I thought of him as a man.

One day we stopped near some farmhouses to watch some tanks going down the road, one after another. I asked a German soldier, I mean a real soldier, where the "HKL," or *Hauptkampflinie* (the frontline), was. The soldier looked at me and, chuckling, said, *"Da gibts nichts mehr zu HKLen."* ("There is no more frontline.") Then he pointed out to the street on the other side of the railroad about fifty yards away. We could see it all from where we were. "Those are the Americans," he said.

"What?" I asked. "I thought they were the Germans coming back."

"Those are American tanks," he said, laughing sarcastically.

Then something happened that gave me insight into American precision and consciousness. Suddenly there was a rifle shot. One single shot. The whole column of endless tanks stopped. They closed the hatches and about two or three minutes later, planes came. They destroyed the single house where the shot came from. In an instant, the planes pulverized the house. Then the soldiers opened the tank hatches, looked outside, waited to see if any more shots came, and moved on. I sat on the other side on the banks of a creek and marveled at the tremendous resources and weapons of the American troops.

Later my companion and I went into a town. We were in civilian clothing, but we never knew what to expect. We saw some Americans driving a jeep. I was scared because I thought I would be killed. We had always been told that Americans did not take any prisoners, that they just shot everyone. The jeep had a machine gun on it, and they were patrolling the town, one person driving and one manning the machine gun. We could not run, so we just stood there hoping they would not shoot us. But they just went by. That was my first close-up encounter with Americans.

Not long after, we were walking through a forest. We avoided the streets. It was evening and we were looking for a place to sleep when a patrol of Frenchmen who had recently been released from prison camp came. We later learned that the Americans gave the released prisoners armbands and told them that for every person they could capture and bring in, they would get cigarettes. The currency at that time was cigarettes. You could buy anything with cigarettes. So those Frenchmen captured us.

They took us at gunpoint to the Americans and said, "Here we have prisoners. Give us the cigarettes." I expected to be shot, but about thirty of us were gathered together in a fire station in a village. An American soldier guarded us. He fascinated me because he was completely different from German soldiers; he was relaxed and funny. His shirt was open. We always had to dress formally. He was sitting on his steel helmet, which was unbelievable. No German soldier would ever have been permitted to do that while on guard. The guns the Americans had were smaller than we had, and they had clips with multiple shots in them. They were much better than our big guns. The soldier was holding his gun like an imaginary guitar, and he was singing something. I do not remember what, but it was very funny.

When he saw me, he asked, "How old are you?"

Elder Busche as a young boy, before he ever imagined that at age fourteen he would be a prisoner of war in a fallen country.

I could speak a little English because I had learned it in school. I said, "I'm fourteen."

He said, "Good grief. Are you hungry?"

When I answered, "Yes," he said, "Well, I can't feed the whole group, but I can feed you. Why don't you get to the window at ten o'clock, and I'll bring you something. Don't tell anyone else because I don't have enough for everyone."

At ten o'clock, I went to the window and he gave me a whole loaf of bread, typical Wonder bread, and a cup of coffee in a tin can. Of course, as soon as I got it, the others came and it was gone. But I had one slice of bread. It was my first taste of American bread, and it was very different from the German bread I knew. It tasted like heaven—the first bit of food I had eaten all day.

That soldier was so normal and friendly with no animosity towards me. I had always felt, even as a little child, that America was a country I could learn something from. I did not know why, but everything I heard about America was always fascinating, especially the principle of freedom. I found my opinion confirmed by the American troops that occupied Germany. They were fair and tried to help us and establish dignity. Every little courtesy we received from our American conquerors was deeply appreciated.

The day after I received the bread from the American soldier, we were taken to a bigger building, a barn, where about three thousand people were pressed. It was terrible. We could only stand, not sit or lie down. There was no way to go to the restroom, and people were very distressed about that. We stood there the whole night, and I thought, *This is it. This is the final day of my life.*

Then they selected everyone sixteen and under. We were pulled out of the group and taken to another prison camp or, rather, the small town of Oberviechtag in the Bavarian forest. There were about thirty of us, and we were placed in an empty house. We were not permitted to leave the house except at one o'clock in the afternoon, at which time we had permission to go out and beg for food. The Americans obviously did not have enough food for us because of the large number of prisoners they were watching. They warned us: "Don't run away or you'll be shot. Stay within the walls of the old town. We have guards at all of the streets that go outside of town. If they see anyone running away, they will shoot. Go and ask the people to feed you and come back in an hour."

So we were locked in the house except for one hour a day. Nobody wanted to disobey. In the meantime, we came to realize that the war had already ended, although we did not know anything for sure except through rumors.

For the first few days, the people of the village had compassion and gave us food because we were thirty young kids. But after three or four days, they did not have any more food to give, so they locked their houses. They knew that at one o'clock, a horde of us would come, so they closed everything down and we got nothing. Some stole. I never did, but it was a miserable situation to be without food for several days.

When the Americans saw that we were getting nothing from the villagers, they gave us each a little piece of bread and some watery soup every day. They did what they could, but I think they were out of resources. After about three weeks, they took us to the school grounds. An officer was there who had us raise our hands and swear that we would never again in our lives take up arms. We were glad to swear that. We were given a document that stated that we were on our way home and were no danger or threat. Unfortunately, they gave us only one document for the whole group, so that forced us to stay together.

Home was about three hundred miles away, and there was still nothing to eat. We had to beg for food from farmers. And, of course, we were not the only ones begging. There were thousands of people trying to get back to their homes and families. There was no infrastructure. There was no transportation system. Most of the people were just walking trying to get where they wanted to go. It was a very, very difficult situation.

During this time, an experience from my childhood came back to haunt me. I grew up in a time when food was scarce. We were able to manage, but we did not dare throw food away. We had the same food day in and day out—bread in the daytime and potatoes in the evening. Sometimes we had eggs or a few vegetables, mostly spinach. There was practically no meat except sausage once in a while.

My mother sometimes used bacon to fry the potatoes. She cut the bacon into little pieces and mixed it in with the potatoes. I did not like the bacon and picked the pieces out of the potatoes and set them aside. I called them spectators in the soccer stadium and used to say to my mother, "There are too many spectators again today."

Years later, as the other boys and I were on our walk home, we had been without food for three days. In the evening, we came to a farmer's house and asked to stay overnight. They let us sleep in a room that had formerly been used for the farmhands. It was a very simple room with a bed of straw. The farmer's wife had compassion on me and brought me a little piece of raw bacon. It was about two inches wide, three inches long and a half-inch thick. I remember how grateful I was for that strip of bacon. I cut it into little pieces and put them one by one in my mouth, holding each piece on my tongue and rolling it between my cheeks and teeth, savoring the flavor as long as possible. It tasted like the most delicious food I had ever eaten.

Suddenly I remembered how, earlier in my life, I had disliked bacon and had refused to eat it. I knew then that the German saying "Hunger is the best cook" is true. I have never forgotten the realization of that moment that food is the greatest miracle. Anyone who has never been close to starvation is missing out on this awareness. It is wise for the Church to invite members to fast one day a month in order to give them an experience of hunger and the appreciation of food.

Often, as we were traveling, we could not find shelter at anyone's home, so we would sleep in little triangle tents that had no floor and provided little protection except from the worst rain. We slept three to a tent. I remember one night, as I was crowded in a little tent sleeping on wet ground, that I set just one goal to achieve in my life: I wanted to have my own tent. It didn't have to be a big one, just a small one with a rubber floor so that I would not have to sleep on wet ground. I could never imagine that life would return to normal because everything had been destroyed. The highest goal I could think of was to have a tent of my own. When I remember it now, with all that I have, I marvel that it was the best I could dream of. Through the years I have never since gone to bed at night without being thankful for the privilege of having my own bed. I cannot sit down for any meal without expressing my gratitude.

I was the only one in our group who could speak a little English. I had liked English in school and could communicate with the Americans. I learned to see them as human beings and not as enemies. We needed to get home, and at one point, there were some American soldiers nearby. I went to an American guard and said, "We have a group. We need to go to Würzburg." At the time, we were near Nürnberg. Würzburg was the biggest city near where we wanted to go. Today, it is about one and a half hours by freeway from Nürnberg to Würzburg; but at that time there was no freeway, and the bridges had been destroyed.

I asked the American, "Do you think that an army truck could take us there?"

"Sure," he answered. "Just a minute and I'll see if I can find someone." And he did. He asked a man who was driving an open-load army truck if he could take us to Würzburg, and he said okay. So we climbed in the truck. He threw a box of a hundred cigarettes to us. We got to Würzburg that same evening.

The next day, after a night on a hard floor provided by some friendly people, we separated. I went to Bad Kissingen, where I had left my mother and sisters behind. The buildings of the city were still

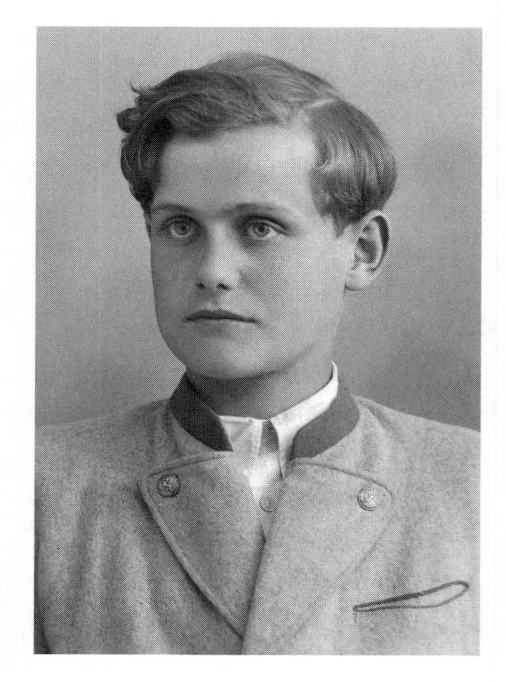

A young Enzio's passport photo, taken in June 1945, after being released as a POW.

intact because there had not been any air raids in the immediate area. We later learned that this had been planned because the Allies wanted Bad Kissingen, a lovely old spa town, as their headquarters. The population had been evacuated in order to make room for the headquarters of General Eisenhower. When I finally got there, after a two-day march, the city was off limits. Nobody could go in.

My mother and sisters had been evacuated to one of the surrounding villages. A couple of weeks after the war ended, my mother began to hear from soldiers who were starting to come home. She hoped that I would also be coming home and thought I would likely return to Bad Kissingen because that was where I had last seen my family. To watch for me, she placed one of my sisters at each main road going into the city. One of my sisters found me when I came and brought me home to the rest of the family. They were living on the outskirts of the town in one room in a house they shared with many other families.

During the war, the vast majority of the cities of my homeland had been destroyed, including my hometown, with all its suburbs and my own family's house. For the next three years of my life I had no roof over my head. My mother, my four sisters, and I slept in the ruins of our house, not knowing whether our father was still alive or not. For the better part of three years after the war, physical survival was the only thing on our daily agenda.

During these years I was in deep emotional pain and unfit for any kind of academic training, even if there had been any available. Everything seemed empty and vain to me. In the midst of these feelings and my own destructive self-pity, I turned my attention to the world of Buddha, inspired by reading works from the poet Herman Hesse. My father finally came home more dead than alive, after having spent two years in a British prisoner-of-war camp. Soon he became very alarmed by my self-centered, destructive behavior borne out of my perceived concept of Buddhism. I owe it to my father's loving, caring patience and wisdom that I gradually let go of this school of thought and got back to the pragmatic tasks of survival.

About two and a half years after the war, I became seriously ill with spinal meningitis. This disease killed many teenagers in my neighborhood, including a brother of my later-to-be spouse. Somehow, I was saved from it and recovered without much help since there was no medication or cure. At this time, I had a period of spiritual awakening. Because I survived and managed to come through the dangerous disease without any visible lasting effects, I felt that someone unknown but close must be watching over me.

2

A Terrible Time to Grow Up

I HAVE LONG FELT THE NEED TO WRITE down some of my childhood experiences. In doing so, I reflect on the political and spiritual situation in Germany at that time. From my vantage point today, I can see that the general population of the United States, and maybe even of Europe, has come to understand very little about the terrible time of Hitler's Germany and the Second World War. It is painful to hear people discussing the period without understanding reality, at least the reality that I and many people I have known in Germany were part of.

I have no memory of anything before Hitler was in power. I was born in 1930, and Hitler came to power in 1933. For me the only political system was the National Socialistic Party of Workers. Its symbol, the swastika, the social greeting with the raised right arm, the uniforms, the music, the talks and proclamations—all were a regular part of the fabric of my childhood life.

My father was very interested in politics. One day he brought home a radio, and it became the center of our family life. Because he always listened to the news, I also became involved in the elements of politics. In the evenings, our family sat around listening to the radio and talking about what we heard. We listened to the talks of Hitler, Goebbels, and others, all of whom were very convincing. They built their arguments in such a simple way that someone listening today might ask, "How could you have fallen for that? How is it possible that you did not understand?"

But Germans were not a politically savvy people. The French and British states had existed for many generations. Germany had not. German territories existed historically as little kingdoms, duchies, and counties. Germany, as a united country, was not established until 1871. It is a surprise to many when they learn that the United States has a longer history than the country of Germany.

It always puzzles me when I read a history in English in which "Germany" is discussed as a country any time earlier than 1871. There was no Germany. There was Prussia. There was Bavaria. There were Westphalia, Saxony, Mecklenburg, Hannover, Württemberg, and many others. There were about thirty different little kingdoms and duchies and shifting boundaries. The rivalry between Bavaria and Prussia still persists today, even though Prussia does not exist as a state anymore. History is very interesting. I learned only later in my life how important history is and how little most people know about it.

I am not saying that the system was good; what I want to carefully explain is that the system had expressed a moral goal that was very successfully portrayed to the population. Everything that happened, we were told, was in pursuit of achieving that moral goal. My father, together with most German people, believed in the basic premise of Hitler's alternative to the chaos that had occurred in Germany's past. There had been inflation, prostitution, starvation, terrorism, anarchy. My father told me that there was a time when there were 30,000 prostitutes in the city of Berlin alone. Corruption was devastating German society. When the new system began, there was a growing hope and a vision of purpose. There was meaning and an understanding of the need for order and discipline.

It is not easy to talk about this, knowing what I know now, but that helps explain the background of our society in that time. We believed what we heard. The magic of the music and the uniforms, the philosophy and talks—all were very powerful and convincing.

Perhaps the strongest proclamation of the party was that of the need for unity. The slogan was "One for all and all for one." All of the adults I knew in my limited circle were grateful that Hitler had come to power in Germany. My father told me often how terrible life had been after World War I. He told me how millions of people had been unemployed and hungry. He talked about the anarchistic terror organizations that threatened the core of society, my father included. I was told that the new regime brought law and order and the establishment of respect for the dignity of human life.

An effort was made to educate people towards trustworthiness, chastity, respect for the work of others, and gratitude for the small things of life. No detail of society was left untouched. There was an educational drive for the beautification of the country. The need for the individual to sacrifice self-comforts in behalf of others was emphasized. We were also specifically educated to honor the profession of the farmer and blue-collar worker, to respect their work and greet them with dignity, and to view farmland as sacred ground. Only farm workers were permitted to walk across plowed farmland.

There was an additional effort to teach sensitivity to the needs of the poor, politeness, and honor to women and motherhood. The family was proclaimed as the center of human life, and women were seen as the head of the house who needed to be magnified. Women

Elder Busche's parents, shown here on the day of their silver wedding anniversary, did much to teach Enzio about honor and goodness.

were expected to be modest and not to use cosmetics or wear ostentatious jewelry. In fact, there emerged a new style in fashion, which had its roots in the folk fashions of earlier centuries.

Selfishness and greed were considered the roots of all evil. Liberal democracy was considered a source of selfishness that could eventually lead to anarchy. Another enemy was the dictatorship of dialectic materialism presented by the USSR.

A self-ruling code of honor was put in place in which it was impossible to indulge in vices such as homosexuality. Youth were encouraged to live worthily and prepare for a good family. The youth organization was one of the most coveted organizations a young person could belong to. To finally accept the uniform and the code of honor, and to participate in the pledge of allegiance was the fulfillment of all dreams when a young person turned ten years old.

We were told, as young people, that the world was in a state of corruption and moral decay and that Western liberalism and Eastern communism would destroy the roots of human civilization. Democracy was described as a plutocracy where the wealthy ruled by dictatorship of money. Our other opponents were the Bolsheviks who enslaved people for their own gratification and gain. The only way to establish a society of righteousness, we were told, was to elect honest leaders, people who did not work for personal gain but for the welfare of their society.

There was a great deal of talk about a world conspiracy with secret combinations. Certain names of rich families were mentioned as well as members of many royal families in Europe. Supposedly, they wanted to establish a world government that would use democracy and communism as tools to fulfill their own purposes. We were told that Germany was the last enemy standing in their way, so they wanted to destroy it permanently.

This idea always seemed very far-fetched to me. And, surprisingly, similar rumors tend to surface year after year, even in America. I do not believe them any more today than I did then. But I have observed with interest what long lives rumors and lies can have and how they can destabilize the comfort and peace of societies.

From my viewpoint today, I am amazed at how successful the ruling party was in bringing, in a short time, the whole nation behind a cause. We were told that it was our role to establish a banner of hope for all people in all nations of the world. It was the desirable goal for the individual—and for the nation—to be independent, to respect the laws of life, and to make it a matter of personal honor to be industrious, reliable, and dedicated to helping those who were weaker. We were invited to fight against everything that carried even a hint of decadence. The heroes of society were those individuals who had sacrificed their personal well-being, or even their lives, for the sake of the people, or *Volk*.

We were told that everyone had the right to own a home. I remember my father discussing with us children the model homes that would be built for people who would not normally be able to afford their own homes. The houses were small and modest but very attractive, with flower boxes and vegetable gardens and room for small animals. I remember that in 1938 my father showed me the first of such newly built suburbs. It was also very appealing to learn that the government felt that every family should have one car. The Volkswagen factory was established to build a car designed to give even the least affluent family the opportunity to afford a simple means of transportation.

The idea that no one should ever freeze or go hungry again was repeated over and over. Youth were invited to participate in collecting "fast offerings" on the first Sunday of each month. The entire population was supposed to fast and give the equivalent in money to the collecting youth. I still have a photograph showing me at the age of five with a "money drum" in my hand, serving the "cause" with a neighbor.

It was expected that all citizens would want, naturally, to support the cause of the government. If anyone elected not to support the cause of the people, he was considered a parasite—someone who wanted to draw his strength from others. We were told that such individuals would not be tolerated and would have to be "re-educated." I cannot remember any case, though, of anyone in our neighborhood qualifying to become "re-educated." I later learned that these "re-education camps" really existed and were officially described as rehabilitation camps.

Also very appealing to the people was the idea that everyone had

Enzio at age 5, collecting offerings in his money drum as part of a nationwide program called WHW (help for the needy in winter).

the right to a decent job, free health care, a guaranteed retirement, and adventurous recreation. There were many places established where entertainment, sports, and everything that would please the masses of blue-collar workers were easily accessible. Big ocean liners were built for the low-income people to go on Party-organized ocean cruises. The Party and the state took many initiatives for economic development where it was felt that the free enterprise system would fail.

The unions were abandoned. Each larger company was facilitated with a controlling board where party officials and entrepreneurs ensured that working conditions were in harmony with the labor laws and that the company did not produce undue profits. There was also a very strong system established to prevent corruption. Bribes or even tips were not tolerated.

Each company had to sustain "voluntarily" the goals and visions of the government. There were regular inspections and reviews where companies could get medals of honor when they were in complete compliance with the goals of the state. A company could be officially reprimanded if it was found to be out of harmony. We came to believe that such a situation would have created an undesirable loss of honor.

Divorce was practically unknown. Before a divorce was granted, numerous conditions had to be met, including endless counseling sessions. We were taught to be hard on ourselves, to overcome self-centered lifestyles, and to care for our fellow citizens. Everything was made a matter of honor, and to lose honor was considered the greatest loss in life.

We were always told that Germany had a lot of enemies and that our neighbors were envious of our beautiful country and the beautiful, clean cities we had. We were also told that it was our role as a Germanic people to come to the rescue of all righteous people in all nations of the world. We were taught to believe that the Germanic race had the role, historically, of preserving the virtues of Christianity. We had to learn about the ancient Roman historian Tacitus, who described to the astonished Romans the virtues of the Germanic people and their hard-working reliability.

We were told that we did not need lawyers because we would say what we meant and stay true to our word even if it meant forfeiting our lives. A poem from Friedrich Schiller was memorized by every youth. The poem told the story of how, in ancient Greece, someone forfeited his life because he had given his word and would not break it. We learned, over and over again, that the world would fall into

Enzio with his mother and three sisters in happier times before WWII.

decay, promiscuity, and chaos if the German cause should fail. We were taught that the righteous in all surrounding nations were hoping our cause would succeed.

Historical Germanic figures were held up as role models. The Frankish Germanic king, Charlemagne, for example, rescued the Pope in Rome from threats by surrounding counts. He was then crowned by the Pope as protector of the Christian church and emperor of the Roman Empire (800 A.D.). Martin Luther, a German monk, became concerned about the corruption of the Catholic Church and, we were taught, saved Christianity from decay. Suggestions were made that the Germanic people were the elect people of the New Testament and that Israel had lost the position because they had killed Jesus Christ. It is clear to me now that we were living in a time of "sound-bite" philosophies issued in simple but convincing forms.

We were taught to believe that, in order not to become decadent, we must stay within our bloodlines when it came to marriage. For this reason, Hitler's Germany had great affection for Native Americans and the original African tribes that had thus far withstood colonial civilization. There was also open admiration in Germany at that time for the people of Islam, as described in the Hitler Youth Yearbook #5, which by chance is still in my possession.

I faintly remember one night when the Jewish synagogue in the city of Dortmund, ten miles from where we lived, was burned down. I heard my father say, the next morning, that it was a terrible act of barbarism done by the "furor of uncontrolled people." I heard him express gratitude that the police had stopped the violence and that everything was under control now. I learned later the irony of this situation, that an organized group within the Nazi Party had initiated the barbarism the government was now claiming to have "under control."

Another memory I have is of the Olympic Games in Berlin in 1936. In German newspapers and radio, it was made clear that the leadership and youth of the world had come to celebrate the festival of sport with Germany. We heard nothing of the misgivings, caution, and even anger expressed by visiting athletes and nations. Many of the youth, myself included, were huge fans of Jesse Owens, favoring him above our own Luz Long in the long jump competition (Owens won the gold medal).

When the International Jewish Federation in New York declared war on Germany before Britain or France, it seemed natural to Germans that drastic measures be taken to expel—or to bring into internment—citizens who were openly opposing us. In the early years of the war, it was unthinkable to me that any German authority or military entity would tolerate crime or acts of cruelty. As the war lingered on, especially in the last two years (1944–45), we began to hear rumors of the atrocities committed by Germany; but we believed they were just rumors. We knew that anyone who would spread such rumors would be considered an enemy and would be reprimanded.

We were told that our enemies were ruthless and decadent and that they would tell all kinds of lies about Germany in order to destroy our ability to stand united behind the cause of the government. Therefore, if anyone was caught listening to an enemy radio station, he could be sentenced to death. Most of us were so intimidated that we shuddered if we accidentally came across an enemy radio station. In every way, we trusted the information system of the government.

I remember the summer of 1944, about eight months before the war ended. I was attending a boarding school in Garenfeld, near my hometown of Dortmund. Fritz Adler, a classmate of mine, had been saying that the Germans were inflicting terrible cruelties on innocent people in concentration camps. He was confronted by school leadership and the Party. He had to stand in front of all the students and teachers and admit to spreading rumors that he had picked up by listening to enemy radio stations. He expressed regret for his foolishness in believing anything that our enemies would say about us.

In the beginning, the German people felt tragically misunderstood. The society I was a part of had the conviction that, sooner or later, our enemies would find out what we really stood for. Then, we were convinced, they would gladly stop fighting against us. In 1941, the fact that Rudolf Hess, Hitler's second-in-command, was flying to England to clear up misunderstandings in person seemed to confirm our opinion. Until 1944, the German people more or less stood behind the government and were ready to sacrifice anything, even to the point of giving their lives. When I look back on this with my current understanding, it seems unbelievable that so many could have been this naive and uneducated in the political realities of the world.

It was during the last six months of the war that I heard people raise questions; however, they were asked more out of frustration and fear for the coming final disaster than to find out the truth. Only after the final collapse did the complete reality sink in. In the ashes of our destroyed country came the awareness of the real tragedy: the awareness that Germany was the villain, the aggressor, the barbarian, the cruel slaughterer.

When people say now that Germans knew what was happening, it is because they simply were not there and cannot understand how a dictatorship functions. There was no alternative view possible because the radio broadcasts came from the government. The newspapers came from the government. All information came from one source. I must, therefore, leave questions about the involvement of the general population open, although I am now, of course, painfully aware of terrible atrocities done by Nazis in the name of Germany.

With the defeat came the reports about the concentration camps. The horror stories of criminal acts done by our own people were first met with disbelief. Finally, a feeling of indescribable shame came as reports were openly documented over and over again. With it came the awareness of betrayal—that the best of our feelings and desires had been trampled on and misused. *We had been had.*

We thought we were establishing a banner of life. Instead, Germany became a symbol of cruelty and barbarism. The German people would have to live with that stigma from then on. The leaders who had brought this upon us disappeared. They committed suicide or were brought to the Nuremberg trials. Those of us who had to live with the shame were not prepared for it. We were grateful for

America and the Marshall Plan, as well as the programs from CARE, the Quakers, and many other charities. Without them, Germany would have ended in chaos.

History is written by those who win the war. The truth is much more subtle, much more complicated, and generally unwanted. Those who lose the war are not willing to discuss what they know and experienced because it contradicts the victors. They are afraid of ending up on the losing end again. In my experience, very little is known about the whole complexity of that period. I have always been reluctant to talk about it because I have never wanted to be blamed or branded as a "Nazi." In truth, my whole soul rebels against what was done by the Nazis.

In my view, one of the real disasters of the war, beyond all of the atrocities, pain, and suffering, is the fact that the people of Germany seem to have lost the capability to believe in anything that reaches higher. After Hitler, no one in Germany could stand up and fight for traditional values. Values, such as being chaste, faithful, and industrious, or willing to sacrifice or unwilling to cheat or lie, were labeled as goals of the past that we needed to leave behind us. If someone mentioned anything about virtue or honor, he was frowned upon and suspected of "wearing a brown shirt underneath," referring to the Nazi uniform. Rebels against the established society became the heroes. The once-so-orderly Germany became a haven for criminals, lawbreakers, and terrorists.

What is called "Nazi" or "neo-Nazi" in Europe or America today is not even close to the real thing. When I see people who wear the swastika now with their cruel, brutal faces, I think they are imitating what they have seen in old war movies as the portrait of the Nazi system. No decent person anywhere could have sympathy for such people.

I believe it is a tragedy in the history of mankind that so many

Enzio, left, and a friend in front of the ruins of the Dortmund Reinoldikirche in 1948. Physical destruction after World War II was surpassed only by the spiritual and emotional destruction that took place in the souls of Germans.

lack the desire to get to the roots of truth and to look at facts without an agenda. Many things that are politically correct may not have anything to do with truth. Hitler succeeded, in many dimensions, to tap into the dream of Zion that seems to be intrinsic to us human beings. He created a mock Zion with the look of righteousness but without its truth.

Because of what I have experienced, I feel able to say that matters of righteousness and of wholesome goodness can be developed only under the unconstrained influence of the light of Christ in the soul of human beings. The awareness of the light of Christ empowers the individual to try to live in harmony with divine principles. Human attempts to enforce those principles by power and force have too easily led to failure and disaster.

The historical hunger of the people for righteousness and salvation was betrayed by an aberration of truth. The results were horrific. The Hitler regime, much the same as the fallen Soviet system, functioned as a vaccination to immunize the vast majority of people, once and for all, against divine principles such as chastity, family values, sacrifice, honor, and integrity. It hurts me when I see that Hitler turned out to have been, in some way, prophetic when he suggested that if Germany loses the war, the last chance for a decent society of law and order would be over.

As an adult, I found what I was looking for as a youth. The true vision of Zion stems from the fact that we were with God before we came to this earth. The adversary uses pompous usurpers of truth, such as Hitler, to confuse us and destroy our hopes. It is only the gospel of Jesus Christ and the righteousness of the members of the Lord's restored church that can fill the vacuum that Hitler left behind in Germany. Only the establishment of the kingdom of God on earth, through living prophets of God, will take the mantle of prophecy from Hitler away.

3

FATHER

I CANNOT THINK OR SPEAK ABOUT MY father without having feelings of reverence and respect. He was, in some dimension, one of the most spiritual men I have ever known. My father was a man of principle. He did not care about advantages unless they were built on truth. He was a man of organization, hard work, and discipline. He never allowed himself any weakness or excuse for anything. He was raised to be full of honor, discipline, dignity, and honesty. He was a perfectionist and would not tolerate mediocrity in himself or others.

Because of this attitude, he would drive his children absolutely wild sometimes. He could be very harsh, very precise, and once in a while without control when his expectations for perfection were not fulfilled. I do not know whether it helped with my own education, but he left a powerful impression upon my life, specifically with regard to feeling the need for law and order, accuracy, perseverance, and problem solving. He was relentless in his pursuit of taking care of every minute detail. He was equally tireless when it came to caring for other people, placing his own wife and children first, but always caring for the people of his business, people he had known from earlier days, and even strangers. No one in need of help would go away without his caring.

Proof of his integrity can be verified by my name—Enzio. During the First World War, he was taken as a prisoner shortly after the war began and spent four years in a French prison camp. A German count known by the name of Enzio was a prisoner with him. His full name was Graf Enzio von Plauen. Enzio is an Italian name, coming from the nobility of the Middle Ages. My father and this count became very close as they endured deprivation together for several years. They made the commitment that if they survived the prison camp they would name their first son after the other person. My father, of course, kept his word. Even though it was many years later and he was in a completely different environment, my father named his first and only son "Enzio." He told me once that the name was not part of his own family tradition and was somewhat alien in Germany; because of that, he said, he would not have given me that name had it not been for his promise. I could see that it was impossible for him not to fulfill a promise. I have always felt great pride in my name because it typifies the honesty and integrity of my father.

In 1933 my father was able to build a house for his family. He built it in a rural area about ten miles outside the city of Dortmund. He still had memories of his experiences of mass starvation after the First World War, so he built his house on ten acres of land where he kept a cow, chickens, and sheep during the first years. A hedge about

The doorway to Elder Busche's childhood home—rebuilt after the war.

seven feet high surrounded our land. We had a vegetable garden, fruit trees, a little forest, and even a small creek running through the far corner. As a child, I always believed that we were rich people compared to our neighbors. With my understanding now, I can see that my father had to fight hard to keep up his dream of a spacious house and land for his family.

My father was a pragmatist who was interested in ethics and causes of righteousness and honor. He was completely devastated when he found out after the war about the crimes and destruction attributed to Germany during the war. It was something he could never understand—how such cruelties could be committed and a regime get so out of control when everything, in his eyes, had started with good intentions and good desires. He himself helped two Jewish men flee Germany when it was obvious that Jews were not welcome there any longer. He did not risk his own life, but he made the effort to provide necessary transportation and paperwork for a poet he knew by the name of Leifhelm and another man by the name of Munk, who escaped to South America and who later returned to Germany after the war.

When my father came home from the Second World War, after having spent two years in a British prison camp, again narrowly escaping starvation, he was in a state of shock. He was not willing to become politically engaged in anything. He could not understand the world anymore. Today, I can see that he was raised in a generation that did not understand the principles of democracy. But I know that he wanted me to understand it. Not many years after the war, in fact, when I was twenty years old, he gave me a book about Abraham Lincoln.

The world that my father understood needed to have a righteous leader who was sustained by the people. He understood his own family and business in the same way. He considered himself to be the first servant of his own family, and he established the same principle with his employees. I saw him many times silently go the extra mile. He gave out of his own pocket when people were in need, not letting anyone know what he was doing. Most of his charitable life's deeds came to light only after his death, as people came to me and shared what my father had done for them.

My father had a tremendous interest in his ancestors. He respected every detail he learned about his own and his wife's ancestors. He initiated an exploration of the lineage of our forefathers—not just several generations, but as far as research could go. He had a

Enzio with his father and two sisters in 1938.

man working specifically on this line, and my father put it together, spending much of his time organizing a pedigree chart. I have a reproduction of this chart that I value highly.

He also did something very unusual. He worked together with a man who came from the same small village from which the Busche family had come—the small village of Heinsen in Lower Saxony, located by the river Weser. Research as far back as records were kept revealed that none of the Busche family was prominent; all were peasants, farmers, laborers, and fishermen. Some lived in the most difficult of times. The man from this village and my father compiled their information, writing, editing, and publishing a history of the village. They were told that it is the only village in Germany with its own history book, covering every little detail, including pictures and name lineages. Every story that was reported was kept for the descendants.

After my father printed the book, he made sure that the

Protestant minister from the village personally delivered one book to every family in the village so that it would be in the hands of the firstborn and each family would establish a feeling of kinship with their ancestors. It was mind-boggling for me, as a young man, to think that a person would be so unselfish, dedicating so much effort and making such a financial sacrifice to accomplish such a project. Needless to say, my father's research made it easy for me to establish my own genealogy and to produce the names for my own family history.

Much later, I learned from a man who traced the genealogy of the first Latter-day Saint convert in Pennsylvania (the convert's name was Bushey) that the first listing of an immigrant passenger from Germany by the name of Bushey was originally spelled the same as mine—*Busche.* It is very likely that one of the members of our line in Heinsen emigrated from Germany, as many people did during those years after the Thirty-Year War in the late seventeenth century.

In the course of my membership, I have found some ten to fifteen individuals who have approached me with the fact that they have the name of Busche in their lines. Considering that the name Busche is very rare in German society, I have a feeling that several of our ancestors and relatives have accepted the gospel. This has given me a feeling of humility and great anticipation that one day I shall meet my relatives on the other side.

Because of the great respect and admiration I had for my father, one of the most difficult aspects of my decision to be baptized was, of course, the question of how he would react towards my baptism. I had a testimony strong enough to proceed with being baptized without asking for his permission, but I wanted to have his understanding even when I could not ask for his blessing. Having this desire in my heart, I went to him. Perhaps it was a couple of days before my baptism when I told him I had come to an understanding and was planning to be baptized. My father had already observed some of my interest in the Church as he witnessed my search for the truth in my early childhood and youth. He had also witnessed, very closely, the experience of my diseases and healing, which will be discussed later in the book. He had met some of the missionaries and was touched, in some dimension, by their honesty and sacrifice. He liked the fact that I was choosing their company; but I still had no idea how he would react when confronted with my decision to become a baptized member in the restored Church of Jesus Christ.

My father's attitude was very serious and sincere when I told him. He said, "Before I say anything, let me sleep on it and I will talk to you tomorrow." He came into my office the next day and said, "I have something that I want to tell you. I have three questions for you." First he asked me, "Have you really investigated this?"

I answered, "Yes."

Second, he questioned, "Have you really taken enough time? Did you look into all corners and read everything you could find, even the literature of its critics, or has someone pressured you?"

I replied, "No, there has been no pressure. I have done everything I could to investigate and I have read also the 'anti' literature."

He continued, "Then, here is my third question: Are you really convinced that this is true?"

Without hesitation, I answered, "Yes."

He said, "Well, then you have no choice. You have to do it. We have to follow our convictions in our lives. Otherwise, we will not be able to stand. Even when it is not popular, and even when people sometimes can't understand us, it is necessary to stand by our convictions. Otherwise, we are unable to stand."

I was completely overwhelmed by my father's final statement. It was so unique. I knew of so many people who made compromises for all kinds of reasons, but here was my father who was concerned that I might have been brainwashed or coerced in some way. When it came to the final analysis, however, he respected my decision and was willing to support me. No matter how much I strive, I feel that I will never be able to equal him in his relentless pursuit of righteousness and of standing by principles of value.

Soon after this experience, something very important happened that had a profound impact on my life, as well as the life of my father. Both my father and I were working at that time in his printing company, which we reestablished in the aftermath of the war. One of our regular customers in Hamburg was a cigarette manufacturing company, the largest of its kind in Germany. It was a very powerful organization well known throughout Europe, and it had a tremendous influence on our business. Because of its need for quality and accuracy, we could provide the service it required even though we were, at that time, a small company. We were always afraid that a bigger, better-equipped organization would take away this company's orders, which basically were the bulk of our business.

Not long after my baptism, my father went to the very top manager, the CEO of this company. He was a highly respected man who, earlier in his life, had served as assistant in the Ministry of Economy in the German government, even serving in Washington, D.C. My father went right to this man, with whom he would normally have had no business, and told him that I had become a member of The Church of Jesus Christ of Latter-day Saints and that members of that church do not smoke. My father said that he wanted to inform the CEO before our competitors could provide such news in an effort to undermine our business relationship. My father, in making this visit, showed tremendous courage and determination to be a leader of destiny rather than becoming a victim of circumstance.

The CEO's reaction was a complete surprise to my father. He

said, "I congratulate you for the decision of your son." My father was overwhelmed and asked, "Do you know this church? What do you know about it?" The CEO explained that during the time he was in Washington, D.C., he had become acquainted with a man by the name of Ezra Taft Benson, a leading man of the LDS Church. Through Elder Benson he had obtained insight and some understanding of the beliefs of the Church. He said, "If your son has embraced this church, then I can only congratulate you." He then said, "I would pay my own son 100,000 Deutsche Marks [at least $100,000 in today's money] if he would become a Mormon." He then told my father of his great concern for his own son.

You can imagine my father's feelings as he returned home and the degree of relief and joy I experienced when he shared this conversation with me. The example of Ezra Taft Benson had such an influence that it was a blessing for me even though at the time I hardly knew who he was. With that kind of introduction to the CEO of that company, my father was not afraid, from that time on, when he made required visits to that customer. I personally had a very successful relationship with that company all during my business life.

When the gospel came into my life, my father allowed me to become his teacher to a small extent. He would come with an endless list of questions for me, asking what "my church" would think about a certain issue. He was fascinated by my responses. Through the Spirit, I was permitted to find all the answers to the questions he asked and was able to explain the beautiful nuances of the gospel of Jesus Christ.

He specifically had questions about the role of families, the relationships to our ancestors, the responsibility for one's actions, and what the methods of discipline might be. He also had questions about practical things, like architecture. He was very impressed when

I showed him a picture of the Lion House. He said that it was a house he could have built himself. My father was, by profession, an architect and was always designing something. Whenever I picked up a newspaper he had been reading, I would always find a couple of drawings in the corners of the pages.

My father asked many practical questions, but he did not have many questions about the doctrines of the restored gospel. Whenever I started teaching him concepts of the doctrine, he would interrupt me and apologize, saying, "I'm too old to change." He admitted that he had been very naive in his life in religious matters and probably needed to be more open, but he also made it clear that he felt it was too late.

He gave me the greatest honor that a young man can receive from his father. After my conversion to the gospel of Jesus Christ, he placed total trust in me. At the age of twenty-nine, just one year after my baptism, he put me in charge of his company. He did not agree with many of the things I wanted to do, but he trusted me enough to let me do them anyway. This humbled me and made me very careful in what I did.

When my father grew older, he took a special interest in the paintings of the nineteenth-century German Romantic period. He loved those paintings very much and was interested in the spirit of that period and the different painters and their contributions. At that time, I did not understand why anyone could become so involved in something that had so little connection with our business.

My father came to the point where he was more interested in those paintings than in running the business and, basically, let me do the job. He was so interested in them that he became an expert, even though he had never studied that period in any school setting. I saw experts from leading universities in Germany and art academicians come to my father to ask for his opinion on the quality or authenticity of certain paintings.

He had a special light he would shine on a painting and just stand in front of it for hours pondering it and moving up and down the hallway, going back, and looking again. Although this seemed boring to me, this was the joy of his life. He also loved to read the biographies of the painters and had a whole library full of books of descriptions of them. From knowing their lives, he could read their paintings and immediately, intuitively feel which period in their lives they came from and whether something was a forgery or not.

Later, in my growing understanding about the importance of the nineteenth century in relation to the salvation of mankind, I realized what his interest was. He loved this period because it was a period of honest self-reflection and searching for meaning and truth. He saw the world with the same spiritual sensitivities that so many thinkers and artists in the nineteenth century did. The dawning era of a new understanding had brought hope as the structures and shadows of the long-past Middle Ages were finally thrown off. Also, with the growing industrialization, there was a fear that men would become slaves of materialism. My father loved the reflection of these feelings in the paintings of that time period.

The painters of the Romantic period lived in a time where it was acceptable to feel close to the elements of the spirit and recognize its eternal value and harmony. My father became an expert in these painters' lives and gained the respect of professionals, who often had only their scholarly learning. Without the involvement of their hearts, they were unable to understand many of the things my father understood because of his love for those people and that period. I learned, from my father, that we have to be lovingly involved in all the elements of our lives, caring only for the true substance, looking through the outside appearance. Only then can we stand on a firm foundation. This is one important lesson my father taught me through his intense love and caring for the painters of the Romantic period.

My father was forty years older than I, and, when he came home from World War II, he was already not feeling well. He had several heart attacks and periods where he could not spend much time in the business. Early in 1964, just a little over six years after the time of my baptism, he was afflicted with another heart attack. His doctors felt it was not so serious, though, and that his life was not in danger. I had planned a skiing vacation with my wife and children. Before I went, I visited him in the hospital to say good-bye. It was in the afternoon, and he was alone in his room. He asked if I could sit with him for a while. I said, "Surely." He told me that he wanted to speak to me. I could see that he was wrestling with something, and that this conversation would be somewhat different from our ordinary talks.

Finally, quite straightforwardly, he said, "Can you promise me something?"

I said, "Yes, whatever it is."

He then went on, "Can you promise me to always be faithful to your church?"

I was completely overwhelmed and I, of course, said, "Yes, Father, I can promise that. But why do you ask?"

He said that he had watched me carefully and that being a member of "your church," as he called it, had helped me. He said, "Everything that was good in you became better but, most important, you became a happy person. I have a strong feeling that as long as you stay faithful to your church, it will be well with you."

I was totally overcome because he had never really been interested in the message of the Church, in spite of the sometimes many questions he had asked me. He would listen carefully and say, "Well,

Enzio walking with his father in 1955, shortly before his wedding day.

that is the best answer I have ever heard for this question." Then he would always walk away. He did not want a follow-up; but I could always see that he was impressed by the message he heard from me.

When he had said what he did about the Church, I asked him, "Father, we have never prayed together as a family or as individuals. Would you feel that this would be a good time to have a prayer together?"

He said, "Well, Son, that would not be fair. You see, I am an old man who is close to dying. What would Heavenly Father say to a man such as I who has never prayed in this life, and then when it comes to dying, he begins to pray? That is not good style. While I felt that I could live without prayer in my life, I must live without prayer in my death."

At that moment, I was prompted by the Spirit to tell my father, "Father, I don't believe you. I believe that you have always prayed, but that you haven't told anyone."

Then tears came to his eyes, which was very embarrassing to him. He said, "My son, you are right."

We talked about many things, not all of which I can remember. But I do remember that he said, "It could be that you are called, like the missionaries, to leave everything and preach the gospel. Then, of course, you will have to obey, but you must promise me to always care for your mother and your sisters and never forsake them." I promised him that. It was a great comfort later when I was called to be a General Authority that I felt my father had foreseen something and that, in some way, he had already given me his blessing. The fact that the company was still functioning very well during my mother's lifetime is one of the great blessings of my life. Without the help of the Lord, it would not have been so. The continuous income derived from the family's interest in the company has been a tremendous blessing to my mother and sisters.

In that wonderful spirit of communication in sacred matters, I said good-bye to my father. Just a few days later, when my wife and I were in Austria for a short skiing vacation, I received a telephone call that my father had passed away. A nurse had come to check on him in the morning and saw him reading a book. When she checked on him again, just thirty minutes later, she found him in the same position and realized that he had passed on. He had not even closed his book. Peace and serenity showed on his countenance. I immediately returned home where a new dimension of life without my father began.

Shortly after my father passed away, I was very surprised by one experience I had that I treasure highly and one that comforted me a great deal.

One night, about seven months after the death of my father, I had a very powerful dream, the impact of which has never left me. In this dream, I was sitting in my office when there came a knock at the door. The door then was opened, and I saw a man standing there whom I had never seen before—a young but mature man with a very serious expression of urgency. There was nothing in his countenance to indicate any light-mindedness whatsoever. Looking directly at me, he said, *"Wir sind bereit"* ("We are ready"). As I was pondering the meaning of his words, I was shocked to see my father standing some distance behind this young man, obviously not having permission to accompany this man to the door of my office. I saw my father standing there like a pleading beggar, with an expression on his face that was completely unknown and unfamiliar to me. He had always been a man with self-confidence, respect, and dignity. Now, I saw him standing there as a poor beggar, pleading with his eyes as if to say, "Please, don't forget! This is important—the most important thing that can ever happen to me!"

It was a tremendously humbling experience for me to see him standing there in the posture of a beggar, needing to ask something of me. I felt so unworthy! Then the vision was gone and I was left alone with the understanding that I had been permitted to see the missionary who taught my father the gospel and helped him to see the urgency of this work for his own salvation.

I too feel like a humble beggar as I think of the greatness of people who have gone before us. The revelation about the need to build temples is one of the remarkable tokens of truthfulness of the restored gospel in our time. How very grateful I am that I was able to receive this personal witness that my father had accepted the gospel and that he was asking me to go to the temple for him.

4

Illness and Awakening

The experience I want to relate in this chapter is a very sacred one and perhaps the most important of my life. Shortly after I was married, and before I had begun investigating the Church, I developed a liver disease so severe that we were told it was terminal. In the first days of my hospitalization, my situation worsened to the degree that I felt life was about to leave me, and I was confronted with the certain expectation of my death.

I remember the impossible feeling I had when I faced the end, because up until then, I had had options. I could say, "Well, if I don't like this, I can do something else." However, when I embarked on that road where there is no other option and no return, I felt indescribable panic. What started very slowly suddenly erupted into complete recognition of who I was. I saw myself confronted as if in a sharp, focused mirror. I could not escape being confronted with absolute truth. I felt unclean, completely unfinished, and unprepared to leave this life for the unknown. I felt the nearness of something

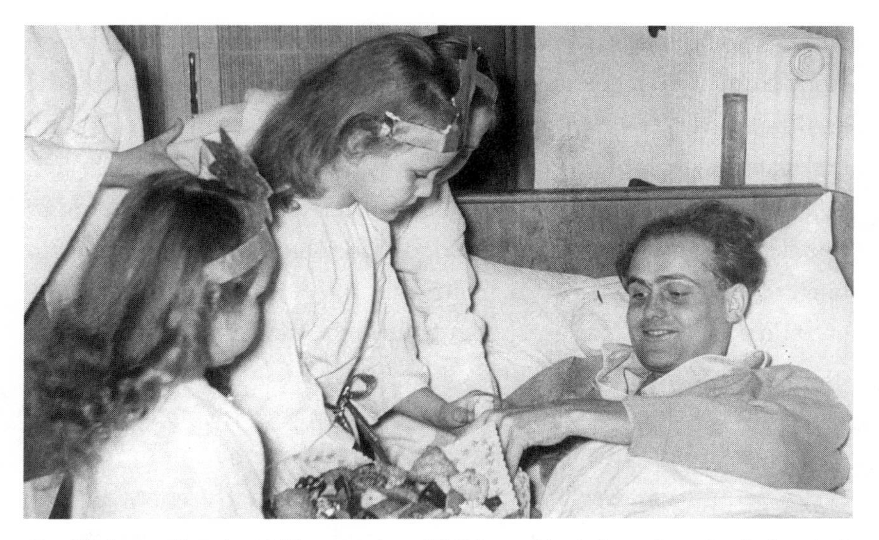

On Christmas Day in 1955, a number of children visited the patients in the hospital, including Enzio, bringing gifts and cheering up the patients with Christmas songs.

so holy, something so pure, and of such indescribable beauty and authority, that I preferred to become extinct rather than to meet that dimension of eternity in such an unprepared way. I was full of panic as I saw myself stripped of any protection. It was such a shocking awakening that I wanted with every fiber of my being to escape.

My panic was so acute that I made what I would now call a covenant. I said, "If there is the possibility that I might receive another chance and make a recovery, I will never be the same. I will live in complete awareness of my conscience, in complete awareness of the need to report about everything—every word, every feeling, and every thought of my life!"

I promised myself that I would live differently, that I would not be the same person as before, and that I would never submit myself to an insensitive lifestyle. It was not that I had lived in terrible sin. I did not commit adultery or steal or rob. But in the light of that experience, every little incident of not living up to my true potential became an unspeakable burden: my lack of gratitude for even the small things I had received in my life—the air I was able to breathe and the flowers by the wayside. My feelings towards my parents and the teachers I had had throughout my life all changed as if I were able to see them in their true character and understand their positive desires. It became impossible for me to comprehend how anyone could live, as I had been living, without this new, full awareness of reality and truth I was experiencing. I, therefore, made a commitment to myself and to the unseen authority I felt was near.

On the wall of my room was a cross with the crucified Christ on it. It was the only object on the wall, and as I focused upon it, I developed a tremendous hope: *If it were true that there was a Son of God named Jesus, who died for me also, then this was the greatest news ever spread in the history of mankind.* I knew that I needed someone to do something for me that I could not do for myself—to wash me clean. For even in my greatest commitment to become totally clean, I could not see myself ever achieving the same state of purity, harmony, and beauty that I felt in the moment that I seemed to approach the other world.

Exactly one week later, as I continued having these feelings—terrible physical and emotional pain, as well as thoughts of unpreparedness and unworthiness—something again happened. I was alone in my room on a Sunday morning. Suddenly there was a flash of light in the left corner of the ceiling. It penetrated my soul to the very core, frightening me, and creating in me an awakening I had never had before. I was totally numb, totally shocked, when I heard a voice speaking loud and clear, in German, "Wenn du jetzt beten kannst, wirst du gesund." ("If you can pray now, you will recover.") It was just a flash of a few seconds. Someone had told me to do something with an audible voice of penetrating authority and amid a clearly visible brilliance of light. I was actually invited to pray!

I did not know what it meant to pray. I did not have any religious background. Praying was not a part of my thinking or a part of my knowledge. It was clear to me that a prepared prayer, such as the Lord's Prayer that I had memorized in school, was not what was asked for, but that I should give of myself in communication with the highest authority imaginable. It seemed to be more than I could comprehend, and I was confused about what I should do. Then it was as if someone were helping me to formulate a prayer—one that, for me, was the most honest prayer I could ever pronounce. In German it consists of only three words: *Dein Wille geschehe* ("Thy will be done"). I said those few words with the full understanding of the meaning behind them and immediately felt an electric impulse course through my body so powerfully that all pain, panic, and agony changed into feelings of joy beyond my ability to describe.

After that there came about a total change in my existence, one that has always been very difficult to explain. Many people are hesitant to listen to matters concerning the spiritual world because they feel they have no control over such things. There is, therefore, a level of spiritual awareness that most people seem to have closed themselves to. But when spiritual eyes have been opened, circumstances change. I found that I could hardly talk about my experience because it was so private and sacred. Yet, I felt, and still feel, a tremendous responsibility to testify boldly because, with that understanding, I have recognized that I have something to share of utmost importance with the spiritually sleeping human family.

This world we live in is not the real thing. The actual world—which is closer to us than we sometimes realize—is full of truth and capable of bringing us to a higher level than we can understand. Indeed, it is more beautiful and majestic than a human can imagine. My spiritual insight let me see that we as human beings live far below our potential from day to day. One day we will be confronted with our true potential; and we will see what we have missed because we have not embraced the ultimate help offered to us from our Creator. Life is not worth living if we walk around in it without really knowing that every choice we make defines our lives in the eternities. Nothing can be hidden, and even every thoughtless spoken word will be brought to our painful awareness one day.

With this awareness, I felt a joy of indescribable dimensions—a joy that made me want to jump up, dance, sing, hug everyone, and never be sad again in my life. I had the sure knowledge that I would recover. It was so astonishing that, although close to fifty years have passed, I can recall those feelings in the same intensity as at the time of the experience, and I feel the same silent urgency to testify of it.

From this time forward, the dimensions of my life changed and deepened. During the time that my physical body was so weak that I could not read or eat or even speak, I learned to understand that our mental and emotional capabilities can be nurtured by divine spiritual forces. I realized that it is possible to receive an awareness of our true origin as pure, innocent children of that being we call God. The key to this sacred awareness comes through self-reflection, pondering, and meditation. It comes after our efforts to look inside and to contemplate.

The long hours and weeks in the hospital were, at first, unbelievably tedious, and the physical and emotional pain alone seemed to be unbearable. But as time went by, I learned to turn my thoughts away from myself. One day, as I was looking at my bed, I saw more than the white linen bedspread in front of me. I saw the individual thread, and I saw the field where it originated. I saw the sun, the rain, the wind it was exposed to. I saw the soil from which it took its nurture. I saw the people that came for the harvest. I felt their sweat and diligence. I felt their goodness. I felt their love. I saw that if every act of labor were done with love and care, this world would heal. There would be light, even divine light, in the heart and soul of every man and woman enabling us to grab one another's hand and to dance like innocent children, filled with the exuberance of never-ending joy.

My mind traveled from there through the various stations of the blanket's production. I saw all the men and women involved in the labor of love it took to make the bedspread ready to give me comfort and protection. As I looked again at the simple bed cover in front of me, I was overcome with joy and gratitude and love. I could not hold back my tears, and I started crying and weeping. Days suddenly became short, and I enjoyed every minute of my life.

In addition to the promise I made to change my life, I felt an urgent need to make two other commitments. I felt so overwhelmed from my experience with the Eternal that I made a covenant with myself—in front of this unknown, sacred authority—that I would never deny or belittle my experience and that I would testify of it as often as I felt prompted. I promised to share with others the truth I learned: that we are watched over and that we are accountable not only for what we have done with our lives but even that we are responsible for every word we speak.

My third covenant was that I would seek out the Author of this experience, the Being whose nearness had overwhelmed me so dramatically. I wanted to become His disciple, no matter the cost.

I knew that I would recover. I was miraculously healed. Exactly one week after that second experience of inner enlightenment, my blood test showed remarkable improvement. Everyone in the hospital felt, at first, that something was wrong with the test; but I knew that I was recovering. Finally, the doctors had to admit that a complete miracle had transpired.

When the day came that I had the energy to read again, I asked my wife, Jutta, to bring me a Bible because I felt that this book

Enzio in 1954, as a critical searcher of meaning and purpose.

might have the answers to my questions and that I should familiarize myself with it. She was very surprised because it was not typical of me to be interested in religion. Nonetheless, she brought it to me, happy that I wanted to read again. I read it from the first page of Genesis to the last page of Revelation. My only interruptions came from eating and sleeping.

I was completely surprised by the Bible. The beauty of its thought and the magnitude and wisdom of its contents overwhelmed me. Especially in the New Testament, I learned that we are all children of a loving Heavenly Father, that we are free, that agency is our destiny, and that, in exercising our agency, we are in danger because we have to learn to make right decisions. I learned that Jesus Christ, the Firstborn Son of the Father, came to this earth to give His life—even to sacrifice His life—so that the children of Heavenly Father, who exist here in a fallen state, can grow by making righteous decisions in the middle of adversity. I learned that anyone who desires to become eligible to go home may do so by becoming His disciple in obedient, true fellowship, constantly learning from Him. I came to see that coming home with honor was the ultimate purpose of life. But the Bible left many questions open, all of which gave me the understanding that my questions could be answered only by the Living God Himself. In spite of the Bible's shortcomings, it became a sacred book for me.

In the Catholic hospital, there was a nun whose name was Irrenea. She was the most angelic human being one could ever imagine. Although she was in her forties or fifties, she behaved like a little girl. To see her walking, one would think she was almost dancing. To hear her talk was almost like hearing her sing. I never saw her discouraged or overly serious. There was always some merriment in her eyes and a sincere interest in the well-being of the patients. During the five months I spent in the hospital, I learned to admire Irrenea greatly. I watched her because she was of the caliber I wanted to achieve in order to be acceptable to the other world, and I benefited from the daily exposure to the authority and dignity of this wonderful daughter of our Heavenly Father.

One day when she was not busy, I took the liberty to ask her if she could spend an extra minute by my bedside. She gladly agreed. I asked her, "Sister Irrenea, can you please give me the answer to just one question—just answer with a 'yes' or a 'no.' Tell me, is the Catholic Church the true church of Jesus Christ?" She was somewhat, but not overly, surprised. She looked off toward the horizon and, after some time, her gaze turned toward me and she said, quite matter-of-factly and without any apologies, "No, it is not. The church you are looking for is the church of the living Christ, and the Catholic Church is a church of dead traditions. You can only remain a member if you have grown up in the church, for then you are so caught up in it, it is difficult to leave it." I was completely overcome by that statement. She stood up and left the room. She was not disturbed. Her dignity remained. I so admired her dignity and honesty that I probably would have become a Catholic if she had told me "yes."

Even after all these years, I still feel tremendous gratitude for that sister. It would probably be difficult to find someone of that charming depth again—a free spirit, a happy, Christlike person who served unselfishly day and night. Her example meant so much to me that I have never forgotten it. Anytime I see a person complaining because of too much work or being overburdened, I remember this selfless, unconditionally loving person. With her courageously open honesty, she was a motivating force for me to continue in my search to find the Living God.

Through my illness and experience in the hospital and through the time spent studying the Bible, I received a spiritual witness of the Lord Jesus Christ. I came to know that He was the source of the miraculous experience that had come to me. From then on, the direction I should follow became clear. I wanted to find Christ. I wanted to become His disciple.

5

CONVERSION

I WAS RELEASED FROM THE HOSPITAL about five months after I was admitted. I developed a tremendous appreciation for many things that I had never noticed before in my life. For instance, I had to learn to walk again. Every one-year-old child has the same experience; but we adults have forgotten how rewarding it is to finally walk without assistance across the room or how beautiful and overwhelming the first outdoor experience is after months of illness. The sky, the flowers, the shrubs, the trees—they all look as if you are seeing them for the first time.

As soon as I felt comfortable walking, I went to the minister of the church I belonged to by registration, the Evangelische Kirche, to begin my search for Christ. I visited him in his office, and I can still remember its specific smell and atmosphere. Surrounded by his library of books and dressed in his official robe, he aroused within me a feeling of respect and admiration. I felt a strong desire to learn from him and submit to his leadership.

As I told him of my disease, my experience in the hospital, and my three commitments, I asked him what I could do to become a disciple of Christ. He looked at me calmly and said that I had come to the wrong address, that I should go see a psychiatrist. I was not offended by this remark because I was so filled with love, understanding, and forgiveness from my recent experience in the hospital. It was as if I was still surrounded and protected by a special spirit, so I merely felt a bit sorry that he, acting in his holy capacity and bearing the mantle of his position, did not really understand the eternal dimension of our existence. I persisted in asking him what I could do and, as a consequence, he invited me to participate in all the meetings held for members of his church. I remember the wonderful feeling I had when I went in the church for the first time as a conscientious visitor with a desire to be close to God, to worship, and to learn.

The first day I was overwhelmed by the newness of attending church and by the fact that I was doing something to show that my life had changed. I was also a little bit disappointed to find the church relatively empty, with only a few participating. Those who were there seemed quite casual in their interest, doing things more or less out of a routine, without a very deep, individual understanding or commitment.

As I continued to attend church services, I developed confidence in my new status as an active, participating churchgoer. Still, the dimension of spirituality that I had felt in the hospital was far removed, and I could not be satisfied with what I was experiencing. I realized that without more involvement, I would soon be in danger of not living up to my commitments. I began to listen to the claims of many other church groups, such as the Jehovah's Witnesses and the Seventh Day Adventists. I read everything I could find about other churches and other messages without being particularly attracted to any of them.

After several months of church participation, I became very restless and desired to move on in fulfilling my promises. Quite unexpectedly, the minister visited my home. He was a very fine, sensitive man, and I had developed a feeling of closeness and admiration for him. He apologized for his initial statement directing me to see a psychiatrist and for his insensitivity during our first visit. He said that in his daily life he saw so many people who told him so many different stories that he had learned not to take anything too seriously. However, in my case, he had witnessed that I participated every Sunday and was really committed.

He invited me to join a circle of members who supported him by visiting various member families. He mentioned that the parish was very large—up to 13,000 people—and that he was not able to visit everyone. He asked me whether I would like to accept that responsibility. I felt overwhelmed with joy and gratitude that he would feel I was worthy to serve. I was finally in a position to do something to prove to the Lord that I adored Him, that I had become aware of Him, that I had changed my life, and that I was willing to do everything I could to build His kingdom.

On the first evening I went visiting, I was furnished with the name of a family and invited to return to the minister's office after the visit to discuss my findings. I remember my feelings of anxiety and nervousness as I approached my assigned family's apartment. I found them to be a typical German family. The man greeted me casually, with a cigar in his mouth. I told him that the minister sent me, and he immediately asked me, "What do you want from me? Do you want money?"

I tried to establish a relationship of trust with this family and to bring the message, as I saw it, from Christ. The man confronted me with his ideas and told me he was not very impressed by the Evangelische Kirche. To my great surprise, I had to agree with many of his points. For instance, he did not approve of how the church had given its blessing to the Hitler regime and the actions of war. He mentioned many details that I was either not aware of or with which, as I became aware, I also had to disagree. I was so surprised by my own feelings that I felt I was not fulfilling the trust the minister had placed in me as his representative.

In the evaluation meeting, I shared my observations and disappointments with the minister and told him that I really wanted to first learn what an Evangelical church member believed in before I could go out as his representative. He felt that would be an excellent idea, and he suggested that the members of the visiting committee come together in my apartment and teach me the beliefs of a church member. Again, I was very excited about something like this happening, and I felt very grateful that these people would take me so seriously as to come and visit me.

I prepared for their visit with great expectations. Yet, when the evening came and then wore on, I was again stunned and disappointed; they talked about everything and nothing. With various opinions and feelings mentioned, there was very little harmony. One quoted theologians who questioned whether certain parts of the Bible were authentic, and others even questioned the authenticity of Jesus Christ. Some were more conservative but also not very sure. I was completely surprised to learn how weak the foundation was upon which these members stood.

I was not willing to let them go in that spirit. I did not interrupt their discussion. At the end of their visit, however, I told them I was disappointed. I had thought from reading the Bible, specifically the writings of the disciples of Christ, that there was some purpose in becoming a disciple of Christ, that there was some objective goal

Enzio and Jutta in 1954, about one year before their marriage and two years before two LDS missionaries found them.

present in building a new society with a new system of values and of dealing one with another. I told them that the impact of reading the entire Bible was still with me and that I continued to study and read from the Bible on a daily basis. (I still have that same Bible, and it is very interesting to see what I underlined and focused on in the early days of my studying.) They were surprised and even shocked. I still remember the looks they gave me when I told them frankly of my disappointment.

That evening, after the visitors had gone, my wife and I knelt down, but instead of reciting the Lord's Prayer, we called upon Father, pleading with Him and asking Him to help us learn how we could become His disciples. In my prayer, I remember I said, "If your disciples worship together in only a small room, and if they are persecuted, ridiculed, and isolated, that would not matter to me." I just had this great hunger and desire to find His disciples. If there were any authorized people serving His cause with a purpose, then we wanted to find them and we wanted to become His disciples. As I was pouring out my heart, I was completely overwhelmed with a beautiful feeling of joy, confidence, and satisfaction. I was no longer afflicted with distress, for light and hope entered into my soul.

About three weeks later, on a Saturday morning when I was at home (which was very seldom because, at that time, I worked six days a week), the doorbell rang. I answered the door to find two young men wearing dark suits. They told me they came from a church with a long, long name. My immediate reaction was to greet them casually with the comment, "Tell whoever sent you that the name is too long. That is not good for sales." It took me quite some time before I could remember the name and before I could say it without getting confused.

The message of these young men was very strange to me. As I listened to them, I actually felt sorry for them. I could not comprehend why anyone in their right mind would come from such a far distance with such a message and hope to find anyone who would be able to believe that somewhere there were some golden plates guarded by some angels. The whole message of the Restoration seemed to be too far-fetched to take seriously.

So, at first, it was not the message itself that I was interested in, but the messengers who brought it. They were completely different from any church representatives I had seen before. They had a spirit of innocence and purity and the willingness to sacrifice. They also seemed to have made a painstaking commitment to the essence of truth, one that was favorably different from people I knew, including myself. Their style of behavior represented a moral authority that took away my ability to say no to their requests and invitations.

They were a little shy. Sometimes I had to encourage them and invite them to say something or to go on with their presentation. At the time, I felt superior because I knew the Bible better than they did and often quoted from it. In a way, I felt that it was my assignment to help them. I felt sorry for them, yet I was completely overwhelmed to see that they were willing to leave their homes and come without pay to bring such an outlandish, far-fetched message to the world.

I was very touched when they talked about their own homes, their families, their brothers and sisters, their parents and grandparents in a way that I had never before seen among young people. They were so full of respect and love that tears would flow down their cheeks when they talked. That impressed me very much because, for me, family was something very important, and I was always very unhappy with the casual approach I had seen people take about families. I liked these young men. I liked their spirit and their personality, and I had them come and visit.

I continued to go to my church. It was clear that the members could not agree among themselves as to what a church member believed, so I suggested to the minister that those who had visited my home might come together in the same circle again and I would invite two missionaries I had met from The Church of Jesus Christ of Latter-day Saints. I told the minister that these missionaries really believed in something and were united. My hope was that in a confrontation with a group who was united we would also find the common denominator of our faith and thus establish some credibility for our message. The minister enthusiastically accepted my idea, and we worked out a special appointment.

When the evening came, the two missionaries did not come alone. They were accompanied by two other missionaries, both of whom were so new that they could understand very little, if any, German. The minister brought the same group of people who were there before, but he also brought a stranger, a minister from Frankfurt. This minister's name was Fuchs, a specialist acquainted with the doctrine of various sects, especially Mormon doctrine. I was a little disappointed because I admired and was accustomed to my own minister, with his nice style and approach, but with this stranger, I did not expect a fruitful discussion.

My expectations proved to be completely correct. The new minister immediately took the initiative and began to speak in a very high, agitated voice that was both offensive and direct. He attacked the missionaries with words of disrespect, questioning their integrity and their good sense. I immediately felt distressed about what was happening. He went on and on. I felt so sorry for those young men whom I had invited that, after awhile, I interrupted the minister and said that I felt it would be an act of hospitality to give the other visitors a chance to say something. Reluctantly, he stopped his tirade and gave them the floor.

I expected the missionaries to get on their feet and fight back and attack the Evangelical church. I was completely surprised to hear the leading visiting elder—a young man from American Falls, Idaho, by the name of Glen Walker—just bear his testimony of Jesus Christ and the restoration of the gospel. As he did so, peace came into the room. I was very much surprised to find that this young man was not intimidated and continued to radiate this wonderful spirit that was palpable enough to be felt by everyone in attendance.

The minister then resumed his attack, even more rudely, furiously, and relentlessly. I grew more and more uneasy about his rudeness. I do not remember all of the details of that evening, but there are two main issues that remain vivid in my memory. The first was the authority of this young man, which soon came dramatically into place. The minister emphatically suggested something about the Mormons, as he called members of The Church of Jesus Christ of Latter-day Saints, believing the crazy idea that Heavenly Father lives somewhere in the universe and has millions and even billions of children. Then he screamed, "How can you think such nonsense?" Elder Walker got on his feet and, with a calm voice and a peaceful countenance, looked at the minister and said, "Sir, are you not a child of God?"

Everyone looked at the minister at that moment, shocked and surprised and aware that this would be difficult for him to answer. If he claimed he was a child of God (which he probably would not deny, being a minister of the Evangelical church), then he would be admitting that God has children and that the minister would not be the only child. The minister was shocked and well aware of the situation because, for quite some time, he hesitated, stopped, wanted to say something but changed his mind, and then he suddenly changed the subject. I was impressed that these young missionaries were in a position to silence this learned man.

Then the minister began to talk more and more about the belief that one does not need to be baptized and does not need to have any ordinances, that all that is needed is faith in Christ in order to partake, through His mercy and His grace, of salvation and eternal life. That issue was picked up by Elder Walker, and he said, "Sir, we do not understand why you are so upset, because in your own words, we are saved. We believe in Christ. We have left our homes and our families to testify of Christ and to preach His gospel. In your own words, we don't need your baptism to be saved. But could it be that you are so upset because, deep down inside, you fear that this message we bring to you today could be true? We realize that you have read many books and have studied many elements of the restored gospel. One must have faith in the Lord and must take his faith away from the world and turn it in awe towards Him and be baptized by immersion by someone who has the authority to do so from Him. Deep down inside you fear this may be true; therefore, you are so upset. Could it be that you are driven by fear?"

At this point, the minister completely lost his control. He jumped to his feet and declared he was unwilling to listen to any more of that kind of nonsense. He then faced me with much antagonism, grabbed the lapels of my suit firmly, and shouted at me, "You are the one who started all of this!" He made a prophecy as he waved his finger at me and threatened me, saying, "If you do not send these missionaries out of your apartment right now, you will become a Mormon!" As he shook his finger at me and gestured in such a threatening manner, a penetrating thought struck me. It was as if a voice inside of me said, "Why not?"

We came to a close after the minister, without asking anyone, offered the Lord's Prayer and thus ended the meeting. Everyone was leaving. The missionaries, too, wanted to leave; but I said to them, "Not you, you stay." That evening I made a commitment to listen to these missionaries regularly because my spirit was impressed by their calmness, their peace, and how they radiated love, understanding, and forgiveness. I had felt the authority they possessed and knew it was different from everything that I had experienced thus far in the Evangelical church. I wanted to become a disciple of Christ and so, that evening, I made a commitment that I would invite the missionaries over regularly and see what they had to offer.

The missionaries taught us beginning in the summer of 1956. They came on a regular basis every two or three weeks, and so it happened that by and by, I came to know the doctrine of the gospel. But the more I got to know of the doctrine, the more overwhelmed I became with its unique, vast completeness. The next step was fear, even panic. My mind was filled with the thought that if their message was true, I would be confronted with something I could not push away.

How ill prepared I was for this message as I saw myself in comparison to its ultimate demands! I felt that I was too far away, with

Enzio and Jutta, with their first two children in 1958, about ten months after their baptism.

too many casual attitudes and bad habits. I became aware of my thoughts, which, I found, were filled with prejudice, empty phrases, and vain ambitions. There seemed to be, between my own life's performance and the vision in the message of the missionaries, an abyss over which no bridge could be built.

We did not make much progress, in spite of everything that had taken place in my life. I continued to pity those boys. I even warned them that there was no hope, that they were just wasting their time, not only with me but also with everyone else I knew. The power of my traditional thinking and my laziness in spiritual matters were so overwhelming that I saw no possibility of reaching the level of these young men from America. Doing so seemed even laughable to me—so hopeless that I did not want to start thinking about making the necessary changes.

Then one day, the missionaries were taken away from our town of Dortmund and, suddenly, in the absence of their regular visits, I felt a tremendous loss—as if something very special and precious had been taken away from me. As happens in life, we often don't appreciate things until they are taken away from us. So, I learned to appreciate the weekly visits we had had with the missionaries, and I began to develop a longing for the missionaries to once again visit our home.

I do not recall exactly when it was, perhaps in the first half of 1957, that I heard a rumor. I learned that once again there were missionaries in Dortmund. To find out for myself and make contact with them, I had to go to their church. I looked at the back of the little pamphlet that had been stamped with the location and time that church meetings were held. The members met in a very poor section of our town of 650,000—an older, industrial area where decent people would not normally venture. To reach it required traveling through the off-limits "red light" district. My parents had never allowed me to go near this area, but there I was, driving through this unsavory part of town on a Sunday morning, looking for the old schoolhouse that served as the meeting place for the branch. I even remember the weather that day—foggy with a little rain, which is typical of central Europe.

I found the building, but there were no signs to indicate where in the building the meetings were held. I found a small group on the second floor of the old school. There were several humble-looking people, mostly elderly and mostly speaking with an accent indicative of East German refugees. I remember the feelings I had as I stood there in that hallway—feelings of tremendous satisfaction with myself. I had the thought of how proud the Savior would be of me for going to such a humble place in order to worship and in order to find the truth. As I considered myself in relation to this group of people, my attitude was that the Mormons could be very grateful that a man like me was coming to their Sunday School.

At the end of the hallway were stairs leading to the first floor. I could easily identify two young men approaching from there as the missionaries. One was the taller of the two—a very mature-looking young man who radiated enthusiasm, to say the least. He had a broad smile on his face. I later learned his name was Bob Thompson, and he was from Malta, Idaho. With great vigor, he shook the hand of an elderly sister standing at the stairs, greeting her with a loud "hello" while pumping her arm up and down with a firm handshake. I was appalled by such straightforwardness and immediately formed a dislike for him. I felt uncomfortable and wished I had never come. There surely would not be anything I could learn from him, so why should I waste my time?

I wanted to disappear, but I could not without being conspicuous because the only exit was the stairs at the end of the hallway. My next thought was to make my visit as brief as possible, so I withdrew as much as I could to the other side of the hallway while we were waiting for the janitor to come and open the classroom where the Sunday School meeting was to be held. Even though the light in the hallway was dim, this missionary did not lose track of me. He bypassed all the others and reached toward me to shake my hand with the same fervor I had just observed. In a reaction of defense, I pulled my hands behind my back. He addressed me with a loud, "Hellooooo, brother!" Somewhat perplexed, I stammered, "I am not your brother." I hoped that would deter his aggressiveness and make him pull back with an apology of some sort or another, but that did not happen.

Quite spontaneously, he clapped his hands loudly together and said, "That's wonderful!" I was again quite surprised. Out of curiosity I asked, "What is so wonderful in my not being your brother?"

He immediately responded, "I've only been in the city two hours and I already have my first investigatoooor!" He pulled out a little appointment book from his pocket and, with a pencil in his hand, he boldly asked, "What's your name? Where do you live?" I told myself that I couldn't escape telling him or he would probably follow me the whole day, so I gave him my name and my address. Next he asked, "When can we come and visit? When do you have time?"

Not until then did he give me an opportunity to explain a little about myself. I took my planning book from my pocket and talked about my schedule of meetings, travels, and responsibilities as I tried to convince him of my importance and the pressing duties that would fill all my time for the next four weeks. He listened intently with a little grin and responded without hesitation, "How about tonight?" I had to take a deep breath. Because no business meetings were held in Germany on Sunday nights, I had nothing scheduled for that evening. So it ended up that those missionaries came that same evening for their first visit.

At the time, we were living in small quarters on the top floor of an apartment building. My wife had prepared an evening meal to share with them. They arrived at the appointed time and, as I greeted them at the door, I was surprised to see that both were extremely serious, without a trace of a smile on their faces. I invited them to come in and told them, "We have dinner ready. We'd like you to eat with us." They did not move. They just stood there and said, "We did not come to eat." I was shocked and disappointed because we had deliberately waited dinner until they came and, in a tone reflecting my disappointment, yet trying to make conversation, I said, "Are you angels? Don't you eat?" Elder Thompson said, "No, we are not angels, but when we come to you, we do not come to eat." Still frustrated and disappointed, I said, "Why did you come?" He looked right through me and, with power and without any hesitation, he said, "We came to baptize you!"

I was so completely shocked and somewhat offended that dinner was not important anymore. I wanted to express something that would teach him respect. I wanted to tell him something that he would never forget. "Sir," I said, "I understand that you are new in town. You don't know me yet. I am one of the few that is friendly to the missionaries. I invite them to come visit and I talk with them, but, so there will be no misunderstanding between you and me, I want to make it clear: I will never be baptized in your church." My saying this in such a straightforward way came as a surprise, even to me, and I was almost afraid that he would react in a way that I had read about in the Bible—that he would wipe the dust from his feet and would leave a curse and slam the door.

It didn't happen that way at all. A big smile came upon his face and his great spirit led him to say, with tremendous enthusiasm, punctuated by gestures, "That's wonderful!"

Again, I was dumbfounded and asked, "What is so wonderful about that, that I will never be baptized into your church?" I began to wonder a little about whether I was not humble enough or perhaps not pure enough or educated enough. I was curious, and I asked him that.

With no apparent forethought, he shouted with a big grin of joy, clapping his hands, full of enthusiasm, "Well, that's what everyone says before he is baptized!"

So, again I was shocked to think that I could not shake him or destroy his great enthusiasm for his message.

I became strangely curious about this missionary. I questioned him, "Sir, what makes you so sure?" At that time he became an instrument in the hand of the Lord to call me to repentance. How are we normally called to repentance in the Church? I have not

Three of the missionaries who taught the Busches in Dortmund, including Elder Bob Thompson, right.

heard many straightforward calls to repentance, but through the spirit of Christ and the inspired words of testimony, the Holy Ghost typically becomes the catalyst to call us to repentance. As I asked, "What makes you so sure?" he looked at me in all sincerity and said without hesitation, "Because you are an honest man."

When I heard him call me "honest," I was completely astonished. I felt like a two-edged sword had pierced my soul from the top to the bottom. I was confronted with an agony of soul and an overpowering awareness of my arrogance, haughtiness, pride, and lack of honesty. I saw myself completely unprotected. I was by far not the person I had committed myself to become as I lay in the hospital, for I had promised I would be honest and mindful and sensitive of what I would say and what I would do. It was as if a bright, shining light was hanging over me, showing my nakedness. I became so ashamed and embarrassed that I wanted, with all my heart, to become worthy of the judgment of honesty from that man. I told him, after being choked up for quite a while, "Sir, I am not honest, but I beg you humbly. Could you please become my teacher on my road toward self honesty?"

With that experience, I saw this young man in a completely different light. Maybe he really was a messenger of the Living God. I gave away my reservations and began surrendering my fate into the hands of this man, whom I learned to admire with my growing understanding of the gospel principles that he taught. Everything that is important to me in the Church today I initially learned from this man—through him, the Holy Ghost etched every fundamental principle and every true concept into my soul. He is still somewhat like "the president of the Church" for me because the authority and power with which he bore testimony to me was of an eternal dimension, and I shall never forget it.

Yes, he was the one who finally baptized us—not just that evening, of course, but after we began for the first time to listen seriously to the teachings of the gospel of Jesus Christ. However, I had many questions and was not an easy person to teach. Most of the time, I would anticipate what would be discussed, and I had more questions than he was able to answer. I was always offended and bewildered by any memorized explanations or impersonal proof of a concept, for I needed to look into the heart to find what was honest and true. As I finally realized that the integrity among the missionaries was genuine, I made progress in my investigation.

All during this time, I was engulfed in anti-Mormon literature furnished to me by my minister. It was an interesting test. The context of the material was challenging and dreadful. I felt the evil design of this anti-Mormon literature, and the Spirit helped me to see, in contrast, the beautiful, wonderful feelings I felt in reading the materials from the gospel of Jesus Christ. I began to place trust in the teaching I received from the missionaries. I threw away the evil pamphlets and booklets I received from the Evangelical church.

That principle of openness to testing various voices has remained with me, for I have come to understand that we can develop trust in the small voice of the Spirit that wants to lead us to all truth when we are humble, meek, and teachable. Following that voice is what we call "having faith." Spiritual truth cannot always be confined to reason. Spiritual awareness of truth goes much further and deeper and must become the foundation of our lives on earth. There is a German poet named Wilhelm Busch who said, *"Nur was wir glauben, wissen wir gewiss"* ("Only what we have faith in, we know for sure"). Our reasoning capabilities will not bring us salvation. Intellectual reasoning can control our lives and give us structure and perspective. It can put awareness of truth into action. But it cannot convert us. Conversion itself will come only by a power from the world of the eternal. That alone can penetrate us and pour light into our souls, giving pure knowledge and intelligence, enlightenment and conviction that goes much further and deeper than any learning that can ever come through the brain.

6

BAPTISM

OUR HEAVENLY FATHER HAS MANY ways to communicate His willingness to help and guide us. He gives us feelings in subtle ways, such as through our conscience. When the conscience is not developed, however, it can be cheated. It can also be soothed to such a degree that it cannot function properly. When we indulge in wrongdoing or follow false examples, the influence of our conscience becomes less and less powerful in our lives. Therefore, sometimes we must be touched in other ways.

I have a feeling that once in a while, Heavenly Father, in His love for us, shows us a situation in a dream in order to help us learn from it. Sometimes, we see in a dream something terrible or bad happening to us, and we become aware as we awaken that it was only a dream. We wonder why we had such a dream, but through such dreams, we can build our defenses so that we will not have to experience the problem ourselves. Through the experience of such dreams in my life, I have been privileged to receive insight and training that I otherwise could never have assimilated. In fact, dreams had a very powerful influence on my decision to be baptized.

One of the powers the adversary has is to fill us with fear. I was sometimes in complete panic as I thought about becoming a member of the LDS Church. I was tortured with wondering what my parents would say, what my customers would think, and how my children might feel later on in their lives. I worried about continuing to achieve a good livelihood if I were considered an outcast in German society. How could I withdraw from all the influential circles of which I was a part? My feelings of panic were so acute that there were periods when I hated the time that the missionaries came because I was not innocent anymore. I could no longer say that I did not know the truth. I hated the predicament in which I found myself, and I almost wished I had never listened to the missionaries in the first place. During this period, I experienced two dreams that had a very powerful effect upon my life.

In my first dream, I was standing in a plane that had a broken wing and was plunging to the ground. I saw a person pressed against the wall of the plane by centrifugal force. He was completely unable to move. I looked closely at the man's face as he plunged toward certain death. His eyes were filled with terror.

I woke up from this dream, my clothing drenched with sweat and in such a state of shock that I could not go back to sleep. As I lay awake thinking about what I had seen in my dream, I suddenly realized that the man whom I had looked upon was myself some time in the future—perhaps at the age of fifty. In my dream, I had been completely powerless to avoid impending disaster in my life. I was overwhelmed by the thought that if I did not accept the gospel, that fate could be mine: I would be unprepared to face death. For me, the dream was a sincere warning that I had to make a decision, and that I could not procrastinate my commitment to the Lord.

Several days after I had experienced the first dream, it began to fade away somewhat, and I began to feel comfortable once again with my pattern of procrastination. But then I had another dream, and this time it was even more impressive and challenging. In this dream, I saw myself on skis on a snow-covered mountain peak. It was actually not too steep at the top, but was more of a rolling slope. The snow was most beautiful, glistening in the sun, and I was skiing down this beautiful mountain feeling immense joy in the beauty of the day.

As I went further down the slope, it suddenly turned into a path that became steep and narrow. I was still in control but had to focus my efforts to avoid a fall. Suddenly, jagged rocks protruded from the right edge of the path, and on the left side was an abyss. I realized that I would have to stay exactly on the path, without any twists or turns, in order not to fall, as a fall would mean being cut by the sharp rocks I was passing or, even worse, plunging into the deep canyon below. As I realized the danger I was in and my inability to turn back, I was shocked to realize I had started this course without sufficient preparation and now had to depend completely upon my own capabilities and concentration in order to survive.

As I descended further down the mountain, the sunlight disappeared in the narrowness of the canyon. Suddenly, the white snow turned into ugly slush. As I concentrated, looking at the gray, watery snow, I realized that I was no longer skiing over snow but over the decomposed flesh of human beings who had lost their lives as they tried to ski down the canyon without falling. Here I was, threatened with falling any second and becoming part of this mass of decaying flesh. I saw the bones and skulls of skeletons, and I was filled with terror to such a degree that I concentrated even more fully to avoid falling as I took one curve after another.

There seemed no end to this terrifying course, but then I saw a valley opening up where there was sunlight again. In the valley was a group of some twenty to thirty people waiting for my arrival. I saw a banner marking the end of the course. The people were not permitted to be close to the finish line, but they cheered with much enthusiasm as they saw me coming, and I could see that I might finish. Just then I awoke and was not permitted to see whether I was able to cross the finish line or not.

As I reflected on the dream, I was amazed to see aspects of it relating to life itself, showing the life of a youth in the sun and the joy and innocence of the new snow. Then life as an adult with its ugly realities, rough corners and edges, and the disaster of almost not making it to the finish line, which I understood to be leaving this life to go home to Heavenly Father. The impact of the dream was so powerful that I knew without doubt that I must no longer postpone accepting the gospel into my life.

Smoking was an additional barrier that kept me from getting baptized right away. Smoking was a bad habit I had developed early in life. When I was drafted into the army at the age of fourteen, I received my ration of cigarettes and started to smoke. The fascination created by smoking is still a memory that can be very strong. It is difficult to explain why it bound me so, but it seemed impossible for me to let go of this habit. Even at the time of my disease, I did not lose my appetite for smoking. As soon as I could get out of the hospital, the doctors gave me permission to start smoking again.

At the time the missionaries began teaching me, I was probably up to forty cigarettes a day, as well as smoking ten or so small cigars and three to five pipes. Smoke enveloped me at all times. In addition, in the printing company where I was plant manager at the time, printing cigarette boxes was the major part of our business.

It was a very awkward situation for me when the missionaries challenged me to quit smoking. My wife joked, "He is good at quitting. He has done it eight times in a row!" She had seen me wrestling with it. Although I knew it was not good to smoke, it seemed impossible for me to break the habit. When the missionaries asked me to quit smoking, they encouraged me to ask Heavenly Father for help. One day, without letting the missionaries know, I asked Heavenly Father to help me quit smoking. At the end of my prayer, I paused to listen. A still, small voice penetrated my heart and mind, saying, "Yes, I can help you quit smoking, but you have to do something for yourself. Read the Book of Mormon in the next thirty days."

I had read the Book of Mormon before, but more to find fault with it and prove it wrong. It did not make a big impression on me, and I was full of criticism, rebellion, and suspicion, all of which were fed by the experiences I had under the Hitler regime and the disappointing awareness I found after the war. I was full of skepticism and full of a desire never to be cheated again.

However, I could not forget the prompting I had received, so that evening I made a decision and an informal covenant to read the Book of Mormon once more, resolving to finish it within thirty days. This time I approached it with a different attitude, with the desire to find out whether or not it could be true. I organized myself to do this by dividing up the pages of the book into thirty parts. As I was very busy at that time in my professional life, I had to begin my day about one hour earlier and make other adjustments in my schedule so that I could make time for reading.

What I did not know was that before I had prayed that evening, I had already smoked my last cigarette. The next morning when I began to read the Book of Mormon, I felt a spirit of strength, comfort, and peace entering my soul that saw me through my first day without smoking. I started the second day in the same way and made it through without smoking. The third day, I was tempted several times to smoke, but I thought, "I have abstained for two days. Why not another?" So I went the third day without smoking, and it was fine.

In the same way, I refrained from smoking one day after another, never expecting to make it through more than that particular day. I was surprised to find that, after seven days, I had not smoked for an entire week. So as I entered my second week, I had additional motivation, knowing that I had made it that far. After about three weeks, my wife reminded me, "Do you realize it has been three weeks since you have smoked?" I was very surprised because I was no longer conscious of a desire to smoke, and I was right on schedule with my reading of the Book of Mormon. Then I had the courage to discard all of my smoking supplies, which were still stuffed all over the apartment.

I have never smoked again since that time. It was a wonderful experience because I learned that, when we pray and listen carefully to the promptings of the Spirit, miracles can happen. The things that seem to be too difficult can be accomplished.

After I quit smoking and became a member of the Church, I had several powerful dreams in which I saw myself smoking again, and I remember how, in those dreams, I felt so remorseful and upset with myself that I could not forgive myself. When I awoke and realized that it was only a dream, what a relief it was to know it was not reality and that I could avoid being engulfed in the misery of resuming the habit of smoking.

During the time I was investigating the Church, I was more and more impressed by the truthfulness of the gospel brought to me by

Members of the Dortmund Branch meeting in their schoolhouse gathering place during 1957, while Enzio and Jutta were investigating the Church.

the missionaries. I was impressed by the uniqueness and philosophical depth of the message. However, I always wanted to have some kind of confirmation or feedback from members of my native country, not just encouragement from the missionaries.

I found out later that, in the first phases of my investigation, the missionaries were reluctant to have me go to the branch. It was a very small branch, and most of the members were uneducated in the academic realities of the world and what someone could call unrefined, even though they were somewhat childlike and humble. The missionaries must have been afraid that we would not accept what we found there and that we might never go back. In my insistence to meet a German member, they finally suggested that I meet a member who lived in Darmstadt, which was at least four hours by train from my hometown. One day, I got in touch with this member, and we met in the town of Cologne, about halfway between Darmstadt and Dortmund. In a hotel lobby, I met a real German member for the first time. To my astonishment, I learned that he was a science student enrolled at the University of Darmstadt and seemed to be well educated. At least his mannerisms and vocabulary showed his background of intellectual and academic training. It was somewhat important to me since I did not want to be directed simply by my spiritual feelings, but felt a strong need to use my intellectual reasoning capacity as well.

Meeting Brother Kissler was a good experience that bolstered my testimony. Yet, even after my meeting with him, there were lingering doubts and many questions. If there were a true message, why would I be the only person really interested? Why should I be the one taking the missionaries' message seriously since hardly anyone else seemed to be doing so? Was my judgment faulty? I had made suggestions to others that they might want to learn the ideas I was studying from the missionaries. But even from religious-minded people, these suggestions had been met with laughter, scorn, and mockery.

These questions were ever present and, one day, in about 1957, the missionaries took me to a German man named Weber. He was an investigator like me, but he had already committed himself to baptism. Several days later, I took him with me to the Ruhr District conference in Herne. Driving home in my car, I voiced my concerns to him and actually talked Mr. Weber out of his commitment to be baptized. He was relieved when he realized that, in me, he had found someone who could help him escape the commitment he had made to the missionaries to be baptized. Later, after I had been baptized myself, I went back to him to share my conviction. Finally, after about three years of dedicated work, he, too, was baptized.

As the missionaries taught me, they were often very frustrated in giving their regular discussions because I immediately sensed when they were providing me with some kind of rote explanation. I would interrupt them and remind them that if they wanted to visit with me, they must honor my rules—they would listen to my questions and answer them. They felt, of course, quite uncomfortable in not knowing what I might want to discuss, and sometimes they just explained concepts in general. I got a little notebook and began to list the many questions I had for which the missionaries had no answers. I was always trying to answer those questions in some way or other. Sometimes the Lord gave me some insight and understanding with a sudden rush of enlightenment that led to a satisfactory explanation for myself. However, there remained thirty or more questions on my list for which I could find no answer.

When the missionaries became more and more aware of their inability to answer my questions, they finally referred me to their mission president, Theodore M. Burton, who later became a General Authority in the Church. I made an appointment with him and went to the mission home in Frankfurt, about a three-and-a-half-hour train ride from my hometown. As I sat alone with him in his office, I was very impressed. He was very disciplined, well-educated, sincere, serious, to the point, and gracious in allowing time for my interview.

I started to ask my questions. He gave answers to each one, but in some way, we did not really have two-way communication. One of his comments made a deep impression on me. He said that the greatest of all blessings was eternal life, without which we would not have fulfilled our purpose. In the restless mood in which I found myself at the time, life for me was a terrible burden—something that was not enjoyable. I surprised him with the remark that I was not looking for eternal life. I was looking for an honorable way to live this life, but I did not want to have it extended into eternity. He looked at me and said, to my surprise, "That is because you have not yet repented." I remember the feelings that I had. I was shocked. I was upset. I was offended. We continued the conversation, but it had lost its value for me.

As I left his office in order to catch my train to go home, I was so upset that I wanted to start smoking again, something I thought I had overcome. I looked for some place to buy cigarettes. Strangely, on that street, Bettina Strasse 55, all the way from the mission home to the main train station, I could not find a store where I could buy cigarettes. Now, that seems inconceivable.

I still had some time before my train left. In order to use that time, I went into a movie, which turned out to be a very good German film about a psychological problem of honesty. I do not remember the title of the film, but it was very popular at the time. As I sat in the show, I had an opportunity to question my own honesty and motivations. Once again the experiences I had in the hospital came vividly to my mind and I calmed down. After the show, I left and caught my train.

During the ride home, I reflected on what President Burton had said. I was still unsettled but was glad that I had not given in to the temptation to smoke again. If I had done so, I would have completely disappointed the missionaries who picked me up from the train station. With great expectations and eyes full of hope and enthusiasm, they quizzed me and asked, "How was it?" It was obvious that they expected that their mission president would have accomplished a miracle with me. I didn't dare tell them what the result was. Now, I can see that this experience was a test of my willingness to take my life in my hands and develop it according to the light of Christ.

As I continued to study the gospel, and even after my two dreams, I was still filled with so much panic and fear concerning the pending change that I tried everything to avoid it. I remember one morning, as I was half asleep, I prayed to Heavenly Father to ask

Him to forgive me for my hesitancy to be baptized. I explained to Him all my concerns and told Him of the challenges I felt I could not master. As I was praying, a little voice whispered, "Yes, I understand that." I was overwhelmed and relieved that He understood me. But then the voice went on, "Yes, I understand. I can see that you are in a difficult situation, but there may be a time when things may not be so well with you as they seem to be now. There may even be a time come when you will be so devastated and challenged in life that you will want to pray to me again." I thought, "Of course, I do not want to give up my right to pray!" Then the voice continued, "If that happens, I can only show you the faces of the missionaries whom you want to send away now, and you would have to start over from the beginning."

I was startled to learn that if I did not make that covenant, I would lose my right and privilege to pray and the ability to communicate with my Heavenly Father that I had already developed. Again, the covenant that I made in the hospital came to my mind, and I was concerned about my lack of trust, commitment, and courage.

That was the final straw. After that experience, I knew I would have to go through with it, and I accepted the challenge of the missionaries to be baptized. But then I said, "I will only be baptized if my wife is with me." My wife had withdrawn most of the time when the missionaries had come. She had not wanted to be in the way when I was discussing what she considered to be my religious hobby. However, after I spoke with her, she accepted the invitation to be taught by the missionaries.

To my great surprise, just three weeks later, she was ready to be baptized. She told me, "That's what I have believed since I was a young girl. There is nothing new to me. I have no questions. I want to be baptized." That was one of the great marvels of my life. One of the missionaries who taught us at that time obviously recognized her goodness. Many years later at a stake conference in Spokane, Washington, a man came up to me full of enthusiasm and confidence and asked, "Brother Busche, do you remember me?" I responded to his question, "No, I'm sorry. I don't remember you." He replied, "Well, I remember you because I was in your home." Then he explained that he had been a missionary when we were investigating the Church and had come one time to teach us.

After he told me that, I could vaguely remember him. He then said that he had made a note in his missionary journal after that visit. He had his journal with him and asked me whether I would like to read what he had written. I said, "I would love to read that." So I read the journal entry he had made those many years earlier which said, "Today we were visiting the Busche family. She is great. He will never make it."

My wife is a very wonderful, spiritual woman, and through her, I have come to understand that women have much easier access to spiritual things and the matters of eternity. I have known my wife since we were children and remember the first time I met her. Our parents had grown up together, and when I was about seven years old, her family moved into the area where we lived, about ten or fifteen minutes walking distance from our home. One day just after Christmas, Jutta, who was barely old enough to walk, and her mother came to visit us.

I had received some wooden blocks for Christmas and had constructed quite a good-sized cathedral in the parlor. My father had helped me, and we had spent a lot of time on it and wanted to preserve it for a while, so the door to the parlor was locked. But since we had company, my mother unlocked the door to entertain them in our best room. When Jutta, who could hardly walk down the one step, came into the room, she went straight to the cathedral and knocked it down, scattering the pieces all over the room. My mother

Jutta, Enzio's wife, at age 13.

was upset and exclaimed, "Oh, my goodness! What in the world will the boy say?"

I was standing behind them and saw what happened, but I remember I was not upset. I thought there was something special about that little girl who would later become my wife. I simply said, "That's fine," because she radiated such a charming authority—the kind that every good man will always admire in a true female. I had no bad feelings at all. I was blessed when she accepted my proposal seventeen years later and am still blessed as she continues to inspire my admiration and respect for her goodness on a daily basis.

When the date of our baptism came, Bob Thompson came to our home. He was the missionary who was going to baptize us, and he was also the branch president at the time. He said something very unusual. He said, "Brother Busche, you are going to be baptized tomorrow. I want you to think about something today. Suppose that

Jutta and Enzio on their wedding day, August 8, 1955.

in a year or two, I came back to tell you that everything I taught you was not true, that I was brainwashed into believing that it was true and I no longer believed it. What would your reaction be?" I was shocked and said, "Are you telling me that you really don't believe what you have taught?" He said, "No, I believe what we have taught you, but I want you to understand that you must not build your testimony on what I have said or upon the words of any other person. You must have a testimony for yourself."

He then asked me how strong my testimony of the Prophet Joseph Smith was. Because I had heard so many anti-Mormon stories, I was not very enthusiastic about all the things that had happened—or I was told had happened—in the life of Joseph Smith. Still, I accepted Joseph Smith along with the beautiful gospel, because he, after all, was the originator of the Church. Before he left, the missionary said to me: "When you go to bed tonight, please ask Heavenly Father about Joseph Smith. Then we'll meet you tomorrow at the baptism."

I did that. I knelt down and asked Heavenly Father about Joseph Smith. I explained that I needed a testimony that was independent of others. Bob Thompson would leave one day. I would probably never see him again, and I would have to stand on my own. As I prayed, a vision opened in my mind where I saw the whole Church disappearing, including all the missionaries. I saw myself completely alone, standing much like Joseph Smith must have stood in the beginning. The whole dimension of the work was unfolded to my mind. I stood and bore witness of the truthfulness of it and of the Prophet Joseph Smith. The vision overwhelmed me to the core of my being, and I was completely overjoyed and satisfied.

My testimony came neither from my brain nor from my own achievements or capabilities, but from a higher source that was so powerful and strong that ever since that time I have continued to grow in my testimony of the Prophet and the Book of Mormon. Today the Book of Mormon is, in some dimension, a much stronger element of my own testimony than the Bible, and the Prophet Joseph Smith holds for me, in some ways, a stronger place than any other prophet. He is the one through whom a dimension of understanding about human life was established, one that is absolutely refreshing and full of hope, especially when we take into account his lack of formal education, his having no mentor, and having no one to help him. The legacy he left had to come only from God. In it, we can find all answers to all challenges mankind is confronted with.

Finally, through the workings of the Spirit, I felt the need to be baptized. Yet the dimensions of the gospel and the realization of my own smallness and lack of spiritual education daunted me. I agreed to be baptized, but only on two conditions: I made the missionaries promise that I would never be called to any position and that I would never have to give a talk. Given what has happened in my life since then, those two conditions seem strange, but I was sincere in my request. I did not want to escape the covenant. I wanted to attend and participate, pay my tithing, and keep the commandments, but I did not feel that I would ever be able to contribute to the work.

I have since learned that Heavenly Father has His own ways to educate us and lead us toward growth. Everything we do has to come step by step, but it does not come without sacrifice. We may feel serving is a sacrifice. However, when we really submit ourselves to the will of God, we learn that, in serving Him, He immediately turns our sacrifices into blessings. When we are on a spiritual plateau, it is necessary for us to understand that we cannot go beyond that plateau until we increase our level of sacrifice and our ability to move one step further. Such was the case with me when I finally gave my first talk, which led to a new level of spirituality and understanding, accompanied by a greater level of faith.

Sister Busche and I were baptized on 19 January 1958 in a public swimming pool by Elder Thompson. The district leader, Elder Rudy Zander, who confirmed us as members of the Church, was a delightful person, originally from New York, whose father came from East Prussia. The elders, like most missionaries, possessed a sense of humor and the ability to make others feel at ease.

Three weeks after my baptism, Elder Zander asked me whether I would like to talk in church. I was shocked and immediately responded, "Brother Zander, I was baptized on the condition that I would never be required to speak, and I expect that condition to be honored," and added, "Or don't we normally recognize promises in the Church?"

He answered, "Oh, yes, we recognize promises. However, this is not a call but a question." I relaxed because I could see the difference between a call from one of the Lord's anointed, which I would have no choice but to obey, and a question to which I could still answer no. Before I was able to say anything more, Elder Zander suggested in all sincerity, "Brother Busche, before you answer, why don't you go in the next room and kneel down and ask Heavenly Father. Then come back and give me your answer."

I felt that was fair and followed Elder Zander's suggestion. I went into the next room, knelt down, and started talking to Heavenly Father this way: "Heavenly Father, hast Thou heard what Rudy Zander has said? I have learned to trust in Thee and speak with Thee as a child speaks to his own father." I explained my fear and my situation—I could not speak. I did not have the capability to address anyone in these matters. For a while, I felt comfortable and validated in my decision, but, as I continued to pray, it was as if a small voice penetrated my heart saying, "Surely, you can." I said, "No, I cannot." Then the voice reassured me, "Surely, you can." "Me?" "Yes, you." Again, I said, "No, I cannot." However, I felt uneasy because I appeared to be arguing with the Lord, and I didn't want to do that.

Finally, I was able to admit, "Yes, I will do it, but under one condition." I felt that I couldn't do it without His being with me. So I agreed, "I will do it if Thou wilt be with me. I will go wherever Thou wants me to go." I went back to the missionary and told him that I would be willing. At the same time I said that, it seemed as if another part of me said, "What are you saying? Now you will have to do it! Now you have made a promise!" I felt a terrible fear come over me. *How could I ever do this? How could I, who never before had given a talk about religious matters, who was still wrestling with all the terminology and was naturally shy about standing in front of audiences, ever do this?*

I started immediately to prepare my talk. I wanted at least to set up the concepts and ideas in outline form even though I probably would not give it verbatim. I had finished my talk on Monday, but on Tuesday, I felt it was not good enough. Finally, by the weekend, I had prepared six different talks. They were all on paper, and I was nervous and undecided about which subject I should speak on or even how to begin.

The missionaries were very kind and contacted us two or three times during that week. When they saw how nervous I was, they suggested that I give my first talk in the other branch over which they presided. On Sunday morning, they held services in Dortmund, and in the afternoon, they presided at an even smaller branch in Soest, about thirty miles east of Dortmund. They suggested this so that, in the event of failure, I would not feel embarrassed before my own branch.

The feelings that I had as we traveled to Soest will always be with me. It seemed that some power wanted to hold me back. I was filled with so much fear, self-doubt, and misgiving about agreeing to speak, that I found myself wishing a flood might wash away the bridge we needed to cross to reach Soest. But we did arrive and entered the small schoolroom where the sacrament meeting was to be held. I saw a congregation numbering only seven, including the two missionaries and myself.

Elder Zander conducted the meeting. I realize now that we only participated in sacrament meeting. We had the opening song, the opening prayer, the sacrament hymn, and the passing of the sacrament. Then Elder Zander announced that I would be the speaker. At the very moment I stood on my feet, I was overcome with feelings of indescribable joy, joy that penetrated my entire being with light and confidence.

All nervousness was gone. I had three talks in my right pocket and three in my left pocket, but I forgot them. I began to speak, but in a strange way I, too, was listening to the words I was saying.

Sometimes I was awed by the beautiful thoughts, depth, and insight that I heard coming from my own mouth. I wished I could interrupt my talk to make some notes because I really wanted to remember what I was saying. As I went on with my talk, I must have forgotten time and everything else around me. When I finally closed in the name of the Lord Jesus Christ, I sat down with a great feeling of joy and deep satisfaction.

I pondered the feelings I had had when, as a young man, I was desperately looking for joy and had discovered how difficult it seemed to be to find. I realized I had achieved the joy I sought through the influence of the Holy Spirit and by submitting my will to the Lord's and actually doing His will. I felt buoyed up by the confirmation that I was finally helping to build His kingdom. After my talk, Brother Zander announced the closing song and the closing prayer. I was surprised and whispered, "Don't we normally have two or three speakers in a sacrament meeting?" He looked at me and replied, "Yes, but you spoke one and one-half hours!"

So I learned a lesson. I learned that we cannot ask Heavenly Father for something through His Spirit without His fulfilling the request. I can testify that His Spirit was with me as I had requested. I felt quiet and peaceful so that I was able to give my talk, but I also felt humbled because I knew it did not come from me. I did not present the ideas that I had scribbled down. They came directly from Him. I made a commitment that from that time on I would not question anything that came from Him or from His servants because I really did want to build His kingdom. I did not want to make excuses. I resolved never to question the sacredness of the covenant I had made with Him. I knew this would eventually lead to brighter light, greater capabilities, and a fulfillment of the purpose of life.

7

EARLY MEMBERSHIP

AFTER MY BAPTISM, WHEN MY COMMITMENT was fresh and I was washed clean, the Holy Ghost helped me to understand the importance of self-honesty in understanding truth. My experiences during this period of my membership were of such magnitude, power, and beauty that it is difficult to describe. Some who have grown up in the Church have probably never had the opportunity to see or feel the new dimension of life that suddenly comes to a person in the moment of conversion.

I was learning everything new. When envisioned through the gospel, I began to see every principle, every historical picture, every aspect of science—even smaller matters like management and business—in a different light. After my baptism, I remember driving and wondering for a moment if I should have a radio in my car. I had absolutely no desire for a radio because the spiritual world inside of me had come into a state of full bloom. I felt so much inspiration and such a new dimension of life that a radio seemed like a nuisance and distraction. I could suddenly not imagine why anyone would want a radio in his car when he had the spiritual world from which to learn about every facet of life.

We had no television. We gave up all of our time-wasting habits, such as playing cards or going to restaurants. We derived joy from simple things, such as going for walks along the city streets or stopping for an ice cream cone.

As for music, I concentrated on listening to classical music. Records were quite expensive and could break. However, when cassette tapes began to replace records, it was easier to surround myself with classical music, which had a tremendous impact on my spiritual education. I am absolutely convinced that the composers of the classical period were inspired as they employed their talents in creating music to help us establish our spiritual foundation.

I am so grateful that the Holy Ghost helped me to grow and understand. I believe one of the greatest challenges for members of the Church is to ensure that our lives are not led by routine. When we are governed by routine, we tend to become insensitive to the need to walk with the companionship of the Holy Ghost. When we are blessed with the companionship of the Holy Ghost, we are protected in dangerous situations, and we become capable of making right decisions and overcoming all fear.

All of our teaching and preaching must be geared toward creating an atmosphere in which the Holy Ghost can bear witness, be with us, guide us, and protect us. If the Holy Ghost is not present in our teaching, no one is edified, even though everything that is said is technically right and in harmony with the letter of the truth. Unless there is a willingness to extend ourselves and our faith, the Holy Ghost cannot be effective in our lives.

Following my baptism, as I was accepted as a member of the Dortmund branch, I found myself surrounded by a diversity of members, some of whom were from very humble circumstances and, to some degree, unrefined. Nearly all the manners, even table manners, that I had been taught to observe from my youth, were lacking among my new brothers and sisters. Many of the younger people had immigrated to the United States after the war. Most of the members were refugees from the East and spoke a dialect that seemed rather foreign to me.

I remember one incident in particular with one of the members as I came into the meeting place soon after my baptism. When I walked into the room, this man looked me over from head to toe then came face to face with me. He took my tie with one finger and predicted casually, "I'll give you four weeks." It was as if he were measuring me by his past experiences and didn't believe I would make it. I realize now that I could have been offended, but, instead of being irritated, the Holy Ghost blessed me with a powerful feeling of calm, satisfaction, and gratitude, and I was not offended at all. I smiled at him and even surprised myself with my answer. I heard myself saying, "Brother, I am so glad that men such as you will be there to help me and prevent such a thing from happening."

This man had gone through many experiences. He was able to bear a powerful testimony. But he was very insecure and was constantly striving to attain recognition in the Church. In many Sunday School classes he had verbal battles with others in an attempt to prove this or that point. In an unpolished and impolite way, he easily degraded others who did not share his viewpoint. Nothing could be done to change this man. We could only give him more love than he earned and try not to be offended by his uncouth behavior.

This man later moved from our hometown. I hadn't seen him for some time when, much later while serving as a Regional Representative, I came across him and greeted him with a warm heart. For the first time, I saw him overcome with strong, but humble, emotions.

He hugged me, squeezed my hands, and said, "I thank you. I love you."

It has become easy for me to recognize that the people who have earned love the least need it the most. And that is, in my humble understanding, what the gospel is really about. Sooner or later, we will overcome our shortcomings if, through the love of Christ, we see in one another only the good, even when there are sometimes only small attempts to put that good into action. The gospel of Jesus Christ is in the process of healing the world; members of the Lord's Church, with the help of the Holy Ghost, can learn to see the goodness and wholesomeness within each of our Heavenly Father's children. Under the influence of the Holy Ghost, each member can treat his or her fellow citizens as if they had already achieved the potential that is shining through them, even if it seems very dim at the time.

As far as I knew, there was no new chapel building in Germany at the time of my baptism. There had been a branch building in Dortmund before the war, but the facilities had been completely destroyed. Were I to point out the places where we as Saints met for our meetings, some individuals would probably be surprised and wonder why we did not mind going there. Had our parents known, they would have wondered if I had been brainwashed to go there with my wife and our firstborn child every Sunday morning and afternoon. However, the Holy Ghost gave me the understanding that buildings and surroundings are not important. As I contemplated the birth of the Lord in a humble manger, I realized that, while the world's wealthy and successful have their own surroundings, the Lord's work would go forth from humble places to serve the cause of salvation. Only the spirit of the work was important.

Enzio (back row, second from right) with members of the Bielefeld District at a district conference in the early years of his membership.

Years later, when I saw the first chapels being built in Germany, I was amazed and humbled.

The members who were active in the Church had to carry several assignments at the same time. One of my early assignments, in addition to other callings, was to be a youth leader. We developed some mid-week classes for the young people, and I was called to be their teacher. The programs that were outlined by the Church seemed very complicated, and we were not able to understand them. Also, we had much smaller numbers, so we were not able to fully implement the programs. We always felt guilty because we were not fulfilling the programs as outlined in the handbooks. It made it necessary for us to rely on the Spirit and ask the Spirit to guide us in what we were doing. Because of that, our meetings and activities were always focused on the Living God's willingness to assist us in the daily struggles of our lives. Many of the mostly inactive youth became reactivated and began to make great sacrifices to attend our spiritual meetings. Soon the missionaries were bringing young people to the classes to hear the gospel.

As I mentioned, most of the youth were originally inactive. They did not have a good understanding of the teachings of the gospel because they also came from families who were less active or not members. Nearly all were completely unspoiled by material things, coming from backgrounds of humble circumstances. Even those who were somewhat active members seemed to have no initial desire to rise to a higher spiritual level. They enjoyed the same jokes and pursued the same interests in life as any non-believer. Of course, as every child of God does, they hungered to be edified by the Spirit. We wanted to help these young people come to an awareness of the existence of the Living God and of His love for each one of them.

I felt we could make an impact on the youth if we had them all together for some kind of activity. A simple get-together, however, was not enough. It had to be an activity that led to a growing awareness of the spiritual power that the Lord wants to endow us with when we learn to focus our lives on Him. We made arrangements for a day's outing in the countryside by a lake called Möhnesee. We were successful in motivating nearly all of the less-active individuals. We finally brought together a group of fourteen young people. We arranged for transportation by car to the lake, where we pitched a large tent.

We had very poor circumstances. It was a holiday and many people were on the road. We could hardly find a place to be together for our games. However, we had prepared carefully before we went on the trip, and, in everything we did, there was a special sparkle and spirit. At the start of the activities, it was difficult because the youth wanted to run around as they had always done, but we were successful in developing their awareness of how much more beautiful life can be when we become considerate of the feelings and needs of our fellowmen. For one day we tested how it feels to be unconcerned about our own well-being and instead concerned ourselves with making sure that all the others in the group received something good from the day.

We started by coming together in a meeting and talking about how God loves all of us and how much He wants all of us to find joy and success in life. We established that the key for that success would be always trying to find the good and positive in our fellowmen and to overlook weaknesses and shortcomings. This became our goal in all the day's activities.

We held activities such as ball games, academic and skills competitions, a hike, food preparation, and cleanup. The ice broke in the hearts of many and, finally, we were united as a group, imbued with the Spirit of the love of Christ, basking in the gospel, praising one another, praising the Lord, and rejoicing in the beautiful plan of the restoration of the Church. The activity culminated with a meeting in the evening where points were given for positive participation. The young people rated each other's behavior and example. The winners of the group (and later several others) were sent to the mission-wide youth conference for free, which became a high point for the conversion process of many of the inactive youth of our branch.

One of those youth, Wolfgang, later became quite a powerful, influential man in the Church. He had a delightful personality, as did his younger brother. The two boys set a goal at our activity to reactivate their father and were successful in achieving that. Wolfgang became a leader of the youth group with his enthusiasm and unpolished faithfulness. He was eager to learn and soon understood the love that Heavenly Father has for all of us. He was able to use his new understanding to completely turn around his life. He later

A group of German youth at a two-mission conference in Hessen in 1961. Brother Busche is in the middle, far left.

served two consecutive full-time missions, one a proselytizing mission and the other a mission to build chapels. After he established his professional life and began his family, he became a bishop, a stake president and, finally, a Regional Representative. We never know what can happen when someone begins to become aware of the love of God planted in his heart.

Wolfgang showed to many what someone can make out of himself—independent from a lack of a formal education—when he finds the Living God. He had completed only a few years of school. He had a difficult time accomplishing even elementary writing tasks, but he possessed a keen desire to learn. He kept a dictionary in his pocket. Whenever he did not understand a word, he would find it in the dictionary and learn its meaning and spelling. His desire to learn became contagious for many others in the group. It had not been many years since the end of World War II, and many of our young people did not have a regular school education. Wolfgang struggled to read the scriptures. In class it was painful for him to take a turn reading aloud. This did not deter him from developing spiritually, however.

Once in our Mutual class, Wolfgang reported an experience he had communicating with Heavenly Father. He told how he was working as an unskilled laborer in a foundry where hot iron was put into molds after it had been melted in huge ovens. He was working in a very hard environment among all kinds of rough and tumble people and felt most unfulfilled in his job. He suffered especially because of his young age. He was only seventeen, and he was the special target of a tall, husky co-worker who teased him whenever he could. This man would deliberately take Wolfgang's tools, then, when confronted by Wolfgang, would gruffly defend himself saying, "Are you calling me a thief?" The man would regularly shove him around and even beat him up.

One day when Wolfgang was again humiliated by that man's behavior, he remembered that he had learned that God is alive and cares to help us when we ask Him in faith. He realized he could ask God to fight his battles with him. When a hammer Wolfgang had just purchased turned up missing and the man claimed it was his, Wolfgang went into the restroom and knelt in prayer to Heavenly Father. He explained with emotions of a soul in despair, "I have this miserable situation, and I don't know how to deal with it. What should I do?"

Wolfgang told our Mutual class how he suddenly felt a great peace come into his soul. Calmly, he went back to the man and apologized to him, saying, "I have accused you of things for which I am sorry. I do not want to accuse you. I have so many reasons to be grateful that I am permitted to work with you. You are a good man, and I look up to you as an example because I need to have an example in my life." Wolfgang said this sincerely because he was also aware of the goodness hidden in that man.

The man broke down in tears and said, "I am not a good man. I am not a good example." The man then admitted to taking Wolfgang's tools and returned them all to him, saying, "I am not worthy to be an example to you but, from now on, I will try." That was the beginning of a solid friendship. I still remember the overwhelming happiness Wolfgang radiated as he described that first experience with the power of prayer and the Lord's ability to help us deal with difficult circumstances, even turning around seemingly hopeless situations.

Following this eye-opening experience, Wolfgang established and followed a principle in his life that became the basis for his success. With the help of Heavenly Father, he would volunteer to do the uncomfortable things in his surroundings. He tackled any task that was uncomfortable or unpleasant for most people. He would invite Heavenly Father to be with him so that he could accomplish the task. Buoyed up by his faith in Heavenly Father, he was able to always maintain a positive attitude and develop capabilities to overcome the challenges of life. He became not only a very successful missionary but later, in his vocation as a salesman, he was always volunteering to do the unpleasant jobs that nobody wanted to do. He finally became the official troubleshooter for his company.

The experiences I had with the youth and their spiritual growth are highlights of the early days of my membership because I was able to see how the Spirit works with all of us as we learn to become honest in our communications with our Heavenly Father. Although I was a new member and did not know much about what I should do, the Holy Ghost guided me and helped me do what was best in every situation. The Holy Ghost has the power to help every person who will ask sincerely and in faith to do things that normally he or she would not be able to do.

As members of the Church, we cannot be satisfied when we simply fulfill our roles according to the letter. We must have as our objective the desire to live by the Spirit, to be guided by the Spirit, to act by the Spirit, to teach by the Spirit, and to decide by the Spirit. Then we cannot fail.

Those first experiences with youth activities helped me a few years later when I was a counselor to Mission President Stephen C. Richards. I was still so new in the Church and in that environment that I was not always sure of what I had to do. I more or less depended on someone else to tell me how I could fulfill my responsibilities. I had just been called when I learned of a conference where the youth of two missions would come together at Edersee Lake in Hessen. When I was called to be a counselor, the conference had already been scheduled, and all the preparations had been made.

I suggested to my wife that we go with our baby and spend the week with the youth at Edersee. When we arrived, we found that the youth hostel had been completely overbooked for our conference. It had 120 beds, but more than 160 people had arrived for the conference. Since we had a car, my wife and I felt that we should drive to another place to stay.

As I was making my way to my car to leave, the mission president saw me and called, "Brother Busche, come over here!" I did as he asked. He pointed out that the organizing committee for the conference was weak, the leaders were inexperienced, and many problems had developed because of the situation. He then smiled, put his arm around me and said, "Brother Busche, with the authority that I carry, I set you in charge of this youth conference." I was flabbergasted. I had seen the young people grumbling about what was happening, saying that nothing was planned and there wasn't anything worthwhile going on. Here I was, completely unprepared, just hoping to have a week of recreation with my family.

The temptation to drive away and forget about the whole thing was very strong. However, the Spirit prodded me, and I was, of course, firm in the commitments I had made with the Living God. I immediately excused myself so that I could find a quiet spot in the forest to speak with Heavenly Father. As soon as I was alone, I knelt in the forest and poured out my soul. As I was still on my knees, the Holy Ghost opened my mind to an understanding of how to organize the conference, what needed be done, and what should be gained from it.

I was astounded. I saw the whole conference laid out in front of me with all the details—every little thing! It was flowing at such speed—a rush of scenes, really—that I regretted I could not record it so that I would not forget any of the details. I did not even say "Amen" at the end of my prayer. I just stood up and ran back. I was so excited and told the mission president I was ready to go. He then told me that he had to leave and that he would be back at the end of the week in time for the testimony meeting together. That was another shock because I had thought that at least he would be there. I was suddenly the sole person in charge of 160 people for a week!

The youth hostel was located right on a beautiful lake in a serene environment, but youth hostels, which are customary in Germany, are without any luxuries. Guests must do their own cooking, wash their own dishes, furnish their own bedding, and organize themselves during their stay. I knew we had to establish an organization or we could not function there.

I took one person who was part of the original committee and made him my counselor. After the youth were all settled for the evening, the two of us came together to develop some vision. Before we could set up a program for the youth, we had to establish a leadership organization. I remembered the scripture found in Luke 14:33 where the Lord says, "Whosoever he be of you that forsaketh not all that he hath, he cannot be my disciple." I did not know these people, and I did not know if all of them were even members. I met individually with several of the people from the group who looked a little more mature, and I read this scripture to them. I asked for a response from that person: "Are you a disciple of Christ?" To my great surprise, about ten people were willing to serve and committed to be disciples of Christ by forsaking all of their personal plans to become humble servants for the week.

We spent the night together brainstorming and discussing the ideas the Spirit had placed in my heart, keeping in mind that the purpose of each activity must be higher than just an activity. The purpose must be to build a testimony, to build enthusiasm for the kingdom of God and the principles of honesty, cleanliness, purity, and the love of Christ, and to learn to see the beautiful, mostly hidden, qualities of each individual participant. Our aim as leaders was to help each participant to appreciate the gifts of the Spirit and to work with the youth as though their conversion would be the key to our own salvation. We felt that in order to complete our assignment with honor, we needed to become the instrument used to convert everyone.

The next morning, we called the group together and announced the plans we had. We explained the organization, the program, and all the details. We had left nothing to chance. There were rotating groups responsible for the cooking, another for the cleanup, and so forth. We needed to instill within each young person a desire to be part of the team.

It went over pretty well, except for one young man. He was sitting on the last row with his arms folded across his chest and a bored look on his face. He was a very good-looking, athletic young man with all the attributes of masculinity, courage, and charisma that make a young man physically attractive. All of the girls had their eyes on him and tried to get his attention. While I was explaining our plans, those in the group surrounding him were just not listening. I felt quite helpless against such competition. I knew just sending him out could not solve the problem. In my frustration, and while still speaking, I turned my mind to Heavenly Father and said, "Heavenly Father, Thou hast a problem here. It is not my problem. I have no relationship with this young man. I have no influence on him. He is one of Thy children, and I need help. I cannot do it alone."

When the meeting was concluded, I learned a little more about this young man. He was a member, although not very active. He was a very capable athlete and a champion swimmer in the state of Hessen. Since we were at the lake, we felt if we could give him an opportunity to excel more fully in swimming events and let him show how good he was, he might have a desire to participate.

We made plans for a swimming event that would take up an entire afternoon, with competition among the various groups. The weather was very favorable, with calm water and a comfortable temperature. However, no matter how enthusiastic we were about the swimming events, this young man refused to be interested. Nothing could faze his boredom.

Finally, I called him by name and said, "Are you with us? We want you to show us what real swimming is!" He did not change his superior stance but said, "I don't even have to take off my pants and I can still beat every one of you!" Everyone in the group was watching him. Some of the girls whispered, "Isn't he wonderful?" Nothing could have dampened enthusiasm for our program more.

Before I knew it, I heard myself saying, "Okay—and I'm going to beat you tomorrow!" At the moment I said that, I wished with all my heart that I hadn't. I said to myself, "Are you crazy? How in the world could you have said that? You don't have a chance!" I was shocked but knew that everyone had heard me. The idea met with their liking. They immediately started to bet on which of us would win. I could see that the believing ones were betting on me. Here I was, over thirty years old and, though I considered myself a good swimmer, I had no experience in swimming competitions and had never trained for speed swimming. This young man was in top shape, the recently crowned swimming champion of Hessen! I could not withdraw my challenge. After everyone had retired for the evening, I was in the lake practicing and speaking to Heavenly Father, saying, "It was not me who said that. I have no power to beat this young man unless Thou art with me."

The next morning, the young people's enthusiasm for the contest was even greater. It was decided that we should start at a certain tree on the shoreline, jump in the lake, swim a distance of about 100 meters, swim around a rowboat that was anchored in the lake, and then swim back. It would be quite a long-distance swimming feat.

I really do not know what happened to me. I jumped into the lake and rushed through the water like I had never done before. I was the first one back to the tree. At this time, the young man made a mistake. He complained that I had cheated by dunking him behind the rowboat. He lost his credibility at that point because it was not my style to dunk a seventeen-year-old behind a rowboat. To my surprise, however, I heard myself saying, "Ok. I'll beat you again."

Again, I was completely dumbfounded. I was exhausted and could hardly stand, but we did it again. This time the Lord helped me in a special way. The young man was so furious that he had been unable to beat me that he tried to swim under water a long distance. He was quite far ahead of me when he surfaced, but he was not aware of the effect of the waves in the lake. He surfaced as he would have in a pool, but as he gulped for air, a wave washed over his face,

Brother Busche reaches the shores of Edersee Lake, after beating his young friend in a swimming competition. His friend is making the waves at the far right edge of this photograph. His wife, Jutta, is at the left, acting as a referee. After the swimming competition, a new spirit came into the participants and the conference became a real success.

and he breathed water into his lungs. He began to cough and could not continue. The rescue swimmers had to come to his aid, and I had no difficulty getting back and winning the race.

This mishap gave me an opportunity to become friends with this young man. When he was humbled, he became willing to be part of the conference. In fact, for the remainder of the conference, he became a positive influence and served as a leader in the conference.

The objective we had set for the conference was that it would be the best youth conference ever held on German soil, and that everyone who participated would leave with the determination to serve a mission and marry in the temple. That objective was achieved. Many years later when I was already serving at Church headquarters, I had a visit from two of the participants of that conference who told me that they had tried to keep track of all of the participants. As far as they were aware, all, with one exception (the champion swimmer) had later served missions or married in the temple.

When we were finally able to get everyone to participate in the conference, it turned out to be a beautiful experience where we reached new spiritual heights and learned from one another to be honest with ourselves and to testify of the workings of the Spirit in our lives. We hardly took the time to eat we were so busy sharing our awakening to the realities of the Living God and our growing love for Him, the gospel, and our new vision of the beauty of His kingdom. This was an experience of overwhelming importance to me. Once again, I had seen that this work is much more powerful than I could imagine. As we place ourselves in the hands of the Lord, He can lead us to master even the most difficult challenges and turn them into success.

Many years later, additional joyous information added to my memory of that early experience. Our German youth conference had been a two-mission conference, and since the young man whom I raced against was from the other mission, I had never seen him again. I later heard rumors that he had immigrated to Canada, but I feared that he had become less active. During a tour of the Quebec Montreal Mission in 1992, the missionaries were introducing themselves as part of their stewardship reports, with which I normally used to start missionary conferences. I became excited when one young man had the same name as the champion swimmer. I asked him where he was from. He told me, "Edmonton, Alberta, Canada." I quizzed him about his family, and he said his father had immigrated to Canada from Germany. His father was the young swimming champion of that event that was now more than thirty years past! He told me his father was a bishop. I simply told that missionary, "I know your father and I am proud that I know him. He is a great man." I cannot describe the feelings of gratitude I had for being permitted to learn what became of that wonderful young man, whose spiritual awakening was still so vivid in my memory.

8

The Chapel Miracle

When I first became a member, our branch met in a very humble room in an old school. Later, we secured some rooms on the fifth floor of an office building above a men's clothing store on Westenhellweg, next to the Petri Church in Dortmund. However, it was our dream to have our own chapel where we could ensure the dignity of our little branch. We began earnestly seeking to build, even against all odds.

It seemed impossible to find land. Land that was not owned by large companies, government organizations, or the two major churches in the area was very scarce. Even if we could find land, securing permission to build a chapel for an organization that was associated with "a dubious American sect" seemed to be impossible. For a period of several years, our attempts were futile.

In our printing company, we used the services of a famous architect. Eventually, I approached him about our need to find land, and he agreed to help in our search. If his efforts were successful, he expected to be hired to construct the church building. Being desperate for any kind of help, I agreed to his terms after I received permission from Church headquarters. This man found a piece of land in a good area, although it lacked transportation accessibility. It had more advantages than anything else we had investigated, so it did not take long for the members to become excited about it. President Theodore M. Burton, who was serving at that time as the European mission president, came to see the land and agreed that it would be feasible.

The next step was to secure a building permit. To everyone's disappointment, the building permit was denied because the city's youth department claimed the land was needed for a children's playground. Even when it was obvious that this was not true, I was dumbfounded that even such a well-established architect was unable to obtain the needed permit. I wondered if there would ever be a possibility for success if his influence was not sufficient.

In my desperation, I went to the head of the youth department, intending to take him to see the land and convince him that, because there were not many children in the neighborhood and there was a school nearby with an already-existing playground, there would be no need for an additional playground. That man was emphatic in denying my appeal. I later learned from one of his relatives, who happened to be a member of the Church in Hamburg, that the man had sworn that as long as he was alive, the "Mormons" would not get any permission to build anything in the city of Dortmund, and that his influence would be strong enough to uphold such a commitment.

Then the following happened: President Burton, who was a very sincere, inspired Church leader, to whom I owe many elements of my own conversion and my own understanding of the working of the Lord and His Church, challenged the members of the branch to bring a special sacrifice to the Lord and show how serious we were in our desire to secure a piece of land. He challenged us to do 100 percent home teaching for several consecutive months and promised that the Lord would provide a miracle.

The 100 percent home teaching was very difficult because the branch was spread over an area of more than one hundred villages and towns, most of which were more than an hour's drive away. Many of the members of the branch had never had a testimony, having been baptized simply so they could obtain food from the Church after the war. The number of Church members on our records was large, but the number of participating members was very small. All of the active priesthood, young and old numbering only about twelve, really had to sacrifice time, resources, and effort to achieve 100 percent home teaching. For instance, in one month my companion and I had to visit twenty-eight households. Our achievement of 95 percent home teaching was celebrated all over Germany as a first.

At that time, quite unexpectedly, something else happened. Brother Weber, of whom I spoke earlier, introduced me to a man named Kurt Kauper who came to my home and asked to talk with me. He first asked me if I was a member of The Church of Jesus Christ of Latter-day Saints. I said, "Yes." He then said he wanted to share an experience with me. He explained that during World War II, he had been a prisoner of war in an American prison camp in Florida for quite some time. The captain of the prison camp, who had had a great influence upon him, was a member of the LDS Church. That influence affected him throughout the remainder of his life. He claimed that one thing he had learned during his prison stay from his captain was that anything worthwhile can be obtained only through the sacrifice of being honest, reliable, and caring for others. He attributed everything he accomplished later to the teachings of that LDS prison camp leader.

He told me that recently, during the night in a dream, he had felt compelled to do something to repay that man. He said that even if he were able to identify his benefactor, he knew he would probably be told, "Give nothing to me but give it to my Church." When he had learned from Brother Weber that The Church of Jesus Christ of Latter-day Saints was in existence in Dortmund, he felt prompted to find its leader. Since I was the branch president at the time, he had come to me and asked me what he could do for us.

I said without any hesitation, "We need a building lot so we can erect our chapel." With a smile, he replied, "That's easy. I am the head of the real estate department of the city." My heart nearly stood still. Here was the very man whom I had tried so hard to contact but had been turned away by his office staff and secretaries several times. Now, on his own, he was coming to me. I realized that he was not familiar with the problems we had experienced in obtaining a permit, and I accepted his invitation to visit him the next day.

When I met with him in his office, he unfolded a map of the city of Dortmund. It was a huge scroll-map, secured on each side by a wooden stick. He then asked me, "Where do you want to build?" I could not believe it! I did not want to offend his generosity, so I pointed out some areas that were quite humble, having in mind that in such areas, a building permit might possibly be obtained with his influence. With a big smile, he looked at me, took hold of my finger, and put it right in the center of the map of the city—the area where recreational facilities were established, such as the sports arenas, the university, the botanical and zoological gardens—where it would be virtually impossible to obtain a building permit. He put my finger right there and, still with a smile, said, "Where is your faith?"

I humbly mentioned that this area was the "green belt" and that no permit would ever be given to build a chapel there. Still his smile did not fade. He simply said, "Trust me." I was caught completely

Brother Busche, second from left, at the June 1966 foundation of the Rhine Ruhr District. In six years, two stakes grew out of the district. Pictured with Brother Busche are Ralph Sebald, Wilhelm Nitz, and Rudolph Burckhardt.

by surprise, but he did what he said he would do. He made a choice piece of land available to us that was accessible by mass transportation, in an area where anyone would really like to go on a Sunday.

He fought our fights and established a respect for the restored religion by bearing testimony of what its teachings had done for him. He gave talks before the whole city council, explaining the influence that one man had had upon his life and how, without that man, he would not have been able to achieve what he had in his life. He explained the importance of establishing an organization in the city of Dortmund that cared for other people—an organization that would teach lessons of dignity similar to what he had experienced. Finally, after many difficult moments, Mr. Kauper succeeded, and we received a choice piece of land for a very nominal price with a permit to build a chapel.

Approvals from the city council would not have been granted, even with Mr. Kauper's influence, had it not happened that the head of the youth department suffered a sudden, unexpected heart attack and died. He was, in a way, a prophet, for he had said, "So long as I'm alive, the Mormons will not get their piece of land." It was easy to think that the Lord removed him and opened up a way for us to acquire the property.

This property is, for me and the others who were involved, a monument to the miraculous power of the Lord. It is also a fulfillment of the prophecies of Theodore M. Burton, who told us, "If you will make a sacrifice to the Lord and prove to Him how serious you are, He will perform a miracle and you will receive your land." President Burton was inspired. He had faith without any doubt. How we rejoiced as we finally secured our piece of land!

We built our chapel under the program of the Church that was in effect at that time: we were to erect the building ourselves with the assistance of building missionaries who were serving labor missions rather than proselytizing missions. Before we could start building, we had to raise 20 percent of the total estimated cost. Raising funds was extremely difficult because active members were few in number and all very poor. I, myself, was struggling in a company in a very competitive business. Although I had a small number of shares in the company, I was not the owner and I was living on a nominal salary. We had to come up with ideas to help us generate the required funds.

First of all, we established the awareness of the reality of the Living God. We concentrated on teaching enthusiasm and love in our classes, that we might be united in faith, with expectations of divine guidance for the successful fulfillment of having our own chapel. We were able to unite the whole branch, under the influence of the Holy Ghost, to commit to ten "Golden Rules," as we called them. We would dedicate our lives to the building up of the kingdom. We would forfeit personal vacations and Saturday outings, contributing any money saved toward building the house of the Lord, among other things.

In my business, I was able to arrange work for members to perform at home that was normally done in our automated bindery. All compensation for their work was put into the building fund. We had been struggling for several years without much progress when my company received a huge order that required folders to be placed in envelopes in a certain sequence. That project had to be done before a certain deadline or the customer would not be bound to pay for it. I dared, against the counsel of my production manager, to give this project to our handful of Church members. Payment for completing this project would increase our chapel fund enough to put us over the top. However, it could be done only if every active member would sacrifice literally every free minute for a week to complete the project.

At that time, one member, a former coal miner named Walter Drieschner, was employed in our company. He was given the responsibility of organizing the members into an effective crew of laborers. If the project was not completed to the customer's satisfaction and on time, there would be no money at all, and my company would be fined.

Under Brother Drieschner's leadership, this mammoth project was set up on the fifth floor in our Church meeting rooms. There were literally tons of paper hauled up to the fifth floor for assembly and insertion into the envelopes. All the active members—men, women, children, even missionaries, my family and me included—came together to spend every free moment in order to complete the task within the week's time.

The Dortmund chapel under construction. Work on the building—which was completed entirely by the members—began August 29, 1964. The building was dedicated by Elder Ezra Taft Benson exactly one year later, August 29, 1965.

Delivery had to be made to Busche Printing Company at eight o'clock sharp Saturday morning. On Monday everything went fine, with everyone working enthusiastically. On Tuesday people were tired and began to make excuses. On Wednesday and Thursday, the response was lagging. On Friday, in desperation, about twenty-five members spent the entire day working feverishly. Still, in the evening when I was able to arrive, it was apparent that we were not going to be able to meet the deadline.

However, we tried to keep our enthusiasm high and continued working into the night without any interruption. At about 2:00 A.M., when we took a count, an overwhelming part of the job was still not finished. Some people were so exhausted they fell asleep on the chairs while others of us continued to work. We all felt numb and overwhelmed with panic and frustrated hopes. At about 4:00 A.M. another count was made. By the time daylight arrived, the impossible had been done. It was all finished.

Some members claimed that, in the middle of the night as many slept, holy angels came and worked to complete the project. The ones who were there will never forget that night. I cannot say that angels were there; but neither I nor anyone else can explain what happened. I do know that when we started that Friday evening, only half of the order had been done, and we were not making much progress. Then, between 2:00 and 4:00 in the morning, something happened that we could not explain. So, I just have to leave it as this—that some members still claim that there were holy angels who came in the night. I would not be surprised because we were completely dedicated and willing to give our lives to get the amount of money we needed to build our chapel.

It is not necessary to say that this was also a time when we were very successful in missionary work. We baptized wonderful people on a regular basis every week. We were especially touched that, just before we started our building, we baptized some men whose skills proved to be invaluable. I was still the branch president. I did not, and do not, understand much about building because that is not my background. One of the new converts was a young architect full of enthusiasm and capabilities. Another convert laid tiles by profession and also knew how to lay bricks. These two men became my counselors and employed their professional skills in erecting our chapel in their free time. In addition, we had a young carpenter in the branch who had just finished his education. Another man was a miner who understood carpenter work.

Despite such able workers, I was overwhelmed by the dimension of building a meetinghouse—not just a small building, but one with a chapel, a cultural hall, many classrooms, and a big yard to be landscaped. We were given the assistance of a delightful couple serving a building mission, Brother and Sister Roy and Erma Hill from Provo. We gave them housing in our home while Brother Hill served as the responsible building director. He was a plumber, and although he did not have much of an understanding of other aspects of construction, with his humility, dedication, and industry, he was able to provide the direction, continuity, and leadership so necessary for our success.

The whole city became very nervous when they heard that we were not hiring any company to do the building for us but that we would do it ourselves. Many predicted that we would fail, that it would never work, and that we would never be able to pass the very strict tests to obtain a user's permit.

We came together shortly before the groundbreaking ceremony at which Elder Ezra Taft Benson, who was by then acting as the European mission president, was to preside. We came together and established again our code of honor and our dedication and commitment that we would give our all, sacrificing whatever was needed to erect our church building. We committed ourselves to build a structure that would be of such quality that it would never embarrass us, our neighbors, or Kurt Kauper, who had helped us acquire the land.

When the day of the groundbreaking arrived, Elder Benson gave a wonderful talk. His brother, Waldo Benson, who was the mission president in Düsseldorf, was also there for the groundbreaking. At that time, Elder Benson issued a challenge. In his talk, he said that the building program in Europe was suffering. Most buildings were taking too much time to reach completion, making it almost impossible to finish them. In our own district we had, at that time, two

Work on the Dortmund chapel corresponded with an increase in successful missionary work, including the reactivation of many.

other building projects, one in Düsseldorf and one in Essen, both of which were well into their third year without being finished.

Elder Benson charged me, as the branch president, and all the members of the branch, to complete the building in one year. It was August 29, 1964. He promised us that if we finished the building by August 29, 1965, we would be fulfilling our part in honesty, and he would be back for the dedication. His words deeply penetrated our souls. We saw ourselves dividing up all of the work over the available days and making sacred commitments and covenants.

In that spirit, we started our building, and the Lord was with us. Although we were moving ahead pretty much on time, I personally was the weakest in believing that we could do it in one year. My counselors and the other workers were full of enthusiasm, but I must admit that during this period, I did not have much confidence. At times, I tried to rationalize that it was not necessary to complete the building in one year, but my counselors and other strong members who would counter always rebuked me: "If you don't believe, we'll do it for you." I knew I would have to repent and bolster my enthusiasm.

Many of us came to work on the building site early in the mornings, before starting our own day's work. Of course, after work, we returned again in the evening to do all we could. With that type of schedule, I felt under a great deal of pressure. My father had passed away just a few months earlier, so I had the full responsibility of the business on my shoulders. Our children were young. My church duties, with all the meetings, reports, and finances, could not be neglected. There was no one who could help me with making the various required reports, so I had the full responsibility to do them. Yet, in looking back now, I see that in some strange way, everything fell into place.

We were assigned six young building missionaries, but as it turned out, a few were not supportive workers but rather young men with some unresolved challenges who were probably not qualified for full-time missions. They were not yet used to hard work and mental discipline. We had a tremendous challenge with these young men because they needed to live by missionary rules, and those rules had to be taken seriously. Of course, the majority of the young men were extraordinary and dedicated to giving their lives to the service of the Lord.

The whole building was made of bricks; even the inside rooms had bricks to avoid maintenance costs. Placing the bricks in the high walls was an endless task. I can still see where I laid the bricks. I was placed in an area where I could not do much harm—in the back. In my desire to be perfect, I laid my bricks exactly and accurately, but I was very slow. Now when one looks at the wall where I was working, it is obvious where my work left off. The few bricks I placed are laid in the right order, one after another, but if everyone had worked at my speed, the building would never have been finished.

The brickwork in the building looks great except for one brick. When one is in the chapel looking towards the rostrum, in the left corner about halfway up, close to the top, there is one brick that is definitely out of place. We must not have caught that brick. Whenever I am in the chapel and see that brick, it reminds me of our time working together and, once in awhile, I break down in tears.

The work began to flow with a certain enthusiasm that was remarkable. Even our wives and children came to spend time on the building lot. The Primary had a great many children attending because, when the fathers and mothers were working, the Primary teachers would take care of the children. We sometimes had twenty or thirty children playing around in the sand and with the bricks. Also, to our great surprise, neighboring children came and loved to be on the building lot to build their sandcastles. We had a tremendous spirit of unity as we worked together, sometimes singing hymns as we dug the ditches, poured cement, or built the walls.

There was one element that was intimidating to us: the chimney. The chimney had to be built according to strict regulations; otherwise, the fire marshal would not give his approval. As none of us were experts, we built everything but left the chimney undone, hoping that through some miracle, we could find someone who could do it. Even our experts were nervous about it because no one had ever built a chimney before. It was becoming a major burden. We already had the woodwork for the ceiling done, but there was a hole in the middle where the chimney was to stand. Finally the leaders of the building committee decided to just get the chimney done.

At that time, we had some very good building missionaries, specifically one young man from Berlin. All the missionaries were on the site on Friday, and when I joined them in the evening, we began building the chimney. We did not make much progress, however. We wanted to make sure the chimney was not a stumbling block to our obtaining a user's permit. When we left for home about 10:00 P.M., it began to rain a little, and we were nervous about how we were going to finish the chimney because we had not even completed the foundation. We would come back early the next morning and work on it.

As we came back to the building lot, we were in for a shock. The chimney was done! Two of the building missionaries, under the leadership of the brother from Berlin, without telling us, had committed that they would not go to bed until they finished the chimney. They had told us "goodnight" and had pretended to leave when we were leaving, but they stayed on to work through the night. They had erected a provisionary tent on top of the building, and the two missionaries had continued to build without interruption.

The missionaries had wanted to surprise us because we had been kind to them and helped them in many ways. This was their way of blessing the members of the branch. These missionaries claimed that, in the middle of the night, strangers came to help them. They could not explain it, only that there were men in white suits who came to finish the work when the missionaries were dozing off from fatigue. I cannot confirm it, nor can I deny it, because the miracle was done. As we came back in the morning, the chimney was there, and the brickwork was beautiful. There was no reason to criticize, and the inspecting experts later said it was the finest chimney they had ever seen built. In that way, we were very humbled again and shown that when we do our part and are in tune with the Spirit, help is available and things happen.

One Saturday we were in the final stages of building. We were putting the wooden pieces where the tiles would be placed. There was singing around, and children were taking part in some of the organized play around the building. I was standing on the scaffolding and was surprised to see a nicely dressed little girl whom I did not know standing next to me. She looked to be about eleven years old and was clutching a paper clipped to a board. She asked me, "Would you please support us in our petition?" I asked, "What kind of petition is it?" She looked at me with her big eyes and with a look of concern on her face. "Oh, don't you know? The Protestant minister doesn't like you. He has invited the whole neighborhood to a big protest demonstration to be held next Saturday. They want to turn people against you and come and tear down the walls of your building. But," she said, "don't worry. Before they can come to you, we, the children from Carl von Ossietsky Strasse will stand in front of your building. Before they can come to you, they will have to run over us."

I was shocked! Here was a little girl working to keep a minister from causing us harm. I added my signature to her list. I was truly worried and questioned why any minister would do something like that. How could we protect ourselves from the prejudice, hatred, and animosity of other churches? Yet in my heart, I thought, "Why should we worry? The Lord is already raising these little children for our protection."

We found out that more than 3,000 people had been invited to attend the protest demonstration. The papers carried notices about it. The Protestant church had a huge hall at their building where the meeting would be. I went and talked with our brethren, and we agreed that eight of us would go to the meeting and sit on the first row. We would make ourselves available for comments and would try to be led in our actions by the Holy Ghost. On that Saturday, after we had prepared ourselves through prayer and fasting, the eight of us, dressed in our best clothes, went to the meeting and sat on the first row. We were there in the spirit of prayer.

The meeting started, although the hall was not filled. There must have been about three hundred people there. The minister stood on the stand and spoke for about thirty minutes, telling lies and half-truths about the restored gospel. He then opened up the meeting for questions. Many questions came, especially about our beliefs. The minister then made the statement that we do not believe in the atonement of Christ.

At that moment, I could not remain in my seat any longer. I stood on my feet with my hand raised. The minister said, "There are some of them among us and one would like to say something. Should we let him?" The people were shouting, "Yes! Let him speak!" I then stood and talked about the atonement of Christ, but the people could not hear me, and they shouted, "Louder! Speak up! We can't hear you!" After a while, they said, "Use the microphone so that we can hear what you are saying." So, at the insistence of the crowd, I went up to the microphone to speak after an invitation from the minister.

I spoke under the power of the Spirit about the atonement of Jesus Christ. I was myself amazed at the depth and beauty of the thoughts I was empowered to express. I talked about the need for the Atonement and for the ultimate sacrifice our Lord had made. I also talked about the need for our commitment to give our lives in building not only a structure but in building a society of caring love one for another.

The Holy Ghost came into the congregation. I do not know just how long I spoke—perhaps about twenty minutes—but when I finally finished, I blessed the people and told them of our love for them and that they were our fellow brothers and sisters. After I finished, the minister stood there quite paralyzed. He could not move. As he stood there without taking any initiative to do anything else, I felt it appropriate to dismiss the meeting. We were then surrounded

Members of the Dortmund Branch in front of their newly built chapel in 1965.

by many people who wanted to learn more. We had some thirty people give us their names; several of them were eventually baptized.

I still remember the feeling of having experienced something most unique: the dedication of the little girl, whom I learned was a child of one of the neighbors; the way in which the Lord handled the matter; the protection offered us by many people; and the disappearance of animosity towards us. From that time on, we enjoyed peace as our building was erected, and the Church developed a high reputation in our city.

As the end of our one-year goal came near, I still felt we could not be finished in the given time. I tried to convince the crew that the world would not collapse if we gave it another month. The building committee, led by Brother Kutschke, Brother Maedel, Brother Ostermeyer, Brother Sebald (the later three all having been recent converts), some building missionaries, and Brother Roy Hill, all protested and said, "No! We will finish it in the given time. If you do not believe it, we have faith enough to do it without you." I had no problem repenting very quickly and kept thinking to myself, *My goodness. What has come out of our struggling little branch in just a couple of years?* We could see the kingdom unfolding, fast and unstoppable.

The building was finished and dedicated on August 29, 1965, by Ezra Taft Benson—exactly one year after he had challenged us to do so. As President Benson was already released from his assignment in Europe, we had to call him and remind him of his promise to dedicate the chapel if we had finished it in one year's time. He admitted that he had forgotten all about it, but he changed his schedule and came to fulfill his side of the bargain. The building still houses the Dortmund unit and, after an additional wing was added, it became the headquarters of the Dortmund stake.

9

Raising a Family

We loved to go to Holland when our children were young. The beach there was only about two and a half hours away from our home. Once in a while when we had a day off, we started early in the morning and took the whole family to the seaside on the coast in Holland. Although it was a long day, and there was often traffic, we had the family together, and we enjoyed the water and the atmosphere of the seaside.

One time, we went to the beach in Noordwijk, a town in the northern part of Holland with a beautiful, long stretch of sand at the oceanfront. Our children were quite small: five years old, three years old, and a baby. It was so crowded; there were thousands of people there. We were fortunate to find a couple of square feet to call our own. We were quite engaged in building little protective walls around the small place that was ours for the day.

As we were working, we noticed that our three-year-old son was suddenly gone. We were shocked. How could we possibly find him among all those people? Where should we go? On one side of the beach was a big freeway with four lanes of cars. On the other side was the ocean. Left and right, there was nothing but sand and people. Frantically, we began to search as much as we could without neglecting our other children.

I saw suddenly, as I had never seen before, what the life of one of our children meant. It was everything. The trivial things that upset us earlier were now all meaningless. Everything we worried about was unimportant. The idea that something could have happened to our little boy was absolutely unbearable. I would have given everything, everything in my possession, to secure his well-being. I became desperate because all of the avenues we tried to take in order to find him did not lead to anything.

Finally, after a long time—it seemed to be at least two hours—we suddenly saw him. I saw him in the distance, and he saw me. He was distraught, but, in the very moment our eyes met, I saw a glow of indescribable, satisfying joy in him. Of course, I felt that same joy in my soul as I saw the little fellow. I ran as fast as I could and hugged him, checking to see if he was hurt. I was the happiest man in the world.

I saw then a little glimpse of what it means to be together as a family. I realized the importance of the promise that we will never be separated but will be together no matter what happens, even in death. I do not know all the dimensions of eternal life, but I can easily see that eternal life means nothing if we are separated from our loved ones. Therefore, everything that we learn in the gospel culminates in the understanding that we need to build relationships of trust and communities that go beyond our mortal abilities as we learn to love, to give, to embrace something that is bigger than we are—the kingdom of God.

Through that experience at the beach, I gained a deeper understanding of the scripture in Malachi 4:1, "For, behold, the day

The Busche family in 1963.

cometh, that shall burn as an oven; and all the proud, yea, and all that do wickedly, shall be stubble: and the day that cometh shall burn them up, saith the Lord of hosts, that it shall leave them neither root nor branch." I felt at that time what it would be like to be without my children, the branches, or to lose communication with my parents, the roots. Life is the time for us to prepare to meet God so that we can be together with families in the eternities. If we forget this, we may lose the opportunity to be with our families, and we will be as frantic as I was when I lost my son on the beach that day.

I am astonished by how the Lord has helped my wife and me in our personal family life. With our baptism, my wife lost almost all contact with her family, and my own mother and several of my sisters, in the early days, became somewhat indifferent toward us. These circumstances of isolation made it possible for us to become very close to one another, uniting us in our need to constantly plead with the Lord. There was hardly a day when He did not inspire us to come together in family council. Learning is never easy, and my wife and I went through many personal learning crises. However, our family finally, through the influence of the Spirit of the Lord, became a strong, proven unit, with a oneness that we both, in all humility, have accepted as the greatest gift and blessing from the Lord.

When we became members of the Church, Jutta and I learned to look at life with an entirely different perspective, especially when it came to teaching our children. The education we had received was the traditional, central European authoritarian one. We were always told what to do and were not permitted to have our own opinions. Discipline was enforced by slapping a child's hands or face. I especially received many disciplinary slaps from my mother. Jutta and I had always felt that such forceful disciplinary action against children was not appropriate, but we did not know a better way, having had no experience with a different method.

At that time, there emerged a popular trend toward anti-authoritarian education, where parents tolerated a child's behavior, however unacceptable. Young parents were advised that this anti-authoritarian method, although an extreme contrast, was preferable, having had its origin in America. Jutta and I felt, however, that order had to be established and that we had to fulfill the needs of our family without following traditional authoritarian dictatorship or trendy permissiveness.

Under the influence of the Holy Ghost, we developed a spirit of partnership in our family. We felt it important to develop the individual's awareness of responsibility to himself or herself, other

The Busche family in 1970.

members of the family, and our Heavenly Father. In addition to family home evening, we had regular family council meetings. At the end of the day, we would express our feelings about the events of that day, listen to one another's concerns and complaints, and tell of joyful experiences.

As parents, we wanted to avoid criticizing our children's behavior yet teach them to distinguish right from wrong. We agreed upon a system that allowed them to recognize and evaluate their own wrongdoing. When they did something wrong, we discussed a punishment. We let the children set up the fine for themselves so they would become their own judges. We instigated a point system where points could be earned and tallied at the end of the day. Through this system, we established expectations that the children agreed to among themselves. This method, although time-consuming, laid a strong foundation and helped us feel close as a family.

Under this system where the children judged themselves, we had some remarkable and wonderful experiences. For example, at one of our family council meetings, our oldest child was found guilty of some transgression. In his honest way, he accepted full responsibility. When asked what kind of punishment would be appropriate, he said with determination, "Four weeks with no television." I was quite surprised because four weeks was a long time for a little child. I wanted to make it easier for him and I asked, "How about two weeks?" Again, with determination, he said, "No, four weeks. This time I need to feel it." So it was that he deprived himself of television for four weeks. When others were watching television, he would leave the room and do something else.

One Saturday about three weeks later, our children went to a birthday party at my mother's house. Because it was raining, after the celebration, my mother suggested that the children watch television. Our oldest son declined, explaining why he was depriving himself. My mother said, "You can watch it here. I won't tell your father." He replied, "That isn't what is important to me. I know that my Heavenly Father would be watching me." My mother shared that experience with me. Of course, I was very touched and proud of our son for his commitment to honesty at such a young age.

Each of our children was honest and had many good qualities; however, our oldest son picked up a bad habit of swearing and using foul language in school. Jutta told me about his inappropriate behavior. I was very busy again during this time and not often at home. When I was at home, this boy seemed to be well behaved, so I did not take Jutta's report of his behavior too seriously, much to her dismay.

One day, I was at home sitting at my desk working on a project when this son came home from school. My room was near the entrance, so I overheard him use abusive, degrading words toward his little sister. He had no idea I was home and felt safe being rude. I was completely shocked and filled with rage at his behavior. I jumped up from my chair to go after him. While taking the few steps necessary to reach the door, I silently asked Heavenly Father what I should do in order to handle the situation.

I opened the door and confronted my son face-to-face. As he realized I had overheard him, his expression reflected shock and fear. My natural inclination would have been to grab him by the collar, shout at him, and maybe even spank him. To my great surprise, however, I felt an overwhelming feeling of calmness and joy, and I saw myself behaving in a way completely different from my nature. With a big smile on my face, I reached out my hand toward him and said, "Welcome home, son!" He was startled by my reaction. For a moment, he must have hoped that I had not heard what he said. Then I heard myself saying, "Would you please come with me to the living room because I want to talk to you?"

We went into the living room. I gave him the best chair to sit on and sat next to him. I heard myself praising him, telling him what a wonderful young man he was, and how I recognized the difficult time he was going through in his life, seeing so many bad examples and hearing so many offensive things at school. Then I talked about the battle that every human being must fight—how inside of us is the "real me," the child of God that wants us to do good. There is another force that prompts us to just let go and do things we ordinarily would never do. I explained that this is a battle that is not always easy to win. I expressed my trust in his goodness and my belief that he would be able to overcome the temptation to use foul language and unacceptable expressions. I told him I would be his friend in this battle and would stand beside him to help the good in him triumph.

Our son began to protest, saying, "You always see me as good, but I am bad! I am awful!" He kept accusing himself of all that was bad, but I assured him, "Because of the good within you, you are now accusing yourself." I again explained to him about the two voices that struggle within us. We had the most beautiful talk. I told him how I had wrestled with such things as I was growing up and what a good father I had had to help me. I was then able to explain the atonement of Christ and why we love Christ so much for making it possible for us to be washed clean from our sins if we are faithful to our covenants. We felt a wonderful feeling of peace and joy. We cried and hugged each other, expressing our love.

Through this experience, I became more fully aware of how our Heavenly Father is always there to help us if we will listen. I thought of how disastrous it would have been if I had reacted with anger and inflicted the punishment I had felt he deserved. What a wonderful opportunity would have been lost to develop a feeling of love and closeness and see through behavior the goodness of a child of God.

The system we developed at home was a strong contrast to that used by schools at that time. Students were expected to conform to the group. Teachers seldom treated children as individuals. Schools at that time enforced harsh rules governing the issuance of grades and the enforcement of behavior, and the children were expected to participate with unquestioning compliance. Our children struggled with this system because at home and at church they were learning through love, warmth, patience, and the voice of the Spirit. There were many times during their schooling in Germany that our children were frustrated and suffered because of ridicule and exclusion, which made them, in some aspects, rebellious about school.

When our oldest was about fourteen years old, he attended a private school because it became too difficult for him to concentrate and succeed in the public school system. This private school also had its flaws, particularly a very liberal biology teacher who, following the trend of the time, taught a sex-education class. Our son came to me explaining that he needed permission to attend an X-rated movie that his teacher required his students to see if they wanted to receive a good grade in his class. He asked what he should do.

The Holy Ghost helped me with this situation. I said to my son, "You are old enough to make your own decision. I suggest you go upstairs to your room and speak with Heavenly Father and ask Him what you should do." He immediately responded, "I will not do that. I know exactly what He would say!"

This was a tremendous learning experience because it confirmed that deep down we know what is right and what Heavenly Father would like us to do. If we hesitate to ask Him, we feel we remain innocent. Of course, we are not innocent because the Spirit wants to tell us what is right even before we pray.

The Lord helped me on another occasion when one day our sixteen-year-old son refused to go to church with us. We had just had our family prayer and were at the door ready to go. But he just stood there and said, "I'm not going with you. I want to stay home. I'm old enough to make my own decisions." I did not know what to do. I was completely stunned, and I could not hold back my tears. Finally, I hugged him and told him I loved him and that we would miss him. Then the rest of the family got into the car. We prayed in the car, asking for Heavenly Father to help us in this situation. When we came back from Sunday School, he was standing at the door and said, "Well, it was a boring morning. Next time, I'll go with you again."

Our oldest boy continued to have challenges in school and was especially confused by the contrast between the message of the gospel and the realities of much of the rest of life. Regardless, he seemed to always be happy and have a tremendous sense of humor. He was not very disciplined in his schoolwork but excelled in sports.

The Busche family home in Dortmund between 1959 and 1978.

In Germany, the final school examinations, which are called *abitur,* are very difficult to pass. Since university study is free, these examinations are used to eliminate all but the most industrious and best students. Much hard work and preparation was, at that time, required in order to receive a high score. In some areas of his life, this son was very dutiful, but in other ways he was very unsettled. Whenever we, as parents, expressed our concern about his preparation for his final exam, he brushed our worries aside, saying that he was very good at sports and his aptitude in sports would compensate for his weakness in other areas.

Shortly before the final examination, our stake was playing a soccer game against the stake in Berlin. Our stake president was young and dynamic. Everyone was counting on our oldest son to play for our stake's team. Because of the importance of the final examination, our son felt he could not risk playing in that game. When the stake president learned about that, he talked to him and explained to him how much he was needed. When our son told him about his dilemma, the stake president promised him that if he would play, everything in connection with his exam would be okay. Our boy believed in priesthood leadership, so he had no doubt that everything would be fine.

The stake team won by a score of 2 to 1, but our son broke his foot. He came home very sober and quiet. He did not blame the stake president; he blamed only himself. Now, of course, it was impossible for him to have the leverage that he had counted on. He flunked the exam and came home very bitter and sarcastic. He said, "I am not going back to school. I will go right on my mission." I told him, "Son, you cannot do that. This examination is important. You will have a chance to do it again in six months. Before you can go on a mission, you have to finish school."

For about three days, he rebelled against my ultimatum. While he did not blame the stake president or the Church, he was absolutely unwilling to do anything else. He was upset with himself and angry about school and life in general. After about three days, his attitude suddenly changed. With determination, he declared that he would prepare himself and take the test again in six months. He made a private commitment that he would concentrate on his preparations without wasting any of his time. His concentration would be on his schoolwork, the family, and the gospel. He told us that he had covenanted with God that he would not watch TV, not go to the movies, not listen to popular music, and that he would have no dates. He said he would keep that covenant for six months, until the day of his final school examination. Of course, I was very impressed and told him I thought it was wonderful that he had come to an understanding of the need to sacrifice in order to receive blessings and come to a greater level of spiritual awareness.

With that commitment, he acquired strength as he had never

had before, and he learned to be sincerely focused. At that time, the change of attitude became noticeable to his classmates. One such classmate was Gerd, a sarcastic, foul-mouthed, longhaired, hippie from our neighborhood, who had also flunked the examination. He asked our son what he was going to do after he finished school. Our son told him that he was going on a mission. Gerd asked, "What kind of a mission?" and our son explained in depth about his testimony of the Lord Jesus Christ and the need to find meaning and direction in our lives. Gerd was deeply touched by this sincere testimony. He mumbled, "I think I need to learn something for *my* life."

At that time, we were hosting firesides once or twice a week for missionaries to teach investigators. Gerd had such a bad reputation that Jutta and I previously had not allowed him to come to our house. We did not want his type to be around our teenage daughter. When Gerd asked how he could learn more, our son, although fully aware of our concerns, invited Gerd to come to our next fireside. He asked, "How can I do that? I am not allowed to come to your house!" Without hesitation, our son said, "I will smuggle you in and you can hide behind a chair."

So it happened that the next fireside brought a very interested group of some twelve or thirteen investigators together in our home to be taught the gospel. I had just finished giving my talk when we heard someone sobbing. We saw Gerd sitting behind a chair, sobbing like a little child. After that, Gerd took the lessons from the missionaries and very soon was converted and committed to change his life. There was one obstacle, however. When he had his interview with the bishop prior to his baptism, he admitted that he had been part of an insurance fraud. He had arranged for his motorbike to be stolen by a friend, and they had then shared the insurance money. The bishop, of course, refused to authorize Gerd's baptism until he reimbursed the insurance company.

In order to earn the money he needed to pay his debt, Gerd took an evening job while preparing himself during the day for his exam. Our son and Gerd became very close during this period and both succeeded in passing the exam. Our son then left to go to the England Manchester Mission, and Gerd was able to go on his mission within six months after his baptism. Gerd was called to the Switzerland Zurich Mission. President Walton was his mission president and always spoke very highly of Gerd.

Before Gerd went on his mission, something very interesting happened. A young lady living in the neighborhood of our chapel had to pass it on her way to school. She was preparing for her final examinations at school one year after our son's examination. She was interested in what kind of church met in that building and asked her teacher some questions, but the teacher did not know anything. Her teacher suggested she go herself and visit that church to find out more about their beliefs and report back to the class. One Sunday morning, she stood in the parking lot of our chapel, and there she saw, to her great surprise, a young man whom she knew as being a menace to the girls in the city. He was dressed in a dark suit and white shirt and had neatly cut hair and a big smile. In surprise, she asked, "Gerd, is that you?"

Gerd said, "Yes, it's me."

She asked, "What happened to you?"

He told her about his change to a life of joy with Christ. She was deeply impressed. Our daughter and others welcomed her warmly as she entered the chapel. Three months later, this young woman was baptized a member of The Church of Jesus Christ of Latter-day Saints.

After our son finished his mission, he met this young woman and, after some time, chose her to be his wife, which made her our daughter-in-law. So, in a very astonishing and fascinating way, the

Elder Busche's oldest son, with President and Sister Alder, arriving in the mission field in Manchester, England.

word of the stake president was fulfilled when he promised our son that if he would play in the soccer game, everything would be just fine. Our son's faith was definitely tested, and many details had to mesh together before that promise could be fulfilled. Without the extra effort he exerted because of his foot injury, he would probably not have been instrumental in Gerd's conversion and perhaps would not have had the opportunity to meet his future wife.

This same son was helped in an additional way by serving the Lord. When I was working as CEO of Busche Company, I found very few people in the business world with whom I could speak about the gospel. One exception was Mr. Westermann. He was purchase director of a worldwide business. When I left the company to follow the call of the prophet of the Lord and become mission president in Munich, he was the only one of my customers to visit me in the mission home. He still did not quite understand what I was doing and why. After I was transferred to Salt Lake City, he came three weeks later "to check on you," as he said.

I had a free weekend and so I showed him Temple Square, the Church Office Building, and the Missionary Training Center in Provo. His English was much better than mine at the time, and he was not shy about asking questions. He wanted to see the dormitories of the missionaries. Mr. Westermann asked one of the elders what they were doing. The young missionary came out and answered with a fresh, confident smile that they were studying Chinese because they had been called by a prophet of the Lord to teach the gospel to the Chinese people. That was enough for Mr. Westermann. He finally began to understand what I was doing and why I was doing it.

He was deep in thought as we traveled back to Salt Lake. After about thirty minutes of silence, he asked me, "What are your children doing?" I said that our oldest son had just returned from his mission in England, that he had finished military service, and that he was looking for an apprenticeship in a good company. He did not feel he had a chance, however, because of his poor grades in school. Mr. Westermann said to me, without hesitation, "Let him apply to our company." I told him that I knew there were 2,000 applicants and only a few positions available. Our son felt that he had no chance, I told him, upon which Mr. Westermann replied, "Let him apply, anyway."

I called this son as soon as possible. Reluctantly, he agreed to apply for the job. As expected, however, three weeks later he received a form letter stating that he was not accepted. A few days later, I received a telephone call from Mr. Westermann. He asked whether our son had been accepted, and I said, "No." He said, "I will call you back." He called me back in about thirty minutes and said, "Your son is accepted." Mr. Westermann had spoken with the personnel department and had asked whether they had seen that our son had served two years in England for humanitarian reasons. They said, "No," and Mr. Westermann replied, "We need to hire him. These are the kind of people we want in our business."

Our second son also went through some challenging times growing up. When he was just eighteen years old, he had his first car. He was wrestling with some important decisions at that time. I had felt quite uneasy about some of the developments in his life, and I was aching for an opportunity to visit with him and speak to him without any confrontation.

At that time he knew a girl who lived about an hour away and who was a little older than he and, I felt, more "experienced." I was not too happy about his interest in her, even though she was a member of the Church. This son knew about my reservations, and he was a little touchy about it, as most teenagers would be.

I was serving as a Regional Representative at that time, and I had to get up Saturday very early to catch a plane to Berlin for a stake conference. On Friday evening, our boy surprised us by saying that he was going to this girl's home to celebrate her birthday. He could see that Jutta and I were not very happy about it and, defensively, he said, "Don't worry. A lot of people will be there and I won't be alone with her." I said to him, "Okay, but I want you to be back by 10:00 because I have to get up at 5:00 A.M." He knew that we had a policy that I would not go to bed until our children got home. I reinforced the instructions: "You must help me so that I can go to bed early." He left us with a happy smile, saying, "Don't you worry. I'll be home by 10:00. I promise."

We had a nice evening together as a family, but at 10:00 this son was not home. By 10:30, my anger was growing. I wanted to teach him a lesson. I put my pajamas on, took my blanket, and sat near the front door to demonstrate my frustration to him when he came in. I read the scriptures to prepare for the weekend. I wondered why he did not at least call. He was not home at 11:00 or 11:30. I felt a growing anger and helplessness and did not know what to do. At about 12:30, I heard a cab come to our door. Our son jumped out of the cab and ran to the door. He asked me, "Dad, can you give me 20 marks? I need to pay the cab."

My first reaction, after I paid the money, was to relax because I realized Matthias was safe but that something must be wrong with the car. After he came in, he was very frustrated and said that he had tried to call all night, but the line was busy. I checked the telephone and it was slightly off the hook. He told me that he had left her home at 9:00 in order to be at home by 10:00, but as soon as he was on the freeway, his car broke down. It was difficult for him to hitch-hike home, and the last stretch he had to take a cab.

Everything seemed to be okay. I could finally go to bed. He had been obedient after all. Then suddenly something happened. The small voice of the Spirit suggested something very uncomfortable. I knew that our son's heart was with his car that was stuck on the free-way. The prompting of the Spirit went like this: "You have wanted to have an opportunity to show your son how much you love him and care for him. You have wanted an opportunity to speak with him uninterrupted. This is it. Take him back to his car and tow it home." I was taken aback. This would mean two more hours before I could go to bed, so my first reaction was, "No, I cannot. I'm too tired. Have you forgotten I have to get up at 5:00 tomorrow morning?" The Spirit responded, "It was just a suggestion."

So I turned and said, "Son, let me get dressed. Then we'll go together and pick up your car." I will never forget his surprised and delighted eyes. "Dad, you can't do that. You have to get up at 5:00." I heard myself say, "I don't mind. I love you and you are more important to me than my sleep."

As we went to pick up his car, we had a most beautiful talk that we both badly needed. Our son made some very important decisions, which laid the groundwork for the person he would later become.

I had, altogether, only two hours of sleep, but the Lord is able to work strange miracles. When I finally got up at 5:00, I was fresh and happier than I had been in a long time, and we had a wonderful stake conference in Berlin.

Although this son and I were closer and he was making progress, he still struggled with challenges in his life. He later had a girlfriend who was not a member of the Church and who lived in our hometown. She was a very beautiful girl and seemed to care very much about him. Our son was torn between the things he knew were right and the things his girlfriend wanted him to do. We were very frustrated as we tried to counsel him. One evening, we probably said more than he could handle. He exploded and did something that we had not before experienced in our family. He yelled, "I'm fed up! I'm leaving and staying the night with her!" Furious, he jumped up, left the house, and took off in his car, tires squealing.

Jutta and I fell on our knees and prayed with all the energy of our hearts, crying for help. About thirty minutes later, our son came back home, subdued and apologetic about what had happened. He had not yet gotten to the main road when he was stopped by the police, who wanted to see his driver's license. When they saw his emotional state, they took the key from the car and threatened to take his license if he did not immediately turn around and go back home. One can imagine how we felt when we learned what had happened and knew that a protecting hand had interferred so he could cool off and avoid making a terrible mistake.

Later, when I was called to be a mission president and we had to move to Munich in southern Germany, our boy stayed in Dortmund to finish school. He still had his nonmember girlfriend, who made a great effort to please us and show responsibility. She was obviously very fond of our son and accepted his involvement in the Church. She also showed some interest, and we all felt very comfortable that sooner or later, she would be baptized. It was clear, however, that our son's struggles were not over.

We did not like them traveling alone together, but they did it anyway. They came to visit us in Munich and stayed in the mission home—after establishing the understanding that there would be no infraction of the law of chastity. One day we felt a strong spirit of contention and knew our son was wrestling with important decisions. We were talking in the living room. Suddenly I found myself completely in the hands of the Spirit, and I heard myself tell him how much I loved him and how much I trusted him. I told him that if it were really his desire to marry this girl instead of going on a mission, he would have my blessing under one condition: that he first go upstairs and kneel down and call upon Heavenly Father and ask Him what to do. Jutta and I would wait and leave him alone for twenty minutes. We asked the girl to stay with us. As I heard myself say that, I was shocked. I did not want that to happen, but I could not take the words back.

Our son went upstairs and, after twenty minutes, he came down in tears. "Dad," he said, "I'm going on a mission." We were also in tears, our hearts rejoicing. At that moment, the girl lost her composure. She cursed us, the Church, and the missionaries who had visited her. She behaved in such an ugly fashion that it was the additional confirmation our son needed to break with her completely and to start preparing for his mission call.

The Busche family in the mission home in Munich in 1979. Their oldest son had just returned from his mission, and their second son had recently left for his mission in Toronto, Canada.

One experience with our youngest son demonstrates my wife's great heart and insight. This son was going to a gymnasium, which is somewhat the equivalent of an American high school. He wrestled, as all of our children did, with complicated issues in the German school system which, at that time, was very mechanical and structured and centered around students who were focused on nothing but the teacher's expectations. We had to keep in mind that, at that time, the curriculum in the schools where we lived was dictated by the philosophies of agnosticism, socialism, and amoral liberalism. If someone said anything different, he could be targeted as being someone from the old times.

This son had always liked his mathematics teachers and was curious to hear what his new math teacher's opinion of him was. At a parent-teacher conference, my wife went to see this new teacher. The teacher, however, was very negative about him. He said that our son was lazy and would never go anywhere in mathematics. Jutta was completely disheartened but was not willing to give that kind of report to our son.

When our son came to her with wide eyes and enthusiastic hope, asking, "Did you see my teacher? What did he say?" Jutta answered, "Well, he was very happy that you are in his class, and he said that you are one of the very few that really has talent in math. The only thing that you need to do is to work hard, and then you will be one of the finest students in the class." With that planted expectation, our son really put time, effort, work, and enthusiasm into mathematics and became, in one year, one of the best students in the class. I felt so grateful for the inspiration of my wife to use the gospel and to do something that the teacher should have done—plant positive expectations, hope, and love into the hearts of the students.

We, like most parents, had other challenges with our children, but we also had an abundance of blessings and inspiration from the Lord. I have felt love and admiration for our children as they have developed beauty of character, uniqueness of personality, and the inner strength needed to tune into divine power. We treated our children with the greatest respect and appreciation, which was not the traditional way of parenting in our home country. Perhaps we were too tolerant, forgiving, and understanding. We have been accused (particularly by our oldest son) of not being strict enough. He has said that he would have been a better student and been better prepared to cope in life if we had been stricter with him. That might be true, but on the other hand, we wonder whether we would

The Busche family in 2000, just after Elder Busche's 70th birthday.

have developed the same closeness, trust, and love for one another that we enjoy now.

Training up a child is the greatest responsibility anyone can have. If there is not unity between a father and mother, or if they are not available to answer a child's many questions or help a child face the many fears that accompany childhood, the child's development is hampered. There is no substitute for loving, caring parents. Schools cannot assume the responsibility of parents. We, as parents, need to be in harmony with the Spirit to know what we should do. The Spirit has a solution for every challenge in our lives, but we need to be close and listen and pay the price. I am eternally grateful for the help the Lord has given us in raising our children.

10

MAKING A LIVING

I HAVE CERTAINLY LEARNED TO BELIEVE that a person who humbles himself or herself will be able to walk with Christ, specifically when tested with crises or difficulties. My father was fifty-eight years old when he returned from a British prisoner-of-war camp. Because he was forty years older than I, he wanted me to join his printing company as soon as possible to help carry his load. I started in the business at the age of twenty-three—without having completed my academic education—and became involved in the technical part of the company.

After my marriage, when I was twenty-five, my father made me the foreman of the printing operation and soon left me more or less alone in that field. After my baptism, when I was twenty-eight, my father demonstrated that he had complete trust in me. He made me the CEO and left the running of the whole business to me so he could spend most of his time pursuing his great interest: studying and admiring the Germanic painters and their works of the nineteenth century.

When he was only 25, Enzio was made technical foreman of the Busches' printing company.

The first years of my membership in the Church were the same years I was struggling to establish our printing business. In desperation, I spent a great deal of time on my knees, and I had a constant prayer in my heart. Before I made a single telephone call, I always asked God what to say. Before I made any visit to customers, I asked the Lord what to do. In all those years, He never forsook me. When I was humbled and focused, asking for the Spirit to guide me, He would take me by the hand and I would be safe. There were many small ways the Lord showed me that I was not alone, and one particular area in which I had great comfort and guidance.

The Lord guided me to make my business decisions based not only on my own ideas but also on the input of the employees. We created employee committees, and various aspects of the business—sales, marketing, production, even spoilage—were put on the agenda, and the people who were most knowledgeable about them contributed to the solutions. At first, the employees did not know what to make of this arrangement. They may have seen it in the beginning as an expression of my weakness. But after a while, they became involved in the fact-finding, problem-solving, creative development, and cost-saving procedures that became the backbone of the company. True, it was time-consuming and nerve-wracking sometimes, but overall there was a spirit in our company that made it unique, progress-oriented, and successful.

Only much later, when I was in America, did I learn that this type of management was taught in universities and is called participatory management. But I can say that the growth and success of our company came from the promptings of the Lord, which taught me how to overcome difficulties, find solutions, be unafraid, and have trust in the creativity and goodness of human beings.

I remember the Lord's influence in even small situations. Being the manager of a company in the tough printing market in Germany challenged me exceedingly. During the years I served as a Regional Representative, the First Presidency trained us for an entire week twice a year at general conference time. I had to arrive in Salt Lake City the Tuesday morning before conference to be trained, and I could not leave until after the last session on Sunday. That meant that twice a year, from Monday to Monday, I was absent from work. My mother (my father had passed away by this time) complained several times that I was neglecting the company.

One Friday afternoon, before I was to leave for Salt Lake, I sat in my car in the parking lot after a visit in town, pondering my need to leave on Monday for a whole week. I knew that many of our machines were idle because of the lack of orders, and a certain spirit of panic had come into the company and my life. I felt helpless, the burden of life seemed unbearable, and I started to cry. I again poured my heart out to Heavenly Father.

Just about thirty minutes later, as I came into the company, I saw smiles and even exuberance on the faces of the sales people. One

Busche Printing as it looked in 1960, after its first major extension. Enzio was in his third year as CEO at the time.

after another, they came into my office and told me that, at about the same time I had been crying in the parking lot, five of our customers had given huge orders to fill the capacity of our company for the next two weeks.

The Lord was a constant support to me in my business, but the adversary also tried to influence me to be afraid and uncomfortable with the life I led, which was so different from most Germans. In taking care of so many things for the Church, I did not have much time left for socials or taking care of business partners or business elements. I was completely absorbed by the Church, spending nearly every evening and weekend—with time only for the most necessary family affairs—taking care of the essentials of my Church callings.

Because I did not drink or smoke or participate in certain activities, it was also difficult for me to approach people outside the

Church because our interests were so different. Other business people, and especially my mother, criticized me sharply for not spending enough time with my business. I had a guilty conscience but did not know what else to do.

One day I was sitting in the lobby of one of our big customers, waiting with people from one of our competitors to see who would receive a significant order. My company was in desperate need of that order. The people from the competing company were very famous, articulate, and clever. I heard them mocking me because I was young and naive. I did not drink or swear or do all of the things that they knew were important for business relations. I must not have appeared like a serious competitor and I thought they felt sorry for me.

I felt hopeless and wondered how I could survive in business being the lone CEO of the company and having such powerful enemies, such capable people who spent all their waking hours with their business, who read all the information concerning the industry—information that I sometimes did not even know existed. When I was at the point of simply giving up and resigning myself to the futility of trying, the door opened. I was called in and given the job.

I have never forgotten my feelings of gratitude and the look of disbelief on my competitors' faces. Their company has since disappeared. Many of my competitors from that time no longer exist. It fills me with humility and gratitude to Heavenly Father for His help and guidance. When we take God seriously and totally accept His influence in our lives, we have nothing to fear.

There was another time in my service as CEO of the company when I was confronted with a very difficult situation. I learned that our largest customer, with whom we did about 70 percent of our sales at that time, was planning to do their own printing because they needed to use some empty space in their own operations. There was absolutely nothing I could do to prevent that from happening. I was completely paralyzed for a while because I knew this could seal the doom of our company, which my mother and most of my sisters depended on for their living. I was also busier than at any other time with Church work. I became more and more paralyzed with panic, fear, and despair.

One night at about 3:00 A.M., I could not sleep yet again. I turned over in my mind the wildest propositions for this company, but to no avail. Finally, I decided to go out for a while. I got dressed quietly so as not to waken my wife. I went out in the streets. There was a light drizzle and a little fog in the air. The cold asphalt and concrete of the city increased the awareness of my hopeless situation.

In despair, I threw myself on the ground, crying and calling on my Heavenly Father. Suddenly something happened. I heard a voice very close to my right ear speak one single word: *Arbeite* (work). At first I was upset because it was just one word; the voice was so near and so beautiful that I wanted to hear it again. I could not comprehend it. I yelled, "More, more!" But nothing more came.

As I pondered the meaning of what had just happened, I realized in this one word there were three distinct messages. The first message was: *He heard me.* This time He realized that I needed something more than just a silent voice; I needed something audible. I was overwhelmed with gratitude and love that I was worthy of that experience.

The second message was: *Repentance.* Everyone might have thought that I was the hardest worker in the company and in the Church because of my long hours. But I knew that I still had a lot of time that I was not using constructively. I was still interested in soccer. I still read a political magazine on a weekly basis. I was even still interested in sailing and read books about that. I made a commitment right then and there that for the next six months, I would get up thirty minutes earlier. I would do nothing else, only Church and business, and I would focus more and make better use of my time. The third message was the most comforting: *Hope.* I understood the Lord would not give me such a message if there were no hope.

When I finally went home, I was rejuvenated. I didn't want to go back to bed, so I went right to the office. On the way, I saw in my mind revolutionary restructuring possibilities for the company that I later put on paper. Basically, I separated the company into little profit centers, an idea that was completely new at the time. I involved the whole team in this new idea, and enthusiasm and hope came into their lives. I already had reason to be grateful to the Lord for the insights and comfort He had given us when another really wonderful thing happened.

It had always been difficult for me to hire competent, successful people because of several handicaps our company had. First, our location was in Dortmund, an industrial town where many people did not want to live with their families. The city's image as a blue-collar town, cold and bare, without cultural or historical advantages, made moving to Dortmund unappealing to many. Second, with the growing success of the business, we had expanded the original building a little at a time, eventually buying the neighboring houses and completing an impressive block. In a decision made earlier by my father, we had a four-level print operation with access from the road, where trucks could easily get in and out. It was the ideal floor plan for smaller operations, but there was no place for additional expansion. These two factors had always been a great handicap for me in finding competent managers, operators, and, especially, successful sales people. Many people who rose through the ranks in our company quit when they became really effective and then found jobs in nicer towns or factories.

Enzio and his wife meeting with Josef Neckermann, a well-known German businessman.

Therefore, I was surprised one day to find one of the successful sales managers of a leading competitor in my office. He said that he wanted to work for me. He was unimpressed when I told him the reasons that working for me would not be a good idea. Furthermore, I told him I could not pay him as much as he was receiving at his current position. He still wanted to work for me, and when I asked why, he said, "I don't know, but I know that if I worked for you, I would feel good. I want to feel good in my work and I don't now." He joined our company, and six of his best salesmen came with him. They filled the capacities of our printing operations to the point that we were forced to find place for expansion.

This man later became the sales manager of Busche Company when I was called as a General Authority. If he had not been with us, it would probably not have been possible for me to accept the call that President Spencer W. Kimball gave me in August of 1977. I have never forgotten that it started with one single word in answer to a prayer of desperation.

When I was called by President Kimball, my first assignment was to be president of the Germany Munich Mission, so I had to move from Dortmund to Munich. I felt that I had done everything I should have done. I had informed my customers, clients, business associates, and the people in my company about my sacred call and my commitment to obey. Most people reacted with silence, and I was certain they would never be able to understand. I did have some nice visits with people who showed some respect, and I had one experience that was particularly moving.

After I had given my letter of intent to move, I was contacted by one of our customers. Normally I dealt only with second- or third-level personnel, but I was invited to dinner by one of this company's highest executives. I had heard about him before, and everyone I knew spoke respectfully of him, but I had never met him personally. One of my managers and I went to the dinner and were taken to the private dining area of the top management. The executive had invited all the staff that had dealt with our company. The dinner was formal, polite, and elegant, and the food was exquisite.

During the meal, I noticed that he wanted to share something with me. He was hesitant and reluctant, as if he had a confession to make. Finally, he said, "As I heard about your decision and your commitment to take your beliefs seriously, I felt I should invite you and share an experience I had. I would not dare share it with anyone else because I would not want to risk being ridiculed, but I felt that you would understand."

He explained that during the Second World War he was captured by the Russians and taken to a prison camp with thousands of other soldiers. They received no food and no shelter but were just left in an open field surrounded by barbed wire. Scores died daily. He realized that he would have to escape or he too would die. He and five other German soldiers climbed the barbed wire and walked under cover of night about ten miles to the front line. Once they arrived there, it seemed impossible for them to get across the Russian line to the German side without being seen. Russian soldiers were everywhere. He and his companions hid in a cave during the day. Their attempts to cross at night were frustrated by a full moon and spectacularly bright nights.

For three nights they prepared to cross the lines but were unable because of the brightness of the night. They ate roots and rats, but they were so exhausted that they knew if they did not get across the next night, they would be too weak to go. When they came out of their cave on that night, they were dismayed to again find the night clear, the moon and stars shining brightly. Everything was visible. "Then," he said, looking at me to make sure I was not smiling, his voice shaking and his eyes tearing, "something happened that I cannot explain, but it is as real as anything I have seen in my life."

"I knew little about religion," he said, "but suddenly I found myself on my knees, crying and asking for help with absolute surrender and desperation in the panic of the nearness of death. I was still on my knees when suddenly a wind came and clouds and fog and it began to rain. It rained with such intensity that the Russians ran to find shelter or rain gear. In that one moment when everyone was gone, we jumped over their foxholes and raced across the Russian lines to the German side. We arrived safely without so much as a scratch. The Germans on the other side were puzzled to see us wet because when we got there, there were no clouds or rain, and the moon and stars were shining as brightly as ever.

He then looked at me and, again hoping that I would not smile, said, "Do you believe me?" I said, "Yes, I believe you. I believe that every human being is a child of God, and as soon as we humble ourselves in the depths of prayer, God will guide us. He will never forsake us." We shared a moment of spiritual communion. Everyone at the table was silent. I had learned in many years of service that there are sacred moments when a human voice can sound foolish—especially when the Holy Ghost is speaking so loud. So I was silent, too, knowing that this was a moment we would not be able to forget.

On my last day in the office, I was thinking about what a historical moment it was. As I reflected on the changes that would come, I felt quite lonely. Just then, Karl Hoell entered the room. Karl had been hired by my father right after the war. They had been in the same prison camp together where Karl worked in the kitchen. Out of compassion, he threw a chunk of food over the fence to my father every night. My father always said that because of Karl, he had survived the prison camp. After the war, my father hired him and put him in charge of the finances of the company, even though he had no pertinent background or education. My father believed that someone with good character could learn everything else. Karl had been head of the finance department of the company for as long as I had been the CEO. He was a very close friend of the family and the only man, outside of the family, that my father called by his first name.

As Karl came into my office, he appeared very sad and, after a moment of silence, he said, "Can't you just stay?" I knew him very well. I knew he was a good Catholic, and so I felt inspired and prompted to tell him, "I cannot because your prayers have been

Busche Publishing and Printing as it looked in 1991.

heard and answered." He protested and said, "My prayers? I did not pray that you would leave. What do you mean?"

I answered, "I know that you are a good Catholic and you probably have prayed thousands of times, 'Thy kingdom come.' Your prayers have been heard. His kingdom has come and He has restored His kingdom on this earth. I have embraced this with a holy oath, and now He is calling me to serve Him full time. I cannot break this oath." We embraced silently, and he never argued with me again.

11

Quiet Heroes

SHORTLY AFTER OUR BAPTISM, JUTTA and I became aware of an elderly sister named Sister Maischt, whose enthusiasm for the gospel and the Church was so extraordinary that the shabbiness of her outward appearance did not matter much. From her looks, she was as close to a fairy tale witch as anyone I have ever seen—always wearing the same, long, ugly black dress, and never clean, always smelly. She simply did not try to look groomed or acceptable.

The missionaries were always very embarrassed by her and tried to prevent her from approaching us, which she often attempted. However, as a young convert, I did not see her outward appearance so much as I was fascinated by her relentless enthusiasm. No one knew her very well, and only later did I learn the whole history of her background.

She was originally from East Prussia, about 1,000 miles east of Dortmund. She had five children who had been killed by the Russians. Her husband was killed. She was raped several times. Her farm was burned down. With a little handcart, she made her way to Dortmund to a piece of land she had inherited there. She lived in a shed without plumbing or electricity and lived off the food she grew on her land. She never talked about the details. When anyone asked her about her background, she would immediately change the subject and talk about the goodness of Christ, the support of angels, and her testimony of the Book of Mormon.

One day, in the early days of my membership in the branch, I was questioning why I was there. There were some people in the branch with seemingly unrefined speech and behavior. I was standing there in our humble meeting place, undecided about whether I would ever come back, when she approached me with a look of determination, thrusting her face so close to mine that I could not avoid her smell. She yelled at the top of her voice three times, "Brother Busche, it is true!" Her words sank deep into my soul, touching my spirit. In a strange way, I was never offended by her smell, or her ungroomed hair, or the holes in her shoes, or the dirt on her shirt, or the wrinkles in her stockings. I can still feel today the power of her testimony penetrating my soul.

One day, as I drove home with my wife and our little one-and-a-half-year-old son, Markus, we discussed Sister Maischt and the fact that she walked two hours one way to go to church. We debated whether we should make the sacrifice and leave thirty minutes earlier on Sundays to give her a ride to and from church. We felt good as we finally agreed that we would arrange our time to do this service for her.

How surprised I was, however, when I presented her with our suggestion the next Sunday. She said, "Brother Busche, you cannot do this to me. I'm an old lady. How can I ever show the Lord how much I love Him, how much I adore Him, how much I depend on His atoning sacrifice for my salvation, and my desire to serve Him?

The Busche family recently after their move to the United States. The Busches' oldest son is not pictured. He stayed behind in Germany and still lives there today with his own family.

I'm too old and too ugly and too forgetful to serve as the Relief Society president or even as a teacher. The greatest joy of my life is on Sunday when I can get up early in the morning, walk to church, and take the sacrament. Yes, it is a long walk and, yes, my legs hurt and my back hurts, but every step I rejoice. Every tree and every shrub is my friend. I know every person behind every window. I greet them all with my heart and with my testimony. As I walk, I sing the hymns and when I arrive, I'm through the hymnbook and my heart is full of joy and gratitude because my walk is a celebration of my Savior and Lord, Jesus Christ. And you want to take this away from me? You can't do this to me. Let me walk."

In a strange way, this woman taught me more about the gospel of Jesus Christ than I may have learned in Sunday School classes. Her commitment was total. Whenever she spoke, she bore her testimony. Yes, she looked funny, and people were embarrassed to associate with her, but the more I think about it, the more I know that she was probably one of the most compelling teachers I have ever had in my membership.

Long before I was able to go to the temple, she told me of the urgent need for each member to go to the temple as often as possible. One time, she reported she had been in the temple in Switzerland at least once a month since the temple had opened. That was much more than anyone else in the branch had accomplished. When she could not get anyone to take her to the temple, which was ten or twelve hours away, she somehow saved the money to go by herself by train. Not a month went by that she did not manage to go to the temple.

When I became branch president, one of the most touching experiences of my service was receiving the tithing envelopes from the members. I was deeply touched by the faithfulness and commitment of even the poorest in the branch, Sister Maischt in particular. When I first received her tithing, my heart was touched, but then I saw, to my surprise, that she had added a very large amount as a fast offering. It was nearly fifty percent of her tithing. In compassion, I said to her, "Sister Maischt, you don't have to do that. This is a lot of money for you." She rebuked me in another outburst of conviction. She stomped her foot and shouted, "Brother Busche, you are new in the Church. You don't understand yet. This fast offering is for the poor and this is serious. We must not let the poor go hungry."

I learned that she did not consider herself poor. I also learned that she refused any help that people offered. I never saw her in any other dress or in any other shoes, and I doubt that she had any. I knew that she lived in a little shack without sanitary installation, but she considered herself rich.

One day, she came to me and gave me a large amount of money. If I remember correctly, it was about 1,500 marks—the equivalent at that time of perhaps $1,000. She came to me and said, "Brother Busche, this is money for my funeral because this will be the last week of my life." I protested and said, "Sister Maischt, you are going to live much longer. You are not going to die." She said, "You don't understand. The Lord told me that my time of probation is over and that I should come to you to arrange for my funeral. This is the money, and these are the songs and speakers." She handed me a piece of paper with the arrangements for her funeral.

When she did not show up the next Sunday in church, the Relief Society sisters visited her. They found her dead in her hovel, calmly and peacefully gone. Yet her influence remains still because once in a while, I feel compelled to speak about her. In my mind, she is a monument of womanhood that I know will stand in the day of her resurrection, in prominence and beauty, and stands for me as a beacon of light in these days when we are so easily distracted by the things of this world.

Near the time that I was baptized, there was another man baptized from a neighboring city. His name was Brother Birkhahn, and he was vigorous, positive, and full of enthusiasm for the gospel in a dimension that I have rarely experienced since. He was a man who never permitted himself to be without the Spirit. If anyone needed to be comforted, he was the one to do it. He was an engineer and worked in the steel industry.

One day he lost his job because of the closure of many of the steel companies in our area. He immediately went to the employment office and asked for work. They told him that they had nothing for someone with his education and background. Normally, people in Germany at that time would use this as an excuse to retire because the state paid about 80 percent of the person's previous income when that person became unemployed. A person could take early retirement and get by without working. But Brother Birkhahn said, "I'm not interested in being supported. I'm interested in serving, so I will take any job even if it is for nothing. I want to help support my community."

After much pleading on his part, they gave him a job sweeping the streets—at first with a broom and later with a little machine. He had such enthusiasm, creativity, and reliability that after three months, they put him over the department responsible for cleaning the whole city. He was able to build up a new career with a higher salary than he had had before. He retired recently as the director of city management.

I saw it as an example that when we are in harmony with the Spirit that watches over us, we become service- and love-oriented. Our caring and simple righteousness will guide our way. The Lord will be able to show us opportunities. The most important element in our lives is to be consciously under the influence of the Spirit. Then we will have no fear, no matter what happens in our lives.

Ingrid Engel is probably one of the most impressive people I saw enter the Church while I was serving as a mission president. I feel deep humility and gratitude that Sister Busche and I were able to meet this woman. The missionaries found her and saw that she was a very sensitive person, interested in all matters of the Spirit. After several months of careful teaching, she was converted and wanted to be baptized.

She was married to a very busy, successful businessman in a leading position. As always, the missionaries needed the husband's permission for her to be baptized, but they were a little intimidated by his forceful personality. They asked me whether I could get in touch with him, and I did. Sister Busche and I went to meet with them. We were immediately touched by the wonderful spirit that she radiated but also noticed a spirit of unfriendliness in him. He was somewhat cold and withdrawn and would not give his permission for her to be baptized. I counseled the missionaries to respect the wishes of the husband and to contact the family six months later.

Later, I made another appointment to visit the husband. He again refused to give his permission for his wife, who still desperately wanted to be baptized and become a member of the Church. In the spirit of prayer, I felt prompted to ask him a question. I said, "Sir, I respect you. You are a leader in the business world with many responsibilities and capabilities. But would you please explain a principle to me that I don't understand? My understanding is that in the sanctity of a marriage, the way to express love would be to support the desires and needs of the loved one, not to enforce limits. Could you please explain what principle you are acting under?"

He was a little shocked and flippant when he said, "Well, I may not give my permission, but I will also not say anything if she wants to have it done." That changed the situation. Sister Engel was very happy, and we made arrangements for her to soon be baptized.

In the final interview, Sister Busche and I visited with her and suggested that she not preach to her husband or tell him what he was doing wrong. We told her that if she followed the promptings of the Holy Spirit, she could love her husband unselfishly and unconditionally. She could see the potential and goodness in his heart and not be concerned about his lack of interest in sacred matters. If she would do that, the Lord would bless her and her family.

Sometimes she felt the need to support her husband in his favorite Sunday activities, but she managed usually to be very involved in the worship services of the Church. It was awkward to leave the family Sunday mornings for three hours and then return home to fix dinner and do all the things necessary for the good feelings of the home. But she did it in a loving way with a great sense of humor, always being of good cheer and supporting her husband in a better way than she ever had before. In so doing, she was able to not only improve her marriage but finally to gain the interest of their children, who were all in their teenage years. They were later baptized—not because she taught them but because they wanted to know where she was going on Sundays and what made her so happy. They wanted to go with her, and the husband finally permitted them to go and they were baptized.

In my most recent correspondence, I learned that the Engels' first daughter has a wonderful testimony and has served a mission for the Church. The husband now escorts Sister Engel to church on a regular basis. He still has not accepted the gospel for himself, but he talks about the Church and feels good about it. This has shown me that even if one spouse does not believe, the family can still be happy by loving each other and following the guidance of the Spirit.

In the early years of our membership, the missionaries wanted us to meet an investigator couple, Brother and Sister Schumann. They lived in a nearby town that had no branch, so the missionaries wanted to introduce them to us. The couple came to visit us in our home, and we were very impressed with them. They were some of the nicest people the missionaries had ever introduced us to.

He was an engineer and a manager in a steel company. He was originally from northern Germany. He had a Scandinavian stature—tall and blonde. He was articulate and had a friendly, positive personality. They had three wonderful sons, good-looking, healthy, and energetic. His wife was a highly educated, vibrant young woman, who understood something of art. We had a painting from the famous Austrian painter, Waldmüller in our home. When she came in, she exclaimed, "Oh, you have a Waldmüller." We were very impressed because no other visitors to our home had known who Waldmüller was.

We had a strong desire to help them find the gospel, so we met with them several times. Sister Schumann was ready to be baptized and complained that her husband was too slow and not able to change. Her husband was an honest, reflective, sincere conservative man that impressed me very much. I knew that if he ever became a member, he would be a very good one because he had all the attributes of goodness inside of him. I had no question about her because she was the one pressing for baptism.

It seemed difficult to get Brother Schumann to commit to this new religion. Finally he felt the Spirit and surrendered to baptism, and they were both baptized. We knew we needed to stay close to them because their closest branch was in Bochum, and it was only a very small branch. I made a commitment to stay in contact with them. I called them regularly and visited them in their branch.

After about six months, tragedy struck. Sister Schumann left her husband and followed a younger man to America. She took all three boys with her, leaving Brother Schumann totally alone. I was overwhelmed with pain and disbelief. I thought the worst would happen to Brother Schumann. I would not have been surprised to see him become bitter.

This painting from Ferdinand Georg Waldmüller (1793–1865) hung in the Busches' home. It was a personal gift to Enzio from his father when he became CEO of the company. The painting is now owned by the LDS Church. © Intellectual Reserve, Inc.

Brother Schumann was, however, exactly the man I had seen him to be at the beginning. Following the guiding voice of the Spirit, he refused to speak negatively about his wife. He supported her in her move to America with the children. When I talked with him about it, he said, "I love her. She's a wonderful woman, and I was probably not the right husband for her. I was always a little bit too dry and too slow. She probably needs something more invigorating. If she feels happy, I will be content."

I was struck by the beautiful expression of this Christlike man. He did not waver in his testimony one bit. On the contrary, he became more deeply involved with all the aspects of the beautiful gospel of Jesus Christ. We became very close friends at that time. We went to the temple together frequently and often served together in Church callings. Later, his company transferred him to a city about 100 miles away, near the Belgian border.

Even though he moved to a different area, we remained close. He has had a very successful life. He was still highly respected in his company although he was old enough to retire. His company did not want to let him go because, they said, "If he goes, the whole company will fail." He agreed to spend a few more years working. Some time after the divorce, he found a wonderful woman in the Church. They were sealed in the temple, and they have four children of their own.

His first wife, in the meantime, did not fare so well. Brother Schumann still does not speak ill of her. He even suggested that I go and visit her during one of my many travels, which I did. She lives in the States with her husband, and Sister Busche and I went to see her once. We saw that the vibrant, dynamic person we had known in Germany had become a more disgruntled, unhappy person in a pitiful situation. We had a nice conversation, but we were not able to rekindle interest in the Spirit of the Church of the Restoration that she now denied and neglected.

An amazing phenomenon is that the boys she took with her to America seem to be active in the Church. They are wonderful young men and turned out well in spite of their circumstances. Brother Schumann recently attended the temple marriage of one of those sons.

We were blessed with only three missionary couples while I was serving as mission president in Munich. The most beautiful and wonderful people anyone can imagine were Brother and Sister Seiter from Heber City, Utah. Both were humble, obedient, loving, and caring. Brother Seiter was originally from Germany. He had a bakery in Heber City and worked in it together with their ten children. We had known one of their daughters, who had served as a missionary in Germany when we were just young members. She was very faithful, committed, and dedicated. We felt blessed to have her parents come to us on a mission.

About a year into their mission, Sister Seiter was diagnosed with intestinal cancer, which was in the advanced stage. The need for surgery was imminent, and I suggested the Seiters go home to have it done there. Sister Seiter insisted, however, that they stay on their mission, and her husband supported her. I remember that I told her, "Sister Seiter, this is not an easy operation. You may find that you want to go home later, and then it may be too difficult." She insisted that the Lord had called her on a mission. If He wanted her to die on a mission, that would be fine with her, but she would not be disobedient to the Lord.

The surgery was done in a Nürnberg hospital. They opened her up and then simply closed her again. The cancer was too advanced, and they told her there was no hope. Any operation would only prolong her suffering. At that time, she suddenly changed her mind and wanted to go home and see her children. The hospital staff and doctors would not give permission to release her and have her travel back to the United States. They said it would be against their Hippocratic oath. She needed to be cared for there or her suffering would become unbearable.

The missionaries, particularly my assistants, loved the Seiters so much that they would do anything for them. They arranged for her transportation without me knowing the details. They found out that Canadian Airlines had been trying to do business with the Church for some time. The representative of Canadian Airlines was a member of the Church who was very helpful and arranged for transportation on a regular flight but on a stretcher behind a curtain.

There was a condition, however, that a medical doctor attend her during the flight. The assistants found a military doctor who was returning home and was willing to help. They found an American paramedic car to drive, at the given time, from Nürnberg to Frankfurt. The assistants explained to me how it would all work, and then they said, "The only thing we need is for you to give her a blessing that she will make it."

As I saw how the assistants had worked everything out and how much Sister Seiter wanted to go home, I felt more or less compelled to cooperate. Nevertheless, I had to force myself to do what I was asked to do without having much faith that it would help. I was particularly aware that we were doing something illegal, taking someone out of the hospital without the doctors' permission.

I had so many feelings of inadequacy as I laid my hands upon her. She was in intense pain and on heavy sedation and was hardly aware of what was going on. I heard myself promise that she would have a safe journey, that as the plane left Calgary for Salt Lake City, the pain would leave her, that all of her children would be at the airport in Salt Lake, and that she would recover. I had such a bad feeling as I finished the blessing. I had put the power of the priesthood under the scrutiny of 180 missionaries.

Sister Seiter was smuggled out of the hospital while the missionaries involved the night nurse in a gospel discussion. Sister Seiter was put on a stretcher by the paramedic and, with the help of the kind LDS doctor, she was taken to the Frankfurt airport two hours away. She made the flight, and as they were approaching Salt Lake City, she woke up somewhat. Her pain was diminished. Her children and most of her grandchildren were waiting at the airport, some of them having come a long distance. She went to a small hospital in Heber City, and after three weeks, she was completely healed.

She insisted on returning to Germany. She and her husband went back to finish their mission. She went to the hospital and testified to the hospital staff and doctors of the power of the priesthood of God. They finished their mission, always acting as wonderful examples of faith, love, and service. Brother Seiter passed away fifteen years after returning from their mission, and Sister Seiter lived even longer.

Walter Nabrotzky is a faithful member of the Church whom we knew from the early days of our membership. For some time, he was our bishop. One day on a temple trip, he told us about his conversion. He and his brother were refugees from East Germany. While he stayed in West Germany, his brother immigrated to Kitchener in Canada. One day Brother Nabrotzky learned that his brother had converted to The Church of Jesus Christ of Latter-day Saints. Brother Nabrotzky, being a staunch Protestant, went all the way to Kitchener to bring his brother back to his former church. He stayed long enough to go to the LDS meetings with his brother and, after a short while, he became converted himself. Later, while we were still in Germany, I learned about a tragedy. Brother Nabrokzky's brother had died of cancer. His wife was left to raise their five children on their farm in Canada.

Not long after, I was called as mission president in Munich. I was surprised and touched when I received a missionary named Nephi Nabrotzky, who was the oldest son of the deceased brother. His mother and four siblings sacrificed so that he could go on a mission. He was a fine young man and served in Coburg for his first city.

One afternoon I received a telephone call from a bishop in Kitchener saying that Sister Nabrotzky, Nephi's mother, had been killed in an accident. She had been trying to clear some snow with a tractor. She had driven it into a ditch and was crushed under it in the water. It was particularly devastating since this would have been one of Nephi's jobs had he still been at home. The bishop asked me to take the message to Elder Nabrotzky.

I was shocked. I knew the family. I knew their background. I knew the sacrifice the family was making. Now I had the assignment to bring such a message to Elder Nabrotzky. I started to fast and pray. I could not bring myself to go that evening. I went the next morning. It was a three-hour drive. I wanted circumstances to appear normal, so I arranged to have a district meeting in order to interview the missionaries.

I started the interview with Elder Nabrotzky. I sat for a while in my chair. I did not know how to begin. Then Elder Nabrotzky came over to me, put his arm around me, and said, "My mother is dead, isn't she?" I was startled and said, "Did somebody call you, because I was supposed to bring you this message." But he said, "Nobody told me, but when I was leaving on my flight for my mission, when I hugged my mother at the airport, a voice told me that my mother would die during my absence but that I shouldn't worry. Everything would be fine."

I realized that he was comforting me. He had known this for three months and felt relief because he had not known when or how it would happen. Together, we called the bishop and learned that the fine members of his ward had already arranged where the children would go and who would take care of the farm until Elder Nabrotzky went home.

Elder Nabrotzky finished his mission successfully and honorably. I later met him in Kitchener, where he was raising his own family. That was a very humbling experience because I witnessed how our loving Father in Heaven prepared that faithful young man several months before the tragedy happened. When we are humble and teachable, He can prepare us and strengthen us to cope with whatever may happen.

I was serving as an executive administrator of the North America Northwest Area and was assigned to go with Elder LeGrand Richards, of the Quorum of the Twelve Apostles, to divide one stake and create another. Elder Richards was ninety-three years old at the time, and I will never forget his excitement. Once you have been with him, you never forget his enthusiasm for the kingdom of God and his constant awareness of the whisperings of the Spirit.

He was very gracious as we organized the necessary interviews. He shared the time with me—one interview by me, one interview by him. We were impressed by the many capable leaders that were there. One of the men was well qualified and prepared and recommended by all to be the new stake president. We finally came to his interview, which was near the end. When he came in, we asked the regular questions and then asked him whether he knew of any candidates who might be qualified to serve as the new stake president. He pondered awhile and then said, "Well, I don't think I have a candidate, but I have some people who would make excellent counselors."

After the interview, Elder Richards said calmly, "Well, Brother Busche, we normally do not call ourselves in the Church." He did not mention the man's qualifications or the fact that everyone had

Elder Busche (back row, third from left) with President Thomas S. Monson and Elder L. Tom Perry and Sister Perry at an area conference in Sacramento, California, in 1984.

suggested him to be the new stake president. All of his credentials, all of his faith, everything that he had ever done were not important. He considered himself great, and that was the disqualification. I have never forgotten that.

When we finished the interviews, Elder Richards asked me who I felt should be the stake president. He did not kneel down to pray. He just asked me. I felt a little bit intimidated. I said, "Elder Richards, I'm here to sustain you. I will sustain whatever you say." I was uncomfortable giving my opinion. I felt very strongly that one bishop was the right person, but I said, "My candidate is probably not the same as yours. He was not suggested by anyone else, but I think Bishop Smart is the one the Lord has in mind." Elder Richards said with enthusiasm, "That's the one I had in mind. Let him come in."

That was it. There was no long discussion or anything. Elder Richards surprised me by confirming my inspiration. As we talked to Bishop Smart, we learned more details about him and his family and as the conference proceeded, we saw what a wonderful man he was. He later became very successful in his calling.

It was a wonderful stake conference. The attendance was magnificent. Suddenly, about halfway through the session, Elder Richards motioned the choir director over to him. He whispered something to her. He told me later that he had felt prompted to have the closing hymn changed. He wanted to have the hymn "The Battle Hymn of the Republic" sung and asked the choir director whether they could sing that. It happened that they had the music, so he requested that the program be changed.

During conference, it became obvious that a new bishop needed to be called because Bishop Smart became the president of the new stake. The new bishop was called and needed counselors, but as he prayed about them the day after the conference, the name of an inactive brother kept coming to mind. He was frustrated because that man had been inactive for years, and he could obviously not call an inactive man to become his counselor. Then the following came to light.

That inactive brother had attended the recent stake conference, the first time he had been to church in many years. He had been curious what the division of the stake would be and who the leaders were. Some of the talks went right to his heart and brought memories back from his own mission and from his earlier commitments. Suddenly, he felt a powerful prompting to repent. He said in a private communication to God, somewhat skeptically, "If you can perform a miracle, I will change my life. If the closing hymn is 'The

Battle Hymn of the Republic,' then I'll know that You are in charge and I'll repent." He felt secure that this would never happen because the program listed a different song.

You can imagine what it did to this man when it was announced that there was a change in the program, and that Elder LeGrand Richards had asked that the closing hymn be "The Battle Hymn of the Republic." He nearly fainted and went home distraught. That night he could not sleep.

The next morning, he had to go on a business trip. On his way home, he stopped near a forest and went into the trees. He fell on his knees and wept and asked the Lord for forgiveness and put all his heart into his prayer. He went back home and was at his desk writing his tithing check for the year when the ward executive secretary came. The bishop had felt so intensely that the inactive man should be his counselor that he had asked the executive secretary to go by and see how he was doing. The secretary found the man at his desk, crying and humbled and writing out his tithing check.

The executive secretary immediately reported back to the bishop. The bishop called the stake president. The stake president called me and asked for permission. When I talked with Elder Richards, we both had the feeling, "Why not? If the Lord is willing to call this man, why should he not be called?" He became a wonderful counselor and a strength to the whole ward.

His fate all depended on the workings of the Spirit and Elder LeGrand Richards being in tune. As I shared the details of that experience with Elder Richards later, he said that he had had several experiences like that in his life. He was a man of great wisdom and faith, and I was impressed by his gift of discernment. When he looked at someone, he was looking for the truth in the soul. He could not be fooled by personal vanities or ambitions. He also refused to write talks beforehand. Even for general conference, he spoke on the thought he was engaged in at that moment. I was very grateful to have been part of that conference and to have worked with that great servant of the Lord. I felt he was a man who was truly guided by the Spirit, like so many other men I have worked with.

Walter Kindt was the mission president of the Düsseldorf Mission at the same time I was called to serve as a Regional Representative. He was from Germany but had immigrated as a young man to the United States and had married a wonderful American woman. He and his family were called from Milwaukee. I was honored to work with him very closely as the district president and also, for some time, as his counselor.

We traveled to most conferences together. During those long trips, we had many opportunities to share our testimonies with one another. The many experiences he shared with me were very instructive and helpful when I was called to move to America years later. His testimony was powerful and his enthusiasm for the gospel so compelling that I always marveled at him and admired him greatly.

One experience he shared with me happened after he had survived World War II as a German soldier, having been protected by many miracles. He was with relatives in Hamburg when he received a mission call from Salt Lake City to serve in the East German Mission. The next day, he received another letter, also with a missionary call, this time to the West German Mission.

He felt that he should take the more difficult mission, so he went to the east, which was known at that time as the Soviet Occupation Zone. He served in that mission five years altogether. He and his companion, Rudolph Poecker, went from village to

Brother Busche with Elder Ezra Taft Benson, who was in Düsseldorf in 1966 to dedicate the Düsseldorf Chapel. Sitting with Elder Benson is President Horace P. Beesley, president of the Central German Mission. Brother Busche was president of the newly created Rhine Ruhr District at the time.

village. They financed their missions by illustrating the ancestral line from Adam to Jesus Christ, which they made so professionally that they could sell it from door to door. Brother Kindt told me about many miraculous experiences from that time.

Because of the closure of the Soviet zone, they lost contact with their mission headquarters, but they went on with their missionary calls, trusting that the Lord would provide. One day, his companion, Brother Poecker, was incarcerated because he was accused of preaching things that were not in harmony with the government's policies. Brother Kindt found himself without a companion, and he wrote a letter to Church headquarters in Salt Lake City asking what he should do. They were shocked to find that they still had missionaries in the east zone. They granted him and his companion an honorable release and told them that they should go home.

That was a wonderful example of the simple faith of my friend and his companion. Rudolph Poecker became the successor to Brother Kindt as mission president and later served as a wonderful counselor to me when I was called to serve as president of the Frankfurt Temple.

One day, when I was in Salt Lake City working in the Church's administration building, security called and said that an elderly woman wanted to see me. They could hardly understand her, but they assumed she spoke German. I felt that I should let her come up. When she did, I saw a woman who must have been from a respectable home and who was trying to be charming, but her clothing was a little ragged. Her manner did not fit her appearance.

Her name was Sister Neuberg. She was a German convert and had immigrated with her parents to the United States after the war. I do not believe she had ever married or had a job. She must have always been with her parents. As long as her parents were alive, she had something to do in taking care of them. When they, one after another, died, she was suddenly alone and did not know where to go. She was in her sixties or seventies. What she had to say was astonishing.

She had $1,500 in cash that she wanted to give me for the missionary fund. She wanted to give it to Native American young men who did not have the money to go on a mission. I was perplexed to see this woman with so much cash wanting to give it away for that purpose. I was reluctant to take her money and asked her why she wanted to do that. She told me that she had talked to the Lord, and the Lord had told her the money was needed for poor missionaries; therefore, she wanted to give me the money.

I asked her why she wanted to give it to me. Why didn't she give it to her bishop? Wasn't she a member of a ward? She said, "Ah, yes. My bishop doesn't think I can afford so much. He always gives it back to me and says I should keep it for myself, but he doesn't understand, and I don't want to confuse him. For years, I have gone to the temple grounds and given it to a person that I thought looked trustworthy. But then the Lord told me I shouldn't do that. He said I should give it to a General Authority who could give me a receipt and who would make sure the money went to the right place."

She told me that she had told the Lord that the General Authorities did not understand German and that she was afraid to ask for an appointment with a General Authority. She said the Lord had told her that the Church now had a German-speaking General Authority, and she could go to him. She had asked the Lord what the name was and the Lord had told her, "It is Elder Busche. You can approach him."

That was her introduction to me. Of course, I was very doubtful; but she insisted. I finally took the money, gave her a receipt, and made sure it got to the missionary department. I was surprised when she came again the next year and the next. Every year, she came with $1,500 and gave it to me. I became more interested and learned to listen.

She told me many things—most of which I do not feel ready to repeat—but one day, she told me the Lord had told her that a big flood would come and there would be a river running down State Street in Salt Lake City. I thought she was a little deranged because we were in a desert. How could a river possibly run through the middle of the city?

Of course, I was shocked when just a couple of months later, there was a river running down State Street. It was the famous 1983 flood, which came practically without any warning. After that, I had more respect for what she said.

One day, she was unsettled by a talk at general conference by one of the Brethren. I do not remember who it was because I did not listen too closely to her complaints. Then she said to me, "Yes, I went to the Lord and complained about that talk and that brother, but," she said, "the Lord told me, 'They are all different, but they are all acceptable unto me, even the least among them is acceptable unto me.'" Then she said, "So what can I do? I have to live with that and stop complaining and sustain them all." I took some comfort from what she said. Of course it is difficult for me to make any judgment about her information, but I was often speechless by her simple faith.

She told me one day that the Lord would soon take Elder Bruce R. McConkie to Him. That was before it was made public that Elder McConkie was sick. Soon after, I learned that he had cancer and then he passed away. I finally had to accept that Sister Neuberg had gifts and insights that were very unusual.

Once when she brought the $1,500, I asked her where in the world she got the money. She told me, without any embarrassment, that she was making a special sacrifice because, she said, "I want to show the Lord how much I love Him and how much I appreciate His atonement for me." She went on to explain that her father had left a small endowment for her to live on. She lived in a little house where her parents had lived. She saved the money for the missionary fund by not using any utilities. She did not use any heating all winter but wore two big sweaters, a big coat, and a wool cap. She did not cook any meals but ate raw or cold food. She said, "It's only a small thing that I can do. The Lord has done much more."

She came with a large sum of money one day, about $6,000, and wanted to give it all away to the missionaries. I asked what she was doing, and she said, "The Lord told me that I do not have long to live. I will be able to go soon, and I decided to give all my money

Elder Busche at his desk when he worked as assistant executive director in the Temple Department from 1989 to 1996.

away to the Church." She gave me a big chunk of hundred dollar bills. I was amazed and tried to persuade her not to do that, but she insisted. "Yes," she said, "you have to take it. If you don't, I will just give it away." I decided I had better do something, so I arranged for my secretary, Sister Baker, to have it put in a safe account for her in the Presiding Bishopric's Office. If she ever needed it, it would be there for her.

I must have been inspired because she did not die as she expected. She came by later and we gave her the money back. Two or three years later, she finally passed away. We learned about it when her bishop came and asked if we still had funds available for her funeral costs.

Except for not knowing exactly when she would die, she told me many events that did occur. She was very alone and had no one to talk to. I was probably the only person that she ever told some of the things in her life to. She said, "People don't understand me. Home teachers don't come to me because they are afraid of me. They all think I'm a little crazy and weird. But I like to have my visits from the Holy Angels. I speak with them and talk with them about the plan of salvation, and they give me comfort."

She surely lived a different life than a regular person. Besides her frequent walks through Temple Square, she spent all day long reading the scriptures and other religious books. All were in German. Though she had been in America many years, her English was so broken that most people could not understand what she said. When I finally realized that I was probably the only living person with whom she felt comfortable speaking, I arranged for her to visit me and my secretary on a regular basis. She was always happy and enthusiastic about Christ and the beings from the other side of the veil. She looked forward to being with them and felt honored to be going home soon.

12

Communion with God

AN EVENT THAT HAPPENED SHORTLY after World War II remains very sacred to me. It was an important learning experience in my life.

November 1947 was a time when many people were dying from starvation. Curfews were still in force, and occupying military forces were directing civilians not to leave their homes after dark. If someone was found on the street after dusk, he could be shot without warning.

I was seventeen years old, and we were in the midst of daily struggles to find something to eat. Somehow or other, a man who was a few years older than I was willing to go with me in a small pickup truck full of coal to the east, to a farm about one hundred miles from my home in the neighborhood of Bad Oeynhausen. I don't remember the details of the arrangement, but we were to trade the coal for food. It was against the law for us to have this coal. In addition, our driving the truck and trading commodities for food was illegal. But it was a time without any real law and order. The military government ruled with harshness but did not have the power to enforce many of their rules, other than by shooting on sight. We were just trying to do what we had to do.

The truck we were driving was an old military Renault. After some hesitation, we decided to use the highway because it was almost empty of cars. Only an occasional vehicle from British military forces could be seen. Soon after we started on the highway, we had a flat tire and repaired it. At the exit close to Gütersloh, halfway to our goal, we had another flat tire. This time it was impossible to repair.

Together, we tried to figure out what to do. We couldn't get help from civilians because if they found out about the coal, they would rob us. If we approached the military police, we would be put into prison and confronted with the likelihood of even more severe starvation. It seemed there was absolutely no way out.

I remember I had an old military raincoat with me, but the man who was driving with me did not have a coat. As dusk was approaching, I finally said, "We can't just sit here. We must do something!" I gave the man my coat and left the car to go look for help. When I was some distance from the car, I realized I was quite alone, and I became aware of my helplessness in not knowing where to go or where to turn. I could not even imagine what might happen in my situation. I had not had anything to eat, and the driver of the truck had had nothing either. I was hungry and worn out from helplessness and desperation. I fell to the earth as though I had been knocked down by an unseen power. I began sobbing like a little child, crying to God with a loud voice.

In the midst of my anguish, I was overcome with a feeling of peace, and I became very calm. I went back to the road and continued to walk. I felt a great relief and, in some amazing way, I felt quite secure. I even began to sing, all the while telling myself, "Are you crazy? Why are you singing? Nothing has changed. Why do you feel happy now?"

I went on walking until the road made a slight turn, where I saw lights from a gas station being used by British occupying forces. Without fear, even though it was dark and the soldiers who were standing there could have shot me without any warning, I started over to the gas station. Before I got there, a small truck stopped. In it was a British soldier who asked me to get in. As he opened the door, I could see that the steering wheel was on the right side, as it is in British vehicles. I was very nervous and apprehensive, but the driver smiled at me and waved me to come in and sit next to him in the car. I finally dared to get in.

It was very strange for me, and I felt very uncomfortable because it had been only two years since the war had ended, and the relationship between civilians and the military was still cold and distant. The man began to drive and then asked me what he could do for me. I was absolutely shocked. Using the meager English I had learned in school, I told him what had happened about the car (which I presumed he had seen on the road) and explained the situation that required me to go see a certain man in Bad Oeynhausen, which was still some thirty miles away. He said, "I'll take you as far as I can."

As we drove, I asked him why he was helping me. I knew he was breaking all kinds of laws. He was driving alone, picking up a German civilian, and making a long detour from his route of travel in order to accommodate me. He was very polite and very nice. He said that, just before he came to that gas station, he had had a very interesting experience, as if someone were telling him that there at the station stood a young man whom he should help. He said he was a believer in Christ, a Christian, and that he felt it was his duty to

Enzio at age 19, one and a half years after his experience on a German highway.

help. At that time, I did not comprehend the whole thing. I was just happy I could make it to my destination.

He took me to a place about six miles away from where I had to go. "This is as far as I can take you," he said, before leaving me alone. I went the final distance on foot, running and hoping that I wouldn't be caught. Once I got there, I managed to arrange for the exchange, to have the car repaired the next day, and to have enough food to make the trip worthwhile.

I remember feeling very lucky to have found someone to help me out. I really did not understand how it had all happened. The way I had been raised and the environment in which I was living, did not give me an explanation for the situation other than luck. But much later, when I became converted, I finally understood that it was not luck at all. Help came because I was on my knees and called upon my Father for help.

Even though many years have passed, I have never forgotten this experience. Whenever a person is very sincere, willing to listen, and ready to obey, dedicate himself, and surrender, the Lord is willing to do anything to help that person. I only regret how little I understood or knew of Who is really in charge and Who is always willing to influence our lives if we will just let Him do it. Later, as I was studying the gospel and after I was baptized, I came to understand how powerful and effective true communion with God is.

The printing business was very competitive, and I always had to fight to develop the company or at least keep it alive. I was especially proud of a customer whose contact I had developed and with whom we did quite some business in spite of the fact that his company was located five hundred miles south in southern Germany. As always, we needed every customer very badly, but especially this one with whom we did business on a regular basis. I had to deal with the purchase director, who was a very charismatic, powerful man. Many companies tried to do business with him. He was what one would call a more worldly person. He was aware of the appeal that a purchasing agent of a large corporation has for hungry salesmen, and he liked to play games with his suppliers.

One spring day, I was sitting in my office when this man called me from Paris. I knew that his company had an exhibit in Paris and that he had to be there for a whole week. He called to invite me to come to Paris because he wanted to talk with me about more business. I knew immediately that the real reason he wanted me to go to Paris was not to talk business but to have me, as his major supplier, pay his pleasure bills. Nevertheless, after taking a deep breath to collect myself, I told him that I would be most happy to come visit with him. We agreed that I would come on a night train that would arrive in Paris the next morning at about 11:00.

As our conversation ended, panic began to fill my soul. I knew the lifestyle of this man, and I could see that this visit to Paris could ruin our relationship if I insisted on staying within the parameters of my sacred covenants with Heavenly Father. I knew how difficult it was to establish relationships with customers, and I knew I could not afford to lose this one. His business was too important for our own survival. I could see no honorable way out of the situation, and I immediately began to pray, "Heavenly Father, I do not know how to solve this." In my soul, I prayed all day long, into the evening, and during the night as I traveled to meet my customer. In the morning, when I arrived in Paris, he stood at the platform with a boutonniere in his lapel and the happy smile of a man who is out for pleasure.

I told him I was eager to talk about business because I had to catch my train in the evening to get home by the next morning. He just laughed and said, "You are not going home tonight. We will have fun together. You take two days of vacation. Our wives are not here and I will show you Paris. This will be the best vacation you have ever had."

He would not accept the fact that I needed to go home that same evening. He just laughed and offered to call anyone who wanted to meet me the next morning. He insisted on showing me the Eiffel Tower and other things in Paris, not listening to my repeated explanations that I had to catch the night train back to Dortmund. After we had been to several places, around 4:00 P.M., he said, "Let's first have dinner before we go out on the town."

I was in constant, silent prayer while trying to make the most charming conversation possible. In a small restaurant, we started dinner, which I knew could last several hours. I felt comfortable just having dinner, so I continued with my conversation, hoping there was some way I could convince him that I had to catch the train that night.

My French is not the best, so he ordered the meals and the beverages. To my surprise, the waiter brought a big bottle of wine, which he placed in front of me, together with one he placed in front of my associate. I, of course, drank only water. The conversation was nice and full of life, and, I thought, full of substance. He was in the best of moods, telling one funny story after another. Suddenly, as he came to the bottom of his bottle, he realized that I had not drunk any wine yet. In a rush of candor, he took the still-full bottle, filled his glass and my glass, lifted his glass and, looking at me, said, "You drink this glass of wine to my health. If you don't do this, I will take it as a personal insult and I will not do business with you anymore."

Exactly what I had feared happened. Now everything was on the line. Now, because of my covenants with God, I would lose my best client, the company would be endangered, and I would be left with a bleak future. I began to feel some rationalization growing within me, when suddenly it was as if someone came to put me at ease, telling me, "Let me handle this. I can do it better than you."

I felt a spirit of joy come over me. With the greatest confidence and a big smile, I found myself putting my arm around this man sitting next to me at the table in this restaurant in Paris, looking in his eyes, and telling him with enthusiasm, "Sir, you are a good man. You are a righteous servant of your company. I know you would not base your logical business decisions on such illogical conditions." Before I had even finished my words, I felt surprised at what I heard myself say and thought, *Oh, my goodness. That was great!*

As I looked at him, I witnessed his stunned reaction. He stopped, slowly put his glass down, and became very sober. I could see he was struggling to hold back his tears. Finally, he stammered, "I'm not good. I'm not good at all. I'm a pig. I'm here in Paris cheating on my

Enzio as CEO of Busche Printing in 1966.

wife, throwing my life away, and the only reason I let you come to Paris was I wanted to destroy you. I could not stand your example of righteousness, and I wanted to prove that I could destroy you. If you had drunk this one glass of wine, I would have made you a pig. I would have made you the dirtiest and ugliest person going to places you would not even believe exist. I'm not good. Don't you ever call me good again. Please, can you forgive me?"

I was shocked, but my soul began to rejoice. My silent prayers turned into great expressions of relief and gratitude. Without the Lord's influence, I would have failed. I would have destroyed my life. But, with the help of His Spirit, this experience turned into a great success. After this, my customer opened his heart and became like a friend to me. That evening, he took me to the train station himself. Later on, when I went to visit him at his office in southern Germany and his staff wanted to offer me alcohol, he always protected me. Until the time I left, his company was one of the best and most reliable clients we had in the business.

I have always been so grateful to the Lord for helping me with my important business decisions. I have done nothing without first asking the Lord for guidance, and He has blessed me with the right words and the inspiration that I needed. He has also blessed me as a father with my family. In one incident when we were in great danger, I prayed for the Lord to help me and again He did not leave me alone.

When our oldest boys were eight and ten years old, I had a sailboat—not very large or heavy, but capable of being used in the coastal waters of the Baltic Sea. Because we lived in a big city, we felt the need to spend time with our children in nature. We had a small apartment on the seaside where we spent the better part of the four weeks customary for vacation in Germany. Our time in the more open country on the Baltic Sea was probably the most productive time for the education of our children.

One beautiful day I planned to go with my two oldest sons in our sailboat from Travemuende to the harbor of Burg on the Island of Fehmarn, some twenty-five miles away in the Baltic Sea, at the end of Luebeck Bay. It was supposed to be a wonderful day with warm temperatures. The weather newscasters were talking about light winds and sunshine. We stayed overnight in the small boat and got up early at 4:00 A.M. so we could make it in the afternoon to the harbor, where Jutta and the two other children would be waiting for us on the pier.

Before we started, of course, we had our morning family prayer. We enjoyed the beautiful sights, the calm waters, and one another's company. The weather was so calm that from time to time we could swim without the boat getting out of reach. For a while, we needed the outboard to make any distance at all. At about 11:00 A.M., we were not halfway to our destination, when, in the middle of the Bay, I saw the weather changing. I saw whitecaps on the water, and we all became excited to have some wind because sailing without wind is not much fun.

As soon as the boat picked up speed, we moved forward with good acceleration. Suddenly, I realized the wind was getting stronger and stronger, and I became a little nervous. Concentrating on not showing my concern, I had to pull down the main sail, and we were sailing only with the jib. Soon I learned that it was still too big and the boat was leaning heavily. I could see that we were heading for the shoreline without any harbor.

I felt my responsibility as a father, and I questioned my wisdom in going on such a trip with my two little boys. I knew that it was important to keep up our spirits. As long as I was in a good mood, they would have trust. Only one expression of possible fear came from the younger one when the waves were high and the gusty winds nearly pressed the mast into the surface of the water. He said, "Dad, I really would rather be home right now." To which I answered, "You would miss a wonderful experience and later you would regret it." This calmed him down.

Soon it turned out that the wind became so strong that there was very little hope we would be able to make it. It became likely that we would be thrown on the reef by the shore. I realized that I needed to turn my whole focus and concentration to my Heavenly Father. With intensity, energy, and total focus, I searched for help for what I should do. I concentrated on every grip of the rudder and the lines of the sail, watching the waves and listening to the promptings of what to do. It was an extraordinary spiritual effort of concentration. As I look back on that experience today, I can see that I was led to do everything perfectly and correctly. I used the right moment to tack the boat in the other direction, and I was able not only to bring it against the wind into the small harbor, I even brought it to the dock safely, maneuvering, finally, into a small canal. I did all of this without causing my two little boys to panic. I did not feel that I had been lucky but that I had been led to finish a dangerous adventure with good results. As it turned out, some people on the shore had watched our boat for quite some time. They told us that they had feared we would never make it.

When we finally got home to our little apartment, I shared the true nature of our dangerous journey with my family. I bore witness to them of the living God and expressed my gratitude for His help and guidance. I was so exhausted, and I realized that being focused in constant communication with the Divine for three or four hours is something that is very difficult for a human to do. But I also gained a testimony that with the intensity of our longing to communicate come the promptings of the Spirit and the guidance of Heavenly Father. As I pondered this experience, I saw the extreme difference between the morning prayer we had in our boat before we left and the complete exertion later in that emergency situation. I thought of the scripture, "Draw near unto me and I will draw near unto you; seek me diligently and ye shall find me; ask, and ye shall receive; knock, and it shall be opened unto you" (D&C 88:63).

Much later in my life I had one of my most powerful experiences with communication with God when I was in Munich as a mission president. At that time, I was plagued with frailty of body—a condition called deep-vein phlebitis. This caught me by surprise because I had enjoyed very good health since my miraculous healing in the hospital. As I established my new life in Munich, the rhythm of my routine was interrupted with a change of pace and movement. Somehow, this started an inflammation of my deep leg veins.

The difference between this form of the disease and normal

phlebitis was that I had deep pain, pain in places where there is normally no pain, according to medical professionals. The doctor that I went to could not give me any answers. I was in terrible pain for several weeks, such pain that I would not have believed it possible for someone to go through pain like that. It happened especially at night when I didn't have to do anything, when the body came to rest and when I was in bed trying to find some sleep. Many times in the night I got up and tried to walk, but I didn't feel well enough, so it was really an uncomfortable situation.

I was not able to just stay in bed and be sick because I was a mission president, and I had to run the mission. So I just did all the things I needed to do—even doing the regular interviewing of the missionaries. I sometimes laid down in the back of the station wagon to give my interviews. It was, in some dimension, a spiritual time, but it was also a very challenging time. Sometimes I really felt I was at the end of my ability to take the pain.

I tried many different approaches. I could not take any painkillers because then I would be drowsy and I would not be able to function as a mission president anymore. I was not used to taking painkillers anyway. One night towards morning, about 3:00 or 4:00 A.M., I was in so much pain I could not stand it any longer. I went down to the living room so I would not disturb my wife. I fell down to the ground and began to scream and shout and cry with all of the energy of my soul to my Heavenly Father. Slamming my fists on the ground, I heard myself say that I commanded in the authority of the priesthood to anyone listening that this pain would be taken away immediately or I would be taken dead.

As soon as I was through with my pleas for help, I felt complete exhaustion come over me. It was like I had finished a marathon. I was so exhausted I could hardly move anymore, and I was just able

Elder Busche walking with his daughter in Munich during the time he served as mission president.

to get myself to the couch. Falling on the couch, I fell asleep immediately.

When I woke up, it was a bright day. It was about 10:00 in the morning, and I was completely refreshed. The pain was gone and it has never come back. I was so happy that I could hardly believe it. I was absolutely humbled. I still had my problems with the veins—the normal problems, but the pain was gone, so I could deal with it. I still deal with it today. It will always be with me, but I can manage it when I take precautions and am careful, and I always watch for the promptings from the Lord about what to do.

My experiences with communication with God have shown me that we really must mean it when we pray. As Mormon says, "And likewise also is it counted evil unto a man, if he shall pray and not with real intent of heart; yea, and it profiteth him nothing, for God receiveth none such" (Moroni 7:9). In praying, we must go to the root of honesty with ourselves because we cannot hear truth when we are not honest to the core. We must express our feelings without flowery words and be willing to accept the consequences of our prayers. When we do, the Lord will be there with us and teach us what we need to know and what is good for us in that very moment.

13

The Sacred Temple

When Sister Busche and I were called by President Ezra Taft Benson to serve as president and matron of the Frankfurt Germany Temple, we were completely overwhelmed and unprepared. I had never thought of that as a possibility for us. By then we had been living in the United States for seven years. Three of our four children had established their roots near us. I was so entirely focused on my various assignments that I was hardly aware of the details of the construction of a temple in my home country.

Before the open house and dedication in 1987, we were able to go to Germany and begin our responsibilities. I remember when I stood in Friedrichsdorf for the first time. The temple was about 90 percent ready. It was beautiful. The architecture, the workmanship, the gardening—everything was just superb. It was such a strange feeling to have this unearthly building in this little, old German town. It looked like an edifice from another world.

As I was there, I listened to stories of the history of the temple.

President Kimball had made the announcement for the temple in the early 1980s, but it seemed as though all the forces of darkness had organized to fight against it. It was very difficult to get the temple built. I learned of the many ways the Lord had watched over the various proceedings and how He had helped to make it succeed, but not without several occurrences that can easily be described as miracles.

Friedrichsdorf is located about ten miles northeast of Frankfurt and is connected with an efficient rail system. In the town there had been an old, decaying noodle factory, owned previously by a man named Theodor Haller and his wife, Luise. The site of this noodle factory was the first location offered to the Church for the building of the temple. But the brethren and the real estate department felt it was a not good place for the temple, especially because it was in the middle of a decaying part of town. They began looking at different sites.

The Church was offered many other pieces of land. All of them were investigated, but there was always opposition raised and obstacles brought up. Eventually, there was so much opposition to the temple project that it seemed like it would be impossible to build it in the area. Local ministers in particular preached against it and gave to the media all kinds of incorrect information about the Church. An atmosphere of hate seeped into the political arena. The whole area seemed to become organized to prevent the temple from being built.

The people in charge of building the temple became desperate. After several years of unsuccessful efforts, they went back to the first site in the city of Friedrichsdorf. By this time, there was so much opposition growing in Germany that even the city of Friedrichsdorf did not want to have the Church build a temple there. The city council voted it down. The Church was left without anything.

The Frankfurt Germany Temple in the city of Friedrichsdorf.

Finally, some of our Church leaders suggested that members of the city council travel to Zollikofen in Switzerland—where, for more than twenty-five years, the only other continental European temple was located—to ask the people there what kind of influence the temple had had on their community.

That sounded reasonable. When the city council returned from Zollikofen, there was a great deal of conflict in the council and between party members. The discord over this and other issues was such that some of the members of the mayor's party left it and created their own party. Then, together with the opposition party, they forced the mayor to resign. The newly elected mayor and the newly confirmed city council gave initial approval for the Church to build the temple.

As soon as that approval was given, however, opposition became even more forceful. Newspapers printed articles full of slander against the Church, the new mayor, and even some council members. In order to appease the opposition, city leaders imposed expensive conditions on the construction of the temple, hoping to make costs so high that the Church would withdraw its request. One of the rulings was that the Church had to give back part of the land it had just bought from the city so that the city could build parking lots—not for the Church, but for the people of the city. There would be no reimbursement for the return. Another ruling was that no protective fence could be built around the temple. All the land had to remain public so the citizens could use the greens around the temple as a public park. The city indicated which and how many trees could be planted. They then chose elaborate trees that could be bought only from companies designated by the city. I will not list the conditions in their entirety, but there were a great many, and they were obviously intended, to some extent, to humiliate and provoke Church leaders.

Then, finally, the city ruled that the original owner's villa, which was a ruin occupied by vagrants and rats, had to be restored to its original beauty and 1890s design. This added a tremendous burden and additional cost to the already overextended budget. The Church had to agree to all of the conditions.

As I stood and looked at the almost-finished temple, I was overcome with emotion. It was like the Lord's birth all over again. The Lord wanted to come to His world and the world did not want Him. There was no place in the inn. As I saw the dimension of that rejection, it hurt me. Church leaders in Germany had the grace to endure all of the needles thrust into their flesh. I was awed by the graciousness of the leaders of the Church in accepting all of the demands and insults in order to establish the Lord's house.

Later on that first day of my visit, I went into a bookstore in that quaint, old, beautiful town and browsed through the books. The first book I picked up was very thick and had no title on the cover. As I opened it, I saw that it had a list of names of the founding families of Friedrichsdorf. I asked the salesclerk about it, and she explained that that year—1987, which was the year the temple was to be dedicated—was the 300th anniversary of the founding of Friedrichsdorf.

I learned that Friedrichsdorf was a settlement of the Huguenots from France. Those people followed the teaching of the Protestant movement of John Calvin. They took their religion very seriously and believed in the need of a follower of Christ to be in complete harmony with the principles of righteousness. They were persecuted, and many thousands were killed on the infamous Night of St. Bartholomew in August 1572. After many more years of cruel persecution, they were all expelled from France in 1685. They moved in great hardship all over Europe. Many of them went to German-speaking territories and found some shelter there in various places. Prince Friedrich from Homburg, a principality in a neighboring town, gave a piece of his own land to a desperate group of the Huguenots. They built a beautiful town in 1687, giving it the name Friedrichsdorf—the village of Friedrich. My first name is Friedrich, so I felt a special affinity to the place.

As I realized that the year of the dedication of the temple was the three-hundred-year celebration of faithful individuals who had experienced a very similar fate as the early members of the LDS faith, it struck me that that could not just be a coincidence. The salesclerk in the bookstore told me that in order to honor the memory of their sacrifice, one man from Friedrichsdorf felt inspired to write down all the names and the family dates and other particularities from all the founding families of Friedrichsdorf and put them into a book. It was quite a big book and there were more than 10,000 names of individuals. I suddenly realized that there were powers beyond our control working to fulfill the vision of our beloved

This villa on the Frankfurt Germany Temple grounds was restored to its original beauty as part of the city's deal to allow the Church to build the temple in Friedrichsdorf. The villa now serves as lodging for the temple president and several missionary couples. Elder Busche is pictured here with his mother and his wife.

prophet. I saw myself as the humble executor of the will of higher sources and realized that those earlier righteous and hardworking people had probably been influential in bringing a temple to their town so that their dreams could be fulfilled. One of the first things our faithful temple workers did was to prepare all of those names for the temple.

One final event concerning the building of the temple brought me to the realization that the Lord has a sense of humor and a gentle, subtle way to let us know who is really in charge. I went to the villa, which had been restored to its original beauty. At the entry was a cast-iron ornament on which the initials of the owner and his wife had been placed according to the original design. Their family name was Haller with her name, Luise, and his, Theodor, so that it read *HLT.* Those initials are the German equivalent of LDS. Latter-day Saints in German is *Heilige der Letzten Tage.* Could there be any doubt that the Lord had known it all along?

With that spirit of introduction, Sister Busche and I started our work in the temple in Friedrichsdorf. We consider this one of the most memorable times of our lives. It was very edifying and in some ways also very challenging, but the whole experience enlarged our vision of the work of the Restoration beyond our ability to explain.

During the open house, many wonderful people came from all parts of Western Europe and beyond. One elderly man especially caught our attention. He was somewhat handicapped and bent and could not stand upright. He had to hold his head up very high in order to have eye contact with the people he met. Despite his handicap, there was always an extraordinary, otherworldly glow in his countenance that was just inspiring to everyone who met him.

The very first day after the temple was dedicated, he spent the whole day in it in order not to waste any time. On one occasion, we met in the hallway. As he saw me, his glow seemed to increase. He took my hands and kissed them and said, "Merci, President. Merci, President." That was all he said. I pulled my hands away as fast as I could because I did not feel comfortable having my hands kissed.

I asked the priesthood leader of that group, Brother Scheen, who the man was. He said, "Oh, you mean Joseph Gilbert. Let me tell you about Joseph Gilbert." He told me that Brother Gilbert had been a life-long clerical custodian for the Catholic Church in one of the cathedrals in Belgium. One of his assignments was to give tours to visitors who came to see the cathedral. Many of the tourists, of course, could not speak French, but many of them spoke English. Brother Gilbert could not speak English but wanted to. One day he saw an ad in the newspaper for free English lessons from American students. He felt that was for him because he needed lessons but did not have much money.

He went there and, of course, he found the gospel. He read the Book of Mormon in three weeks and was baptized. He had a testimony immediately. He lost his job and was in dire circumstances. Brother Scheen said that shortly after Brother Gilbert had been a member for a year, he went to the Swiss Temple. On the day that he was in the temple for the first time, he saw in a vision a great gathering of his ancestors who were looking at him and pleading with him, "Please, don't forget us. It took a great effort to get one of our descendants to embrace the gospel. We have all waited a long time for this."

After that, Brother Gilbert became completely committed to the holy work of the temple. At every opportunity, he went to the temple and did the work for his own ancestors. In the very first week of the opening of the Frankfurt temple, he spent five days in a row there. He was the first one at the temple in the morning and last one in the evening to leave. I never saw him other than in the full bloom of excitement. One day I asked him, with Brother Scheen as translator, "What is the secret of your unending enthusiasm?" He looked up at me with a sparkling smile and answered, "I worked my whole life in a house of darkness surrounded by death. Finally, when I am old, I can work in a house of light surrounded by life." His eyes were just glowing as he went off to another assignment. He was so attentive, reverent, grateful, and untiring. Everyone loved him and saw him as a wonderful example of being under the influence of the Spirit of God.

One day, not long after I had begun serving in the temple, I met a woman in the American military service who came for her own endowment. She was accompanied by some sisters from her ward, as well as a priesthood leader. As Sister Busche and I began teaching her about the temple, I felt that she had a somewhat unsettled spirit and saw a little of that in the sisters who were with her, who were all officers in the military. When the priesthood leader inquired as to when I thought the Church would receive revelation giving the priesthood to women, I was at first so shocked that I felt a strong desire to give a stern response and even question his worthiness to be in the temple.

However, as I momentarily withheld my answer and sought guidance from the Spirit, I was witness to something most remarkable. A calmness from someplace else entered my heart, and I heard myself saying things that were somewhat new to me. As I remember, my remarks, in an abbreviated form, were approximately as follows:

> The priesthood is neither male nor female, although it has a male part and a female part. Through the eternal bond of marriage, built on the divine gift of love, the priesthood becomes complete. The roles of the two parts are, of course, vastly different.
>
> Heavenly Father has given the female the role of bringing new life to this world. She does so in a physical dimension—by nurturing, tutoring, training, and teaching—and in the wearing of the very eternal virtues of chastity, loyalty, and wholesomeness, which are essential for the very existence of humankind. Our Heavenly Father has given the male the role of providing, protecting, and admiring. Male and female are in many ways mysteriously different and, because of that, there is a natural desire to love one another in harmony with

the divine laws as they have been reestablished by the restoration of the gospel.

The best way to gain an understanding of the male and female part of the priesthood is to be reminded of a tree. As we look at a tree, it appears to be complete with its trunk, branches, leaves, and blossoms; but we know that another, equally important part of the tree is invisible. The roots—which, quite unseen, lie deeply embedded in the soil—are constantly nourishing and strengthening the visible parts of the tree. The roots do not argue with the trunk. They both enjoy oneness.

The temple is the Lord's essential instrument used to reestablish a true understanding of the male and female parts of the priesthood. In the temple, both men and women wear the robe of the priesthood and are given the garments of the priesthood. Righteous men and women learn that although women are not physically involved in conducting the affairs of the priesthood, no man can excel in his priesthood callings for long without the blessing and care and guidance of a righteous woman. When we listen very carefully in the temple and learn to understand and accept our male and female roles, we will soon see ourselves in our own limitations. Those who concentrate their efforts in developing the purposes and virtues of their own gender will build tender, bonding bridges between men and women on the basis of mutual respect and admiration, inspired by the divine, miraculous power of love. A society that fails to accept the eternal concept of this godly design must pay an unbearable price of confusion of the individual, which can, potentially, lead to chaos, destruction, and the unhappiness of the soul.

The Frankfurt Germany Temple.

As I spoke, I felt a warm, comforting spirit come over me—a stimulating vibrancy that filled my whole being with light and joy. I witnessed how that same spirit came over the listeners. Their hearts became enlightened and their attitudes became mild and receptive. As I continued my remarks, I observed that they had tears in their eyes. The priesthood leader was so embarrassed that he could not find enough words of regret and apology. Deeply touched and lightened by inner understanding, they were ready to participate in the additional experiences of their temple visit.

In October 1986, before I was called to serve in the Frankfurt Temple, I received an assignment from the First Presidency to host a group of fifteen Protestant ministers from Germany, who, during a trip through the United States, decided that they wanted to visit Salt Lake City and the LDS Church. I was given a letter from them that they had sent to the First Presidency. I was surprised by the style of the letter. It was a directive, telling the First Presidency, without any expression of courtesy, that they had decided to pay a visit to the Church, that they expected to be picked up at the airport, be shown around, talk to a General Authority, have lunch, and be taken back to the airport. I was embarrassed and wished that my "countrymen" had shown the respect and courtesy that are the signs of true disciples of Christ.

We arranged for two brethren from the Public Affairs Department to pick them up in two vans. These two brethren had served missions in Germany and spoke German. They picked the ministers up and took them to Temple Square for a guided tour. I received them for lunch and then felt inclined to show them some of the elements of importance in the Church Office Building.

This was around October conference and, at that time, the Relief Society Building was being remodeled, so there were provisionary offices for the women's auxiliaries in the Church Office Building. Because of conference, there were some open showcases for visitors to see some of the lesson materials and teachers' guides. There were also some live classes, where teachers were meeting with students. This was very unique for the German ministers, so we took some time to pass by the Primary. Little children were sitting there, and the teacher was teaching them in a most caring and loving style. She was well groomed. Most of the ministers (three of whom were women) were in jeans and T-shirts, dressed without any care, and they behaved like a group of uncultured college students.

As we passed the Primary presentation, one of the ministers asked me in a somewhat haughty tone how much we paid a teacher like that. I felt impressed to tell him that the teacher would be offended if she were offered pay. She understood that serving one another was one of the greatest opportunities to show our Heavenly Father and Jesus Christ our gratitude for the Atonement and our gratitude for the blessings of life and the plan of salvation. She would see it as a privilege to teach children the gospel of Jesus Christ.

They were somewhat taken aback but looked doubtful. We went on and saw something similar with the Young Women and then the Relief Society. Then someone out of the group, who had not, obviously, listened the first time, asked the same question. "Tell me what you pay a person like this?" I gave a similar answer, adding that as a part of our membership, we surrender joyfully into the arms of the living Christ. As His servants, we serve in the capacity we are called to build His kingdom. I mentioned that this is part of the dignity of our membership in The Church of Jesus Christ of Latter-day Saints.

They looked at me skeptically. Then someone from the back of the group said, "Now we want to ask you a question, and we want you to be completely honest this time. Those young men in dark suits we see on bicycles riding through our towns, how much do you pay them? But this time, be honest. We really want to know."

I stopped and asked, "You really want to know? Then you need to listen carefully to the whole story." I told them in the form of a testimony how tenderheartedly we look at a child when we are parents. We see it as a gift and a privilege to be entrusted with the watchcare of one of Heavenly Father's choice spirits. Every effort is made to assure the child has all the love and care that it needs for our mortal experience. I talked at length about the nurturing efforts of the Church to help parents be good parents. I explained about the Primary, which is the organization to teach children the principles of life, the gospel, and the atonement of Christ. I described a typical young boy and how he would go through the various phases of his life. I explained the various classes, the manuals, and the substance of our teaching. When he turned eight and was baptized, he would receive the first taste of responsibility and participate in the life of the ward. At the age of twelve, a boy is ordained to the Aaronic Priesthood, and I explained the structure of the priesthood.

By the time the boy turns nineteen, I told the ministers, the whole family feels a great deal of anticipation. Will all their efforts pay off? Will the boy be worthy and be honored by a call from the prophet to serve for two years? The young man may have saved his own money for his mission, or his immediate or extended family may support him. If they were not able, other members may sacrifice to fund him. In such a way, a boy matures, and his mission is a culmination of the teaching and nurturing of his family and the Church. His mission is his great opportunity to testify of Christ. I then bore my testimony about the restoration of the truth, that it had all the answers to all the questions.

There was a sober feeling, and they were quiet and looked like they had been hit. A little later, something very touching happened. One of the leaders, who was a prominent minister in Germany, waited until we were alone, then looked at me and said, "I want to thank you, for as you spoke, I felt the Spirit. It has been a long, long time since I can say I really felt the Spirit." Then he gave me a big hug and said, "I love you." I felt that, at least for that moment, there was some kind of bonding in true humility before the Lord.

All fifteen members of that group came later for the temple open house in Germany when they heard that I was the temple president. We had a wonderful visit. They were more comfortable and familiar. They had a deep respect for what we were doing and had helped calm the uproar against building the temple. Yet, I need to mention one small thing that happened after their visit to the open house. The very man who was so touched by all that he had felt and embraced me at the end of their visit to Salt Lake later had an interesting test. He was a seasoned man, respected by German authorities. The state was making an evaluation of all of the smaller religions and their standing in the public eye. This minister was asked whether the LDS Church could be considered Christian or not. The minister gave a written report culminating in the statement: "They cannot be considered Christian." He was either very forgetful or he was not able to withstand the internal organizational pressure and say what he really felt to be true.

While I was temple president, one of my former business associates died. He had owned a large, specialized news agency. We had been close friends, so I wanted to go to his funeral. It was going to be held in Düsseldorf, which is a three-hour train ride from Frankfurt. I went there and met many of my old acquaintances from before I had become a General Authority and moved, first to Munich and then to America. Some of these people seemed to respect my decision to leave the business world to serve in the way I had told them, but many did not take very seriously my explanation of being called by a living prophet.

Among those who made fun of my decision was a man who was a successful journalist. He had made a name for himself in the political and sports worlds because he expressed himself so well and had a very elaborate way with words. He was so skillful and celebrated in public opinion that many prominent politicians I knew used him as the ghostwriter for their speeches. He wrote many renowned speeches that were given in parliament or on television. His ability to express even sensitive or complex issues was considered by many to be brilliant.

He had been associated with my friend's company and so was at the funeral. As is the tradition, after the funeral there was a social dinner, and I was placed at the same table as that famous journalist. I could see he was uncomfortable sitting at the same table as I was, and even more displeased to learn that I was also going back to Frankfurt afterwards and that we might be on the same train. I decided to avoid any further discomfort for him by taking the train that left an hour later than the one I had intended to go on. He must have had the same thought, however, because when I got to the platform to board the train, I saw him also standing there.

There were not many people on the platform, so there was no way that we could avoid one another, and what neither of us had wanted happened—we ended up in the same compartment together. He, of course, was good with words and made lively conversation. It was at the time of the Olympic games, so he wanted to discuss that. It was fashionable at the time in Germany to be against people who tried for perfection or who, like those in the Olympics, spent so much of their time trying to become stronger and more effective and efficient in order to be just a split second ahead of someone else. He talked about how foolish such ambitions are.

He was surprised when I said that I had no problem with efficiency. He was willing to listen, and I shared my beliefs about the possibility of humans attaining perfection. I told him that the Creator of this world was a perfectionist and was taking care of all the minute details. I said that there were great blessings that came when people learned to understand the laws of nature and learned to keep them with exactness. I talked about the tragedy of wasting life to end up in mediocrity.

I discussed possible human crises that result from the lack of efficiency, the lack of being in complete harmony with the laws of nature and the laws of truth. Then I was prompted to ask him if he knew the original meaning of the word *sin*. He did not know, and I told him that *sin* is derived from the word *hamartia*, which was taken from the world of sports and, in its original meaning, meant "missing the target." I told him there was not much pleasure in taking aim and missing the target.

As I was talking about this, I suddenly saw him in deep reflection. After some time, he was, to my great surprise, wrestling with tears. After another pause, he finally mumbled, "I'm sure one who has missed the targets of his life." I was very amazed to find him making such a statement. There was little else that could be said. His emotions were strong and he was obviously ashamed of them. I did not want to interfere, so we sat in silence together for about an hour. Once in awhile, he looked at me, but I knew I needed to respect his privacy.

We finally got to the Frankfurt train station. As we were leaving the train, he was going in one direction and I in the other. Suddenly, he turned around and gave me a big hug and said, "One of these days, I will come to you and ask you to put me back on track so that I don't miss my target," and off he went.

It is now many years later and I have not heard from him since. I know that he is back in the arena of the grandeur of public speaking. Who knows? Maybe one day he will remember the time of honest reflection on a train ride along the Rhine River after the funeral of a friend.

When we had been serving in the temple for about one year, we needed to call another counselor because President and Sister Fetzer were returning home. We tried to find a counselor from a country other than Germany, as the temple was also serving the Netherlands,

Elder Busche and his wife, Jutta (center), with his counselors and their wives, served as the first temple presidency of the Frankfurt Germany Temple.

Belgium, and France. We were looking for someone from Holland because the Dutch members were very faithful and very enthusiastic about the temple. At first, we were not able to identify anyone who was qualified because the candidates we considered were either not ready to retire or were in some other ways incapable. We received a recommendation for a Brother and Sister Vreeken. We did not know them, but after we met them, we realized that they were wonderful people. We suggested that they become our counselors, and they were approved by the First Presidency and set apart by Elder Russell M. Nelson.

Brother and Sister Vreeken had not been members of the Church for very long. Brother Vreeken had been an officer in the Navy and had always worn a beard. I was very glad to have him serving; but at that time felt that it was inappropriate somehow for a member of the temple presidency to have a beard. The brethren had always tried to discourage leaders from wearing beards, but I did not know how to handle telling him about it. I spoke to him in private and told him I understood how important the beard was to him and that I would not ask him to shave it. I mentioned that perhaps some people might consider his beard to be some kind of statement. The next day, he came to the temple without a beard. That was the kind of man he was. He did not make a big deal out of it or become defensive. He was just a delightful person, and his wife was the same way.

As we were serving together, we heard the remarkable circumstances that led to their conversion. They had a daughter who, in her teenage years, was a fan of the Osmond Family. She had all their records and tapes. She read everything she could about them, and when she found out they were Latter-day Saints, she wanted to know more about their religion. She found a Book of Mormon, became interested, and, with a great deal of opposition from her parents, was finally baptized. Her parents were traditional Dutch people and were absolutely appalled that their daughter would join an American sect. They argued with her about it, but as they saw the spiritual development that took place as she went to Church regularly, they finally quit arguing and just accepted it.

Their daughter placed copies of the Book of Mormon around the house without making a fuss about it. Her parents came across them independently and read them. Sister Vreeken read the Book of Mormon without telling her husband because she did not want to offend him. Brother Vreeken also read it without telling his wife. They both received a testimony that the book was true, but they were both too embarrassed to admit it to the other.

They had a camper trailer and decided to take a trip to Israel. They would have to travel through Holland, Germany, Austria, Yugoslavia, Greece, Turkey, Syria, and Lebanon in order to get to Israel. As they were driving, one of them said, "I believe the Book of

Mormon is true." The other one was startled and said, "Well, I believe it, too." They then admitted that they had both read the Book of Mormon and gained a testimony. They rejoiced, in the middle of their long trip driving in their car, that they had both found the truth, and they planned to get baptized as soon as possible.

When they arrived in Israel, they went to the camping place where they had planned to go but found that it was completely full. They were told of another trailer park a little out of the way on private land. They received permission to camp there and found out that the rest of the people there were Americans. It turned out that the other campers were teachers and students from Brigham Young Univeristy. Brother and Sister Vreeken explained what had happened to them, and they were baptized by the people from BYU in the Jordan River in Israel.

On their way home, they stopped in Austria to visit relatives of Sister Vreeken. They went to Church there for the first time. They had never seen a missionary. They had never met a branch president. They were just baptized and became wonderful members. Because of the housing shortage in Frankfurt, while they were serving in the temple, they lived in their camper trailer, which they brought with them. They served with Sister Busche and myself and were just the salt of the earth.

As a temple president, I heard a lot of stories, nearly on a daily basis, where members told me about experiences that dealt with the manifestations of the Spirit or occurrences that can be described only as miracles. I want to share just a few here.

One brother from Holland, whom I had seen in the temple before, had been planning to come to the temple. It was quite a sacrifice and too far to come for just one visit, so members would usually stay for a week at a time. That always took a lot of money and time and preparation. This brother shared two things with me that had happened to him before his trip.

A couple of days before he was supposed to leave, he had a dream that his temple recommend had expired. When he woke up, he did not believe it because he felt certain his recommend was current. Just to be sure, he looked and found out that it had, indeed, expired. He had forgotten that the year before, he had gotten his recommend earlier than usual. If he would have gone to the temple with an expired recommend, he would not have been able to go inside. He was able to get his recommend renewed before he left for his trip.

Then, he said, another thing happened. He lived in a city in Holland and had no garage for his car. He was usually able to find a parking space on the street near his home. But the evening before he was going to leave for the temple, when he came home from work, he could not find a parking space near his home or anywhere on his street. He had to park his car several blocks away. He was angry because it meant he would have to carry their luggage a long distance to the car.

In the morning when he went outside, he was shocked. During the night, vandals had slashed the tires on all the cars on his street. He said that if his tires had been slashed, he would not have been able to make the trip because he did not have the money for repairs or new tires. He believed the Lord knew that and that was why he had not been able to find a parking space on his street the night before. He praised God for helping him make the trip to the temple.

Two weeks before we were transferred back to America in 1989, a sister came and told us of an experience that happened in the first year after the temple was dedicated. She said that she had heard we would be transferred and she wanted to make sure we heard her story before we left.

She told us how she had been in a wheelchair for many years and was deteriorating rapidly. She said that the members of her ward near Hamburg, which is one of the stronger wards I know in Germany, felt compassion for her and decided to exercise their faith on her behalf. Without telling her, they all went together to the temple in a special act of sacrifice and in the spirit of fasting, to pray for her. They all stood in prayer together and they prayed for her well-being.

At the very moment when they were standing in the prayer circle, hundreds of miles away, sitting in a wheelchair, she felt an exciting, electrifying charge come over her body. She felt prompted to try to get out of her chair, and she did. She was completely healed. She said that since that time two years before, she had been the happiest woman in the world. Only later did she realize that the miracle had originated from the faith, love, and prayers of the members of her ward.

One Tuesday morning, we had a man named Prinzl come to the temple for his own endowment. He came unannounced and without an escort. Normally, in Europe, when people go for their own endowment, members of the ward come also to help them feel comfortable and give them a good experience. This man came all alone from Vienna. It was not even a part of our temple district, but Frankfurt was closer to Vienna than the Swiss Temple, so he came there to get his endowment.

As I interviewed him and tried to prepare him for the experience,

I learned a very interesting lesson. He was a convert of about four years. His wife was not yet a member, and so he had waited for her to become a member so they could go to the temple together. Yet, since he had been baptized, he had had dreams where his deceased mother came to him and said, "Son, go to the temple." He had had the dream several times, but he always excused himself saying that he hoped to go together with his wife.

Then he said, "Last Friday night, something happened that changed my life." He said, "My mother had been married to a man who was not my father. I always knew that my real father was killed in the war, in the Battle of Stalingrad. I had never seen my father because he was killed before I was born. My mother remarried later, and I never really thought about my real father." He continued, "Last Friday night, I had this dream again, this time much more fervently than before. My mother was there, but there was a strange man next to her and he was pleading with me and said, 'Son, you need to go to the temple. Otherwise, we cannot make any progress here.' I was surprised because that was not my father."

"I woke up and looked through some old family documents. I came across a picture that I'd never seen before. It was my real father in uniform as a soldier, and I recognized him from the dream. It had been my real father standing with my mother, both pleading with me to go to the temple for their salvation." He said, "I could not stand to go one day longer without coming to the temple. I got my recommend, took off work, and have come here to fulfill the wish of my parents; otherwise, I could not sleep any longer." So that wonderful man talked to me about his experience and then spent the whole week enjoying the sacred work in the house of the Lord.

While Brother Prinzl was in the temple, something very enlightening happened. After he received his own endowment, he was permitted to see his father in the temple as a spiritual being. A couple of

A mission presidents' seminar for the Eastern European Area in 1997. Among those pictured in this gathering at the Frankfurt Germany Temple are Elder and Sister L. Tom Perry, Elder Charles Didier, Elder Bruce D. Porter, and Elder F. Enzio Busche.

days later, when the sealing was being performed for his father and mother, he and all the others standing in the sealing room were permitted to see both of them. There was a great outburst of joy and humble sharing of testimonies of this additional, great sanctifying experience for the ordinance workers of the temple. Brother Prinzl was united for the eternities with his real father and mother, and received a witness and confirmation from our loving Heavenly Father.

14

Saints of the World

I HAVE HAD THE PRIVILEGE OF SERVING in the Church in numerous places throughout the world. As I have served in various callings, I have met many wonderful people and heard about their experiences with the workings of the Spirit, a few of which I wish to share in this chapter.

In the early years of my membership I had the opportunity to counsel with one young sister who was going to get married. She was about twenty-nine years old and was a refugee. She was very educated, articulate, and talented. She had also been on a mission. She had met a young member who was just twenty-one. He had hardly any education and was a blue-collar worker. Not only was he much younger than she was, but he was also much shorter.

I saw nothing wrong with them getting together because I feel that when two people are committed to the gospel of Jesus Christ, all other aspects do not matter. I believe that under the influence of the Spirit, any marriage can become a success. They were married in the temple. However, about a year later, the sister came to me again and said, "I've made a terrible mistake." She was crying and said, "I cannot go through with this." I was shocked. I felt, in my innocence, that there was no way anyone could get out of a temple marriage, remembering the text that I had read in the scriptures and also the words we receive in the temple endowment. I wanted to help, and so I listened carefully and sought communication with the Spirit.

I was finally prompted to ask her a couple of questions. I asked her, "Sister, do you have a testimony of the Lord Jesus Christ?" She said, "Yes." I asked her then, "Do you keep all of the sacred covenants that you have received in the holy house of the Lord?" She answered, "I think so." I asked her to tell me about her husband. "Does he believe in the Lord Jesus Christ?" Again she said, "I think so." I asked her if he lived in harmony with the covenants of the temple. Once more she answered in the affirmative.

Then I heard myself say, "I remember that we talked earlier, before you were married. You came to me with questions about the purpose of your life as a church member living away from the center of the Church and with no prospects of marriage. I remember that we had this conversation once. I hear you complaining now about your husband, how clumsy he is and how you suffer from his lack of education, how you cannot have a stimulating conversation with him, and how he does not like the same kind of music you like, and other things. Could it be that you have a wonderful opportunity here? Could it be that we are not meant to find ourselves but to lose ourselves?

"Instead of looking at all of the things that separate you from your husband, you have the great opportunity to see inside of him and see the hidden beauty because he is, like yourself, a child of God.

Therefore, he has the potential of a god in him, but the only way it can grow inside of him is if he finds someone who loves him and who looks through his behavior, his lack of education, who sees the beauty of his character and the beauty of his spirit. He needs someone who treats him as if he were already at that level where he would be acceptable to you. Could that be the purpose of your life, to help bring this man into the celestial kingdom?"

I could see that my words did not sit well with her. She took it like swallowing a bitter pill. She was obviously not happy about my counsel. Yet thirty-five years later, when Sister Busche and I were in a stake conference, we saw a couple sitting in the congregation who caught my attention. On both sides sat children and grandchildren. I was touched by the tender love I observed between the husband and wife, and then I noticed that she was considerably taller than her husband. Suddenly, it struck me, *can this be the same couple from all those years before?* I saw them cuddling together, she holding his hand and looking at him with a tender awareness of her partner's strength and dignity. As I continued to be fascinated by them, I recognized that she was indeed the one with whom I had talked to many years earlier, who had left my office so distraught. With the greatest feelings of joy, I was permitted to witness that, yes, she had done it. I could now see that she would not give up her husband for anything in the world.

I learned that he had become successful in his building and construction career. Their children and grandchildren were all together, smiling and happy. We must understand the reality of the Living God and what He, through His Spirit, can do in our lives, when we focus on Him and do the things that He will whisper to our souls. The things that look too difficult for us to master are in reality opportunities for growth. For me, this sister will always stand as an example of how we can turn a challenge into a great success when

Elder Busche walking with Saints in Omsk, Siberia. Members there participated in the Pioneer Sesquicentennial in 1997 by holding their own handcart trek.

we focus totally and completely on the Living God. I wish that we all would learn from that wonderful sister who has glorified her life by not wondering "What's in it for me?" but by asking, "What does the Lord want me to do?"

In one assignment, I was called to watch over what was happening in various temples throughout the world. One of my responsibilities was to safeguard the translation of sacred texts into various languages. At a Christmas social once, I was sitting next to a woman from a recently opened country in Eastern Europe who was in the West for the first time and who was helping with the translation work. She was a convert of a little over a year.

I asked her how she liked America, and she was very enthusiastic and positive and had many good things to say. She told me that she was living with a family in Salt Lake City. She went to Church with them every Sunday and enjoyed the meetings and admired the members of the ward. Suddenly, she stopped and said, "One of these days, I wish I could invite all the members of my Salt Lake ward to come to my home branch." I asked her about her branch.

She told me about the poor circumstances they were all living in and about how difficult it was for the members to get to their Sunday meetings and the many sacrifices that they joyfully made. She said the most inspiring time for the members in her branch was testimony meeting that was held on the Sunday of fasting. They all looked forward to hearing their fellow members report about the Lord's working in their lives. They, of course, would not part until everyone had given a testimony because they were all anxious to share the many miracles happening around them. They could not say enough about the love and most gracious care of the Lord. Then she said, "Once in awhile, we have holy angels visit and comfort and strengthen us." She added with a smile, "Can you imagine? I have found people in Salt Lake City who have never seen an angel." She laughed as if that were the strangest thing she had ever heard.

On my first visit to East Germany, the Communist system was still very strong. All of the Saints were intimidated and suffering from a strong feeling of isolation and even, in some cases, persecution. There was a spirit there that Sister Busche and I will never forget. As we spoke to them, the Saints sat on the edges of their chairs, listening eagerly to every word we said and writing it down. They had no Church literature, no curriculum material. They used only the scriptures for their classes in priesthood meeting and Relief Society, and for their sacrament meetings.

I was deeply impressed by what we may achieve when we teach nothing but the scriptures and learn from them directly without further interpretation. The spirituality and awareness of divine influence were overwhelming. Their singing was enthusiastic and full of deep reverence. The discipline of the Saints and their zeal for life was wonderful to experience. Anyone who was in East Germany at that time can testify of that.

The young people especially wanted to be close to us, ask us questions, and share their testimonies. Many of them had wonderful experiences involving the love of God that they wanted to share with us. One young man was serving in the army and had returned to attend the conference. He told me how he was always the best shot in his company and always won sharp-shooting contests. One day, his superior officer called him to his office and told him, "Tomorrow we will have a sharp-shooting contest. I give you an order to shoot bad tomorrow." The young man asked him why he should shoot badly. The officer said, "Just do what I tell you and shoot bad tomorrow. Don't ask questions."

That was very strange to the young man, and he was uncertain what he should do. Nevertheless, he obeyed and shot as poorly as he could. Later, he learned that all of the best shots from the contest were sent to the border police to shoot refugees. His officer must have sensed the spiritual purity of that young man, and he wanted to protect him. In order to make it uncomplicated, the officer had just told him, "Shoot bad tomorrow." The young man had an enthusiastic testimony that the Lord had protected him and used the officer to prevent him from having to go to the border police and shoot at innocent people.

On a later visit to East Germany, we attended the ground breaking of the Freiberg Temple in East Germany. We had been under all of the restrictions of the tight Communist system where we were told exactly what to do and what not to do. Nobody could guarantee our security. The government had been very skeptical about the activities of the Church. All of the visitors who came had their visas scrutinized and had to surrender their passports while they were there. This visit, however, seemed easier, and the dedication of the temple grounds seemed to signal a major change.

As I was visiting the conference of the Dresden Stake while I was there, I asked the stake president how a temple had come to be built in East Germany. He was a wonderful man—very courageous, very outspoken and loving. When I asked the question, he did not think twice but answered, "Maybe it was our daughter." I was surprised and asked, "Your daughter? What does your daughter have to do with this?"

He explained, "Our daughter was preparing to leave for the university. Before she left, she came to us and said, 'I have made a commitment, a covenant with God, that I will only marry in the temple.'" The president said, "We were very sorry about this because we knew that there was no temple in East Germany and that she would not have an opportunity to leave the country. That would mean she would not marry. We thought that she was going too far. We wanted her to marry and give us grandchildren. But she said, 'No, I have thought about it, and I feel it is not worth marrying in any other place than the temple.'"

So she went to another city to study. She was a pretty young woman, and the young men wanted to date her, but she always said, "I'm not dating." When they asked her what was wrong with dating, she said, "I've made a commitment that I will only marry in the temple. If I date, I may fall in love with someone. Then it would be difficult to keep my covenant." The young men thought she was a religious fanatic and left her alone.

This occurred with all but one young man who was in student

government. He asked her, "What is a temple?" She told him what a temple was. Then he asked her, "Can I marry in the temple?" She said, "No," and he asked why not. She said, "Because you are not a member of The Church of Jesus Christ of Latter-day Saints." When he asked if he could be a member of the Church, she said, "No." He asked why and she told him, "Because you are a Communist; you are an atheist; and you do not believe what we believe as members of the Church." Then he asked, "Can I learn to believe what you believe?" And she said, "Yes."

She taught him the gospel and he listened and humbled himself. The Holy Spirit fell into his soul and he became converted. Then the president said, "My little girl must have prayed very, very hard because that was the time the announcement was made that a temple would be built in East Germany."

I later learned that couple was among the first to be sealed in the newly dedicated Freiberg Temple. The last I heard, he is serving on the high council of that stake. I have no reason to question the statement of the president. Maybe it was his daughter. The faith and trust of an innocent, committed person can change the realities of this world.

Another experience happened while I was on that same trip to East Germany. The members there had started a seminary program just the year before, and I was the first one to check on how things were going. I asked them how many they had enrolled in their program. I knew that transportation was very difficult and people were spread out all over. Very few had cars, and, in order to come to their meetings, they had to endure long rides by bicycle, train, or streetcar.

The stake president was very apologetic and quietly whispered, "I'm sorry we are missing eleven." I asked him, "What do you mean you are missing eleven?" He said, "We only have 89 percent enrolled." I was surprised because even in the United States, 89 percent

Elder and Sister Busche with Meeka Voge (far left), wife of the mission president, and Sisters Susan Warner and Mary Ellen Smoot in the Ukraine.

attendance was considered very high. I excitedly told him, "Oh my goodness, that's wonderful." He looked at me as though I had not understood that they only had 89 percent attendance and were missing 11 percent of their young people.

It hit me at that moment that I was a victim of mediocre examples. The president, who had never known any different, would not accept anything less than 100 percent attendance. He told me, "We will not give in. We will not be satisfied with 89 percent. Every one of our young people is important. We cannot lose even one. Next time we will have 100 percent." Again, I felt a deep respect for the man and his commitment. I also learned about the trap of mediocrity, which we are all so vulnerable to. When we are used to seeing 50 percent, 89 percent sounds wonderful. In reality, anything but 100 percent is a defeat.

Then, I asked another question. I asked how many had dropped out in the year's course. He looked at me somewhat startled and said, "Are they allowed to drop out?" Of course, again I realized the difference in my perception and, wanting to support him, said, "No, they are not allowed. We should encourage everyone and help everyone to stay in." He was relieved because he did not believe that we should allow anyone to drop out.

I owe that president tremendous gratitude for his example of leadership in the early days of the Dresden Stake. I will always remember his faith and commitment and that of so many members of the Church in East Germany.

Once when I was visiting one of the Hawaiian stakes, I invited the members of the stake presidency to bear their testimonies before stake conference. One of the counselors was eager to testify to me about his experiences with the workings of the Living God.

This counselor had not been attending church meetings most of his adult life. At one time, he was working on a construction project on an island one thousand miles away from Hawaii, where his family was. He was grateful for the job, however, because he had been unemployed and money was tight. One day he was on the building project and felt a strong prompting to call home and speak with his little three-year-old daughter. He never called home because calls were expensive, but the feeling was so strong that he could not stay on the construction site.

He left his place and asked for permission to make a phone call. His wife was surprised to hear him because he had never called home before, and it was also an odd time to call since it was during working hours. The man asked to talk to their daughter. She was playing outside in front of the house in a pile of sand. The mother finally called the daughter in. At the very moment the daughter was on the phone talking with her father, a big truck ran off the road and into their front yard, right over the pile of sand where his daughter had just been playing.

The mother was shocked, of course, realizing that if her husband had not called, their little daughter would surely have been killed. The man heard the noise over the telephone, and when his wife told him what had happened, he was completely beside himself. He was so alarmed that he began to ponder his life and finally turned it around and became a faithful member. He became such an example of goodness to his fellow citizens that he was called to serve in the stake presidency.

I heard many such stories in Hawaii where I was very impressed by the special kindness of the people, who are very sensitive to the Spirit and have, like many of the Pacific islanders, a great capacity for love, understanding, and happiness even in difficult circumstances. I was deeply inspired by my visits with Hawaiian members. Probably in no other place, with the exception of Eastern Europe, did I feel so comfortable in touching upon the spiritual dimension of our existence.

After the first Spanish stake was created in the Los Angeles area, I was the first visitor. At the stake conference, a sister from Nicaragua bore her testimony. She told how her husband had been killed in the middle of the civil war in Nicaragua. Her family was living in dire circumstances, and she was always asking God to help her understand the pain and the difficulties they were going through. They were visited by two men dressed in white who told her that she would receive a visit from two young men, and they would give her an answer to her prayers.

A week later, two missionaries came to her door, so she listened to them very carefully. She told them, "I was waiting for you because two men in white announced that you would come." They did not understand what she meant. They told her that there were no other missionaries around and especially not ones dressed in white. The sister, in tears, then bore her testimony that those two men were holy angels who came to prepare her because she would not have listened to the missionaries otherwise. She bore her testimony that through the help of those missionaries, she was finally able to immigrate to the United States and could save her children from the onslaught of the terrible war.

When I was serving as mission president in Munich, I would often get two or three phone calls on Saturday evening from people who were traveling and wanted to know where to go to Church. One evening, I received a call from a man who spoke broken English. As I tried to explain where to go to Church, I was prompted to ask him where he was from. He said he was from Korea. It was interesting to me to find a member from Korea all the way in Munich.

As I was talking to him, the thought came to me that one of the missionaries had been writing in his weekly reports that he was teaching a Korean family. He was not able to teach them very well because they could only speak a little German and no English. I remembered that he often said if he just had a Book of Mormon in Korean, he could teach them better. I was trying to remember from the 180 missionaries which one had written me about that. I finally gave up and realized I could not arrange anything anyway because I was scheduled to speak in Sunday School and Priesthood meeting early the next morning in Aalen, a place several hours from the mission home. It was an isolated place that I had never been to before.

I decided to forget the idea when suddenly, it hit me most forcefully that the missionary who had been writing about their need of help from Korea was serving in exactly the place I would be going the next day. I still remember the feeling in my heart when I realized what was happening. I realized that I was probably the weakest link in answering the prayer of faithful servants of the Lord.

I asked the man on the phone how long he had been a member and what he was doing in the Church. I learned that he was a high councilor. I asked him what his assignment was, and he said he was in charge of missionary work. I asked if he had an extra Korean Book of Mormon. He said, "Of course. I always have an extra Book of Mormon with me." Then I asked him if he was willing to get up very early in the morning and told him a little about the situation. He was very excited and agreed to go.

The man's name was Brother Lee, and he was a delightful person. We met early the next morning and drove to Aalen. Brother Lee was a recent convert and was full of enthusiasm for the gospel. He shared with me how well the work was going in Korea. We finally arrived in Aalen and came to the place where the Church meetings were held—a rented facility in an old German house. I saw the missionary standing at the front door. When he saw that I had an Asian-looking person with me, he jumped up and down and said, "Is he Korean? Is he Korean?" I answered yes and he said, "Oh, what a blessing. My prayers have been answered."

The Korean family was already there. Brother Lee sat next to them during the meeting, and they spent the whole day together. He not only shared the Book of Mormon with them but he also bore his testimony and shared the complete, beautiful gospel of Jesus Christ with them. At the end of the day, the family had committed with full enthusiasm to be baptized. It was a deeply touching experience, and the Holy Ghost blessed everyone in that tiny branch.

Late in the evening when we were going back to Munich, I was stunned when Brother Lee, still in a state of awe, excitement, and humility, told me that he was not supposed to have gone to Munich. His business had been in Monaco, which is in southern France. The travel agency in Korea had made a mistake and instead of sending him to Monaco had sent him to Munich. He had been upset when he learned that there was no Mediterranean Sea and no palace of Prince Ranier there and that he had lost two days on his business trip. We were both in awe as we realized what had happened. The travel agent had made a mistake not knowing that he was an instrument in the hands of God. We both realized that the prayers of the missionaries and their humble Korean investigators had been answered.

I met Brother Lee later when I was serving as Area President in the North America Northeast Area. He had moved with his family to New York and was serving as president of the Korean branch there. Still later, I met him again when he was called to serve as mission president in Korea. Oh, how I wish we human beings would always be awake, understanding that the purpose of life is to find the voice and hand of the Living God in our lives so that we can all unite to build the beautiful and awe-inspiring dimensions of His kingdom on earth.

While I was touring in the Ohio Columbus Mission, I was touched by the spiritual openness of the mission president and his

Enzio once said that he would go to the ends of the earth to find the living God. His travels in the service of God brought him to many faraway places. Here he is in Alaska with mission president Doug Snarr in 1980.

wife. It was around Christmastime, and one evening, as we were together in their home, the president's wife asked me whether I could sing the Christmas song "O Tannenbaum" in German. I told her I doubted it because I had not sung it in quite some time and asked her why. She told me that her grandfather had been a German immigrant. He had lived with her family when he was older. She remembered at Christmastime that he would always put on his best suit and very somberly and emotionally sing "O Tannenbaum" in German, tears rolling down his cheeks.

As a little girl, she had been very impressed with this and it was a wonderful memory for her.

Her grandfather was the second convert in the city of Frankfurt in the 1890s. He worked in one of the factories there. He wrote about all the details of his life, where he was staying, what kind of food he ate, his work, and his hourly pay. He was contacted by the missionaries, who were, at that time, called Zion Elders. They brought the message of the gospel to his life and changed his life completely. He spent his free time with the Zion Elders, going from door to door and having nothing else in mind than building the kingdom and establishing righteousness.

Once he heard that there was a sacrament meeting in Mannheim, which is about 80 kilometers south of Frankfurt. He went there by train and spent hours trying to find the location. When he finally got there, the meeting was just ending. In order to accommodate him, the congregation stayed for another hour and gave him the experience of a sacrament meeting. He expressed his love and gratitude for the gospel and for Jesus Christ and for the opportunity to ride on the train for only two hours in order to meet the Saints and participate in a sacrament meeting.

All the members were saving their money so they could move to Zion. Finally, he was ready to leave. He was going to Antwerp, Belgium, and by ship to Plymouth. In Plymouth, a British group of immigrants joined them. He met a girl from Brighton, England, and although she could not speak any German and he could not speak English, they fell in love and were married on the ship.

They went to Salt Lake City together and there, President Wilford Woodruff commissioned them to start what was supposed to be the last colonization from Salt Lake City. They, together with some others, were sent to the Big Horn Basin in the northern part of Wyoming to begin a settlement named Cowley. They nearly starved in the first three years while they were living in tents, cold and far away from everything. In order not to starve, he took a job in Glen Rock, Wyoming, where the train went from Cowley once a week. In order to save as much money as possible, he only went home once during the whole winter—at Christmastime.

The mission president's wife told me the story her mother had shared with her when she was a little girl. That Christmas, her grandfather's family was waiting in a tiny cabin for him to come on the train. The train came, but he was not on it. There was a big snowstorm, but they waited all day long, through the night, with a candle burning in the window, and into the next day, full of deep concern over what had happened.

The next day was Christmas Eve. Just before it got dark, they finally saw him coming. He was covered with snow and on his back was a Christmas tree. He told them what had happened. As the train from Glen Rock went through the Big Horn Mountains, he saw an area where there were lovely fir trees standing, just right for Christmas trees. He jumped from the train to cut a tree, planning to jump back on again, but he fell down and could not get back on the train as he had planned. He was forced to walk the rest of the distance, twenty-four hours straight, to make it home. The president's wife said that her mother told her it was the nicest Christmas present she could remember when her father came home and brought a Christmas tree. I finally tried my best to sing "O Tannenbaum" in German for her.

Another experience I had while I was serving in the Northeast Area took place in the city of Detroit. It came to our attention that we did not have even one meeting place in the inner city of Detroit—all of the activities were happening in the suburbs. We started a small branch in the downtown area, and we arranged for them to meet in an old convenience store for the time being. One day, I went there with the mission president to visit the branch.

When we got there, we were surprised to find the stake president and several members of the stake leadership in attendance.

I thought at first that it was the branch conference, but I soon learned the real reason they were there was to be spiritually renewed. It became apparent that the greatest spiritual depth of understanding and testifying of the gospel was happening right there in that little branch. The stake president confessed to me that when he felt the need for spiritual refocus, he would go to the Sunday meetings at the Detroit branch.

Let me describe what happened when I visited there. In the convenience store where they met, there was just one large room, a restroom and a small room in the back where the children met. It was in a poor area of town. The circumstances of most of the people were such that they focused on nothing else in life but the Living God. Many of them were recent immigrants. There were about fifty people in attendance. The branch president and his wife were a missionary couple from Utah. He conducted the meeting and suggested that since it was testimony meeting, the members might have a chance to bear their testimonies before I spoke. I gladly agreed.

As soon as the sacrament was passed and they started bearing their testimonies, I noticed that something special was happening. Everyone in the congregation was full of enthusiasm and wanted to get up and bear testimony. Five or six stood at the same time and then had to take turns speaking. We heard the most beautiful expressions of love, gratitude, and praise for the goodness of the Savior—how the gospel had changed their lives for the better, or how the gospel permitted them to survive. It was an endless but never tiring testimony about the reality of the Living God, the truthfulness of the Book of Mormon, and the goodness of the restoration of the gospel.

One middle-aged African-American sister wanted to bear her

testimony but was obviously very shy and not able to assert herself. When the branch president ended testimony bearing and turned the time over to me, I said there was a sister in the audience who really wanted to bear her testimony but had not had the opportunity. I asked her if she would like to take the time then. She was beaming all over as she started to speak with a humble but not shaky voice, bearing a most stunning testimony.

She said that when she was a young girl, about fifteen years old, she had a dream that really surprised her. It was so overwhelming that she could not forget it. She asked every possible person—her parents, her teachers, her minister, anyone she met. She found no one who could explain the meaning of her dream, but she believed it was important, and she never forgot any detail of it.

As she talked about her experience, she was very emotional and had to pause frequently because she was crying. She told how the week before, she had been to Toronto to the temple for the first time. Again she was overwhelmed with emotion and could hardly speak. Finally, she said, "When I saw that house and walked into it, I relived the dream I had had as a fifteen-year-old girl. Everything that happened, all the details, I knew because I had seen them a long time before. Nobody had to explain anything because I knew what would come next." She continued, "What can I do now? I cannot say I believe it is true. I know it is true because the Lord made the effort when I was a young girl of fifteen to prepare me for that important event that would happen much later in my life: finding the gospel of Jesus Christ in its unpolluted form."

We were all astounded by the awareness that such a long time before, the Lord, in His tender mercy, had shown this woman in a dream what she must not miss later in her life. It kept her looking for the meaning of her dream and its purpose in her life.

On 17 April 1990, I received a telephone call from a member of the Church in Pittsburgh. He asked if I would be available to meet Joseph Schultz, a man from Germany with whom he had been working on a business project. The good brother in Pittsburgh said that he had served a mission in Germany. He indicated that he was impressed by Mr. Schultz's honesty and by his spiritual openness. He explained that he had shared his testimony with him. I was told that Mr. Schultz confided in him that he was always looking for the purpose of life and that as a younger man, he had wanted to become a Catholic priest. He had left the priesthood because he felt he could not live the law of celibacy, and he did not want to become a liar.

The brother from Pittsburgh said that Mr. Schultz wanted to come to Salt Lake City the following Wednesday and Thursday to find out more about the Church and wondered if I would be available to meet him. I was given his flight schedule and told that he already had reservations at the Marriott Hotel. I contacted the mission president of the Utah Salt Lake Mission, who asked a missionary couple to meet Mr. Schultz and spend some time with him.

Wednesday evening I picked up Mr. Schultz at his hotel, and we spent the evening in our home. It was a wonderful evening as I shared the events that led to my conversion and he shared his innermost feelings and desires that he had as a boy of wanting to help to build a better world. He was blessed with a fine, nearly aristocratic manner, a sharp sense of the responsibility we, as human beings, have before our Maker, and a strong desire to surrender into the arms of the Living God. He had built a good-sized, respectable business. He was married and had four children.

Elder Busche takes a moment to ponder at a session of general conference in April 1999.

I felt his wonderful warmth and openness to learn about the matters of Christ and the gospel of salvation. He soaked in the message of the restoration with the humble, open heart of an innocent child. I felt a tremendous responsibility not to misuse his trust. Sister Busche and I were touched by the goodness, honesty, and humility of that remarkable man.

He told us that in his business meetings in Pittsburgh, he had been impressed that his counterpart did not smoke. Because of his own habit of smoking, he felt challenged by that. When he heard that the man did not smoke because of religious reasons, he was surprised because all of the priests that he knew smoked. On Friday, Mr. Schultz asked the man where he would go to church on Sunday and if he could join him at church because he had nothing else to do in Pittsburgh over the weekend.

That good brother asked Mr. Schultz to join him for the Sunday meeting. Mr. Schultz reported that during the night in his hotel room, he had something unusual happen to him. He woke up in the middle of the night. It was his habit to light up a cigarette, and he did so. As he put the cigarette in his mouth, he said a voice told him, "Enjoy this one because it will be the last. The church you will be going to tomorrow will change your life." After a moment of shock and some pondering, he reacted by taking the cigarette out of his mouth and saying, "Then I won't have this one either." He reported to us that he had not smoked since that time, which was four days earlier. What surprised him even more was that he seemed to have lost his desire to smoke.

This experience is a good example of how there are powers surrounding us, trying to help us. We do not know how close the other side is, and we are not trained or sensitive enough to understand and listen. Sometimes we say, "I had something funny happen," and we even make jokes or belittle the coincidences or occurrences that we do not comprehend. We do not understand what is happening—that someone from the other side who loves us dearly is watching over us, trying to bring us to a state of awakening and wanting to help us.

On Thursday evening, I again picked up Mr. Schultz at his hotel. We talked as I drove west on the freeway. He told me that the Church meeting had been nice but also confusing to him. So he decided to come to Salt Lake City to find the roots of the Church and gain a better understanding. I explained the sacred covenant that the Lord invites us human beings to commit to. He listened carefully and then became very emotional as he heard about the law of tithing. He told me that he had his checkbook with him and humbly asked me if he could pay his tithing right then. I told him that that would be a part of his baptismal covenant and that it would be appropriate to wait until the day of his baptism.

I continued to explain the plan of salvation and the rest of the conditions of the baptismal covenant with God so that we could become eligible for the atoning blood of the Lord Jesus Christ. We arrived at a place in the middle of the Skull Valley desert where I took a small side road. I was driving aimlessly, wanting to go as far from civilization as possible to avoid distractions. We got out and walked a little way into the desert. It was like we were standing alone in the middle of God's beautiful creations. He agreed to join me in pouring out our souls to our Creator. As we knelt in prayer, I felt such a powerful feeling penetrate my heart that I knew he was one of the special sons of our Heavenly Father. At the end of the prayer, we were both overwhelmed with feelings of joy and behaved like little children, dancing and singing as we praised God.

He wanted to be baptized immediately. He was so innocent, pure, and childlike. Then suddenly, he said, "The Book of Mormon. I forgot about it. I have not read it yet. Tell me, is it true?" I shared my testimony with him about the Book of Mormon. He said, full of enthusiasm, "That is enough for me. I believe you. We can still go on with the baptism." I felt impressed to tell him that the most important element in our lives is our family. I suggested that he think carefully about his wife and commit to bringing the gospel to her so that she could partake of its fruit also. He was excited about the idea, saying that waiting was much better because what would his wife think if he came from America as a member of an American church?

As we continued to talk about the beauty of the gospel of Jesus Christ, Mr. Schultz mentioned his desire to spend one more day with me in order to get a better understanding and to have more of his questions answered. I had to tell him that early the next morning, I had to leave to preside over a stake conference somewhere in the east, the arrangements having been made by my secretary. He mentioned that he also had a business meeting in Canada in Woodstock, a town near Fredericton in New Brunswick, where his only office in North America was located and where he also owned a summer home by a lake.

When I checked my calendar to verify where I was supposed to go, I nearly fainted when I realized I was going to Saint John in New Brunswick, and Fredericton was a city in that stake. I had never been in that part of the world before, and so far, I have never been back, yet I was going to a stake conference to the very place that he needed to go. For a moment, we were both stunned. The stake conference was scheduled to be held in Fredericton because it was the most central city in the Saint John Stake. Without any effort or extra travel, Mr. Schultz attended all of the stake conference sessions.

After the conference on Sunday, he and I were invited by the stake president to have dinner in his home. We continued to talk about the gospel under the influence of the Holy Ghost. Mr. Schultz's enthusiasm, kindness, and joy captivated us all. He did not want to leave, but I had to begin the mission tour of the Canada Halifax Mission. He participated that afternoon in the zone conference at the Fredericton Stake Center. He bore a powerful testimony of the restored gospel, to the amazement of the missionaries. Then came the time of good-bye as he had to leave to take care of business matters.

I contacted the appropriate German mission president, who happened to be a brother of Elder H. Burke Peterson, and told him about Joseph Schultz. President Peterson promised to do everything he could to teach not only Mr. Schultz and his wife but also his adult children who were still living at home. During the next several months, Brother Schultz called me on a regular basis to report what was happening as well as the reaction of his wife and children. It was not as easy as he had thought it would be. As he was given the missionary lessons, the whole gospel with its many complexities produced many questions for him. Yet he seemed to be committed and was just waiting for his wife.

Around the end of October, I received another call from him. He said, "This is the most beautiful day of my life because my wife has accepted the challenge to be baptized, but first she wants to talk to you." I had the privilege of speaking with Mrs. Schultz as she bore testimony in her humble way that she did not feel it necessary to fight anymore against the goodness she found in the gospel and in the example of the missionaries.

When I talked with Brother Schultz later, he said that a problem had arisen. He said that his wife had broken her foot and was in a cast. Her doctor had recommended that the cast not get wet for six weeks. He said, "We do not understand what this means. Doesn't the Lord want us to be baptized?" Upon which I said, "I know exactly what that means. Sister Busche and I are planning to be in Germany over the holidays. This delay will allow us to attend the baptism." Again we were both stunned over the flow of events as Brother Schultz said that he had hoped and prayed that I could be there for their baptism.

The baptism took place on Sunday afternoon, December 30 that same year. Sister Busche and I drove with our two oldest sons to the Schultzs' home where we were invited to stay overnight in their spacious country home. As soon as we became acquainted, we left for the stake center, about a one-hour drive, where Brother and Sister Schultz were baptized and confirmed members of the Church. There were about one hundred members present, including a group of about twelve missionaries who were as excited as they could be.

After the baptism and confirmation, Brother Schultz invited my family to go with his family to a luxurious hotel in his hometown for dinner. We learned the "Hotel Vier Jahreszeiten" was his favorite place and everyone knew him there. He surprised the waiters when he announced that he did not want alcohol served to him anymore. We had a delightful dinner and got acquainted with the Schultzs' four children.

I have kept in touch with Brother and Sister Schultz. From her, I learned what a great blessing the gospel has been in their lives as the behavior of her husband so completely changed that it seemed unbelievable. She talked about the different relationship the family had before the gospel came to their home. Exactly one year after their baptism, they were sealed in the Frankfurt temple and, eventually, the youngest daughter was also baptized. On a visit to the United States, Brother Schultz insisted that I take him and his wife to the same spot in the desert where he and I had knelt and prayed so that she could experience the same feeling.

Joseph and Birgit Schultz have shown a keen interest in bringing the gospel to my sisters. One day they went to my hometown to see my sister, who lives in Dortmund in the home where I grew up. Sister Schultz reported a sacred experience to me that happened when she and her husband visited my sister. Sister Schultz told me that my sister was very friendly and hospitable and that she and her husband listened to the message of the Restoration, basically given by Brother Schultz, politely. Then Sister Schultz said that suddenly there was another person in the room who stood at some distance, watching, friendly and gentle, over the scene. She felt that it must have been the spirit of my father. She was so touched that she did not dare talk about it until she and her husband were on their way back home.

I am very grateful for the opportunity I have had to get to know Joseph Schultz and his dear wife and to share in their wonderful conversion process and see the blessings of the gospel in their lives.

It is very humbling to experience how carefully the Lord is watching over His Church. The following was shared with me by one of the brethren responsible for missionary service in the Church. Soon after the collapse of the Iron Curtain, the Church got a request from the government of Bulgaria to send missionaries to their country. It caught the Church administration by surprise. Nobody knew anyone who could even speak Bulgarian, so immediately a tremendous effort to find someone who could speak Bulgarian was begun. A sister who was a missionary in the MTC was found who listed Bulgarian as her second language. This sister's father was Bulgarian. When asked if he was a member of the Church, she said yes. Was her father active? Yes. He lived in the vicinity of Washington, D.C., so one of the Brethren visited him and found him faithful and active. When he was interviewed, he told of his most interesting background.

This brother lived in post-war Bulgaria. As a young man, he became a dental lab technician. At that time, when the Algerian government became independent from France, they wanted help in developing their own country from other Communist countries. The Bulgarian government was selecting people to go to Algeria to help. This brother's laboratory was assigned to send one volunteer to Algeria. There were seven people who worked in the lab and all volunteered to go. They decided to draw lots to choose which one and made six pieces of paper with "no" and one with "yes."

This brother drew the "yes" paper, but because he was the youngest with the least tenure, the others felt it was not right that he go. He insisted that they had agreed to decide by drawing lots,

Elder Busche with his sisters. His youngest sister, Kerstin (on the left), has also embraced the gospel and was baptized several years after Elder Busche's conversion.

but he was outnumbered, so they drew lots again. Again he drew the "yes" paper, which made the others even angrier. They decided to draw new lots with a new system and made him draw last, yet again he drew the "yes" paper. This happened seven times in a row, each time, he came up with the paper that said "yes." After the seventh time, the others admitted that something was happening that they could not fight and let him go.

This brother went to Algeria, but as soon as he could, he fled from Algeria to Paris. On a street in Paris, he met some missionaries and was converted to the gospel. He immigrated to Canada and stayed there a couple of years before he moved to the United States.

He had been working for the last couple of years as a dental lab technician in the Washington, D. C., area.

As he was interviewed, he mentioned that something strange had recently happened. He said he had just received a letter from the Bulgarian government stating that his apartment, which he had owned but which the government had taken away, was now being returned to him. He said he did not know what to do with the apartment and so would donate it to the Church.

Eventually, this brother became the first mission president in Bulgaria and stayed in his own apartment. It is clear that the Lord was way ahead of His Church, knowing years in advance what would happen and selecting and preparing the man who would be the first Bulgarian mission president. He made a miracle happen in order for a young man to get out of Bulgaria, to find the gospel, and to raise a child who had the faith to go on a mission.

It is obvious that the Lord is hastening His work in the latter days. We must open our eyes to the world of eternal dimensions and learn to listen to that little voice that is always trying to communicate with us. We must learn that we of the human race have to live with the consequences of our own behavior. Therefore, the Lord and His servants constantly attempt to bring us to a state of awakening, to guide us to turn around and embrace the small, narrow path that leads to salvation, exaltation, and eternal life as the final fulfillment of every human hope. The closer we come, the more joy will dwell in our souls, and we may begin to sing the songs of redeeming love.

15

Gentle Greetings from the Other Side

When I was mission president in Munich, a sister from a small branch came to visit me. She said she wanted to talk to me, and I was impressed with her story. She told me that many years before she was married but did not have any children. Several doctors had told her that she should never have children because they would be handicapped, so she took precautions not to get pregnant.

One day she met the missionaries and began to listen to their message. She grew in spiritual understanding and finally received a spiritual confirmation of its truth. Her husband was against any religion, so she told the missionaries they should not come back. As they were leaving, both the missionaries stood at the door and told her that she would not be able to ignore the Lord's message in her future life because she knew that it was the truth. The Lord would continue to work with her and, one day, she may even regret her decision.

The reason she came to me was to ask for the addresses of those two missionaries. Of course, it was long before my time, but I was able to identify the two missionaries, and we brought them back in contact with her. The reason she wanted their names was a very interesting one. She said that soon after the missionaries left, she became pregnant and was terrified because she did not want to have a handicapped child. She pleaded with God that if He would help her and preserve her and the health of her child, she would be baptized in His church and educate her child to become a missionary.

To her great joy, and that of her husband, they had a healthy boy. In consequence of her promise, she was baptized into the Lord's church and faithfully raised her son in it. He had recently turned nineteen and received his mission call, and she wanted to contact the two missionaries who had come to her home years before in order to give them the good news about her family. She wanted them to pray for her son and to thank them for their steadfastness and boldness of twenty years before.

I was very touched by what she said. The power and the reality of the Word given under the sacred influence of the Spirit help people accept responsibility and change their lives for the better. I met her son later. He was a wonderful young man, ready to go on a mission. He is still in southern Germany, and I heard that he recently became a bishop.

One of the difficulties we had when I was serving as mission president was finding housing for the missionaries. In Munich, we had one apartment that was adequate for two missionaries, and we had to house six missionaries in it, which was creating some difficulties. This went on for weeks and then months but nothing could be done to change that.

Elder Busche greets President James E. Faust during a session of general conference in Salt Lake City.

Early one morning, Elder Berrett, who was serving as the finance secretary in the mission office, came and asked my permission to go with his companion to find an apartment. To my surprise, he said that he would not come home until they found an apartment, but that he would be home by 5:00. I gave him my blessing but did not expect him to find anything because no one else had been able to. But this time, it was different and taught me an important lesson.

Elder Berrett came home around 3:00 and had found an apartment. I asked him what he had done. He said as soon as they left the mission office, they talked with a sense of urgency to every person they saw. They said, "We need an apartment. Do you know anyone who may have room available?" They contacted hundreds of people in a short time, with the urgency of a drowning man.

Then they found a man who was on his way to the newspaper

with an ad for an apartment that had just become vacant. The apartment was not far away, only about one kilometer, from the mission office, certainly within walking distance. Elder Berrett was able to persuade the man to rent the apartment to them, and they already had the contract in their hands. It was a great learning experience for many as we saw that when we learn to totally focus on achieving something with a firm commitment, taking away all distractions, we succeed.

Another incident that occurred while I was serving as a mission president gave me a better understanding about the Holy Spirit's ability to fill us with abundance when we humble ourselves and become teachable.

I was concerned about a missionary who obviously came from a good family but who had been perhaps a little too protected in his childhood. He had many good attributes, but he was very shy and afraid and did not know how to survive as a missionary. It was not difficult to love him, and I was pained that he was so insecure and unhappy. He was not doing very well as a missionary. I felt what a blessing it would be to give him an opportunity to have a successful missionary experience. I prayed deeply and was prompted to transfer him to a different area.

How surprised I was when, just a week later, I received an enthusiastic letter from that young man asking how I knew about his companion. He told me that he and his new companion had been best friends when they were children, but they had not seen each other since elementary school. He had not known his friend was in that mission, and, of course, I was not aware of any of that. The Spirit had guided me to transfer him to this one young man out of 179 possibilities. They were very successful together, and the shy elder finally had a very good mission experience. I still think about it and how it would not have happened without the help of the Lord.

The teachings of the gospel have a lasting impact on the souls of us human beings, though that impact may not always be evident immediately. Missionaries may be discouraged and not realize how important their work is, and the effects of their efforts may become evident only years later, as was shown by another experience I had.

After a stake conference in Topeka, Kansas, in the early 1980s, I was late getting to the airport because the meetings were long and we were held up in traffic. I finally got to the plane just as they were closing the door. The plane was full. There was only one seat left in the economy section in a middle seat. I was so exhausted, I just collapsed into my seat. I just wanted to relax and sleep a little.

I pulled out my day planner to make a couple of notes about the conference, as I usually do, when I noticed that the woman next to me in the aisle seat seemed to be taking an interest in me. It seemed that she wanted to talk to me and I thought, *I hope she will leave me alone because I really need sleep, not a conversation.* As I was thinking that, she startled me by saying, "Are you possibly a Mormon?" I was surprised at first. I found out she was not a member and that she had something interesting to tell me.

She said the missionaries had come to her home many years before. She was married with young children. She was interested in their message, but she felt like she would risk her marriage if she continued and sent the missionaries away. Then she told me, "Many years have gone by and my husband has divorced me. My children are all grown and living their own lives. I'm all alone." She said she lived in a small town in Texas and had always hoped she would meet the missionaries again. She did not understand the system and thought the same missionaries would still be there. She watched for them on the streets but never found them.

She said she was on a trip for family business and when she saw me walking down the aisle of the plane, she saw in my countenance the same spirit she had seen in the missionaries. When I sat down by her and pulled out my journal, she had felt that I must be a member of the same Church and, therefore, she had addressed me.

I was so overwhelmed with feelings of joy by her story and her humility and desire to find meaning and purpose in her life. I shared my testimony of the living God with her on the short trip to Denver. The Holy Ghost came right into the plane, and she was just glowing. I gave her all the necessary information. She was so happy she would be able to find the Kingdom of God on earth and the joy she felt while the missionaries were teaching her the gospel.

When I served as executive administrator for the Northern California Area in the mid 1980s, there was an earthquake in Coalinga in north central California, which was in the Hanford Stake. I went there to see the damage and find out what could be done to help. I met the stake president and learned about something very interesting that had happened.

The president had felt impressed a week before the earthquake to have the whole stake membership participate in an emergency preparedness exercise. He assigned each ward a different catastrophe—chemical spills, plane crash, whatever he could think of. Coalinga was the only ward he assigned an earthquake. The bishop of that ward was a geology teacher and teased the stake president, saying, "You need to find another disaster for our town because we are not anywhere near a seismic fault. We won't have an earthquake in Coalinga." But the stake president said, "Let's do it anyway."

Everyone in the stake took the exercise very seriously. In Coalinga, they brought ham radio equipment in and got the operator set up. They went through the emergency exercise with all the

In August of 1977, Enzio was asked to translate for President Spencer W. Kimball in this special meeting at the Berlin Stake Center. After the meeting, President Kimball asked to speak with Enzio and issued him a call as a General Authority of The Church of Jesus Christ of Latter-day Saints.

details. Exactly one week later, the real thing hit. Coalinga was so devastated that it took some time before anyone else knew about it because all of the electricity was gone. There were only two major roads to Coalinga and both were impassable. The only way to get information out was through the ham radio operator and the equipment that was still there.

The president told me another strange occurrence. As we drove through the city, I was shocked by the devastation the earthquake had left. Every building in the city had been damaged or destroyed. The only building within the city limits that had no damage was our chapel. Before the earthquake, however, there had been a crack in a wall of the chapel, and it had been an eyesore. The earthquake had closed the crack. The church was the center for the relief efforts, and the ham radio operator was there. The church had the only kitchen that was still operable. There was still running water in the building. A tent city surrounded the church, and people went inside to wash and eat. It was a great blessing to the whole city.

I was very impressed by the stake president, who was so humble and obviously in tune with the Spirit. I saw him years later after he had been a mission president. He told me that because of his experience in Coalinga, he had been asked to give an emergency preparedness presentation about earthquakes in southern Idaho. A week later, they had an earthquake. He joked that he was not going to talk about earthquakes anymore because people would think he caused them.

During the Sunday session of the Houston Texas East Stake conference held in March 1996, the van of one of the members attending the session was stolen out of the Church parking lot. As I left the stake center, I found a group of about eight people in a panic because they had lost their means of transportation. My heart was aching, and I pondered with the stake president what we could do to help that family.

About a month later, I had occasion to call the president about matters in his stake. I also inquired about the stolen van. He reported that after I left that day, he had made an assignment for all members of the stake high council to make an organized effort that very Sunday to find the vehicle. They had divided the very large city of Houston into sections and, in pairs, had prayerfully begun to look for it. As two of the high councilors were driving down a street, they saw the van. It had no one in it, and, most fortunately, the engine was running. One of them jumped into the van and, without having to confront the thief, took it and drove it to its rightful owner. The president said that the owners and the stake members were very touched by this obviously miraculous event.

Later that same month, I was visiting with a president of a stake in the northern mining area of Arizona. He had been called to serve as stake president ten months earlier. I asked him about one ward in his stake that had not been able to maintain their Primary organization because they could not find even one sister willing to serve as Primary president. The president shared a most sacred experience with me.

He said that the bishop of that ward was very concerned because no sister was willing to accept the call to serve. He spoke about the matter fervently with Heavenly Father. After much fasting and prayer, he received a powerful manifestation from the Spirit that he should call a certain inactive sister. He reasoned against it, but received several confirmations and, finally, he went to see the sister, who told him an interesting incident that had happened.

She said that the night before, she had seen in a dream a manifestation of Hell. A messenger had told her that she must decide whether she wanted to go to that ugly place of filth, or whether she wanted to return to Heavenly Father. In my understanding, this seemed to be a warning vision, as is mentioned in Doctrine and Covenants 76:44–45, which describes the torment of those in everlasting punishment and says in verse 47, "Nevertheless, I, the Lord, show it [hell] by vision unto many, but straightway shut it up again."

She was still in a state of shock, trembling over the experience of the previous night, and was very surprised when the bishop wanted to see her the next morning. She was overwhelmed and committed to the bishop that she would bring herself into compliance with the covenant she had made with God and accepted with deep humility the sacred call to serve as Primary president. The miracle of that incident could not be kept secret. When the other sisters of the ward understood what had happened, it caused such a stir that a completely new spirit of rededication and commitment developed.

The following experience is probably one of the most sacred in my whole life. It happened in the very beginning of my service as a General Authority, after I moved to the United States. I was still very new and inexperienced, and I had to rely completely on the Spirit to be able to do the many things I had to do.

On one trip, on assignment as an executive administrator, I gave a talk on welfare to a lovely group of people. I taught them in a special meeting and spoke about faith and the dimensions of faith and the importance of developing it. I quoted Matthew 17 to explain how the Lord expected his disciples to have faith and how frustrated He was when they did not have enough faith to cast out an evil spirit. I quoted that scripture in order to show our need not only to view faith as a thought or feeling, but also as a power with which we can control or even change the circumstances of this world.

That evening, I began a tour of a neighboring mission and stayed in the basement of the mission home that night. I was very tired when I finally went to bed at around 11:00. I fell sound asleep as soon as I was in bed. I woke with a start when, at about 1:00 A.M., the mission president came into my room. The light was on and he was speaking to me, but I was still half asleep and did not understand what he was saying. I asked him if what he had to say could not wait until tomorrow. I could see that he was disappointed, but he nodded his head and began to leave the room.

By then, I was more awake and called him back and asked him to repeat the problem. I focused on listening to him and was surprised by what he said. He said that in the evening, a missionary had been possessed by an evil spirit. His companion had called the assistants to help cast it out. The assistants had gone and done that, but as they got back to their own apartment, the evil spirit had entered one of the assistants. The other was so shocked that he did not know what to do, so he went straight to the mission home.

The mission president was appalled, of course, because this was not just an ordinary missionary. This was one of the stalwart, experienced missionaries who was speaking gibberish and not in control of his physical movements. The mission president had tried to cast out the evil spirit but had failed. He began to panic, but then he realized that he had a General Authority in the basement. That was when he came down to try to wake me up.

After he told me, it hit me like a hammer that the very day I had been speaking about that scripture from Matthew, I was confronted with the same situation. I was under the watchful eye of the Lord and would have to prove my faith or show my lack of it.

I was very uncomfortable and asked the mission president to give me a little time. I wanted to get dressed first. I immediately began to pray with a deep, fervent plea for help. I felt so helpless because I had never been in a situation like that. Crazy thoughts came to my mind. For instance, I wished I had stayed in a motel, but I knew there was no way to escape.

I finally dressed and had no further excuse to tarry longer, so I went upstairs. As I went up, I heard noises and unintelligible sounds, and fear began to creep into my heart. I felt that fear come from the ground, from below, trying to sneak into my system. I could understand why, when people are afraid, their knees begin to shake. When I got to the living room, I saw the elder sitting in a chair, shaking all over, making uncontrolled movements, speaking with foam on his lips. His companion and the mission president and his family were all staring at the spectacle with shock and fear.

As I entered the room, it was like a voice said to me, "Brother Busche, you must make a decision now." I knew immediately what decision it was. I had to decide whether to join the fear and amazement and helplessness or to let faith act and let courage come in. I knew, of course, that I wanted to have faith. I wanted to have the power, the priesthood power, and I wanted to know what to do to save the situation.

In that moment, two scriptures came into my mind. One scripture was very simple: Moroni 8:16, "Perfect love casteth out all fear." And the other was the same: 1 John 4:18, "Perfect love casteth out fear." But I did not have love. I had fear. What do we do when we have fear but not love? My mind was drawn to Moroni 7:48, where the Lord points out how we can gain love: "Wherefore, . . . pray unto the Father with all the energy of heart, that ye may be filled with this love."

I prayed with all the energy of my heart, "Father, fill my soul with love." I cried from the depths of my being, without wasting any time. It all happened in a split second. After that, it was as if my skull was opened and a warm feeling poured down into my soul—down my head, my neck, my chest. As it was pouring down, it drove out all of the fear. My shivering knees stopped shaking. I stood there, a big smile came to my face—a smile of deep, satisfying joy and confidence.

Suddenly, those in the room looked not scary, but amusing. It was just funny to see them all there. I learned in that moment that when we are under the influence of the Spirit, we can find a sense of humor and the ability to smile and not take ourselves too seriously, and we can laugh at ourselves. Then it dawned on me that the adversary's weapons are sarcasm, irony, and cynicism, but that the Lord's power is a gentle sense of humor. I have learned more and more since then that the adversary cannot deal with a sense of humor. He does not have a sense of humor; he does not even know what that is. He is always dead serious, and when you have a sense of humor, you are in control of the adversary's influence.

I still did not know what to do. I had great confidence, but I did not know what to do with it. As I stood there, it was as though someone came and put his arm around me and said, "Let me do this for you. I can take it from here." I was very happy with that idea. Then I watched myself do something very strange and surprising because I did not know what I was doing. I went to that young man who was sitting on a chair shaking uncontrollably. I knelt in front of him and put my arms around him, pulling him gently to my chest. I told him, with all the strength of my soul, "I love you, my brother."

In the very moment I did that, the evil spirit left. The missionary came to his senses, looked at me and said, "I love you, too." He snapped right out of it and asked what had happened. For about an hour after that, we had a spontaneous sharing of testimonies, jubilantly praising God and singing and praying. It was an exuberant experience of the workings of the spirit of love, which is the Spirit of Christ and by it overcoming all evil.

We later learned the cause of the missionary being in that situation. That evening, at an investigator's home, the missionaries had seen an inappropriate movie against the established guidelines. Because of that, he lost the Spirit and fear entered his soul. The fear allowed the evil spirit to enter. That same fear must have come to the assistant, as he probably had never experienced anything like that before. In his insecurity, he may also have let fear come into his heart so that the evil spirit could enter him after he had helped cast it out of the other missionary. The powers of the love of Christ are real. We can control our lives in our families and in our daily routine only

Many of Elder Busche's prayers have been answered as he has gone into the mountains for long walks. Walking is, in fact, one of his favorite pastimes. Here he is with his wife, Jutta, on a walk in the mountains of Germany in 1998.

when we learn to always be filled with the Spirit of Christ, which is the opposite of the spirit of fear, and which is the spirit of confidence and hope and faith and love. Therefore, in order to be eligible for that spirit, it is so important to keep ourselves away from filth and places of filth.

I had reason to marvel at the goodness of our Father in Heaven. I may have needed that experience of learning in the early days of my service as a General Authority of the Church of Jesus Christ. We are here to learn about the reality of the Living God and also to understand that the powers of darkness are real. We need to know that our lives have a very specific purpose: to learn to make decisions of eternal consequences. A church with the knowledge of all things had to be restored so that all children of our Heavenly Father who are seeking for meaning and reason can find it and can also find the light and power to live their lives with growing confidence and joy.

I needed to have that experience because I learned more about the workings of the Spirit and the workings of the power of the gospel through that incident than I could have learned in any other teaching situation. Today, I treasure that more than anything because it gave me an understanding that I could not have received in any other way. With all the prayers that I was offering, I was still not ready to control my fear until I opened my heart to fill it with love. That was a very holy experience. I am very grateful today that the Lord gave me the opportunity to learn that our purpose is to fill our souls with love. That has helped me in many ways throughout my life, and I believe that truth contains the essentials for mankind's survival.

A Final Word

THERE IS A SIMPLE LESSON WE EACH have the opportunity to learn in life. It is that in each of us is the potential for two opposing situations. A person can experience feelings of joy that become almost unbearable. Or a person can experience unhappiness to the extent that there seems to be no way out.

Shortly after the end of the war, my sisters and I were cleaning up the ruins of our house. We had solicited some help from neighbors and friends. One person who came regularly was a woman who always dressed in the traditional black clothing of mourning. She had been told that her husband was killed in action in Russia years before. One day I was sitting in a pile of rubble, using a hammer to clean the mortar from bricks, when I heard this woman screaming at the top of her voice, a shrieking scream. Everyone ran to find out what had happened. We found her shouting and dancing and finally passing out. Her husband was standing in front of her, just a skeleton, in the poorest of clothing, but he was alive. I don't believe I had ever seen a happier person than this woman in that very moment.

On the other extreme, some individuals reach such a state of depression—or become so empty and hollow—that they want this life to come to an end. Both extremes are within our reach. And both extremes *seem* to be based on circumstance. Many who have not come to a state of spiritual awakening, may, in fact, believe that circumstances are the *deciding factor* in happiness. In the case of the woman mentioned above, that distinction may seem true on the surface. With my understanding today, however, I am aware that this woman had been keeping the memory of her husband alive, maintaining the highest level of admiration and gratitude for him. She lived a modest and virtuous life of dedication and selfless service to others. She lived her life in innocence and purity and, therefore, *she was ready to receive that joy.*

One of the great principles that came to light through the Restoration of the gospel of Jesus Christ is that of agency and freedom. Only when a person has come to the understanding that each individual is born free and that the choices that individual makes determine his future—even into the eternities—can that person begin to understand how important every minute of life is. The situation is, in some dimension, tragic because most people in the world seem not to understand what freedom really is and therefore are more or less wasting their lives. They unwittingly become slaves to circumstance, habits, traditions, or their own lust and greed. They live their lives without understanding who they are, where they came from, and what will happen to them when they die. The lives of many seem to be like that of a football player sent onto the field to play without knowing anything about the rules of the game. He does not know which team he belongs to and does not know which coach to listen to. Soon he will be so frustrated and confused that he won't want to play anymore.

Life is that way when we do not follow the longing of our souls and search for the Living God—when we do not spend all our waking hours under the influence of the Light that emanates from Him. Only under the influence of His Light can we learn to understand the knowledge and truth necessary to fulfill the purpose of our existence here.

We alone decide where it is that we stand on the continuum between total frustration and complete fulness of joy. Nothing can happen that will allow us to progress on that continuum until we come to a state of spiritual awakening and learn to become honest with ourselves, thus allowing the Light of Christ to be felt. To bring immortality and eternal life to man—and to redeem him from the state of not knowing—it was necessary to restore the knowledge of the plan of salvation to the Earth.

Knowledge of this plan comes not as a consequence of human hopes and dreams or imaginations; rather, it is a divine spark, already inside of us, that is in need of awakening. Before we came to this earth, we not only knew about the plan, we also approved it. We can be "reawakened" to its truths if we have learned to humble ourselves and gained an awareness of our own nothingness. Without He who created us and without His Only Begotten Son in the flesh, even Jesus Christ, we are nothing.

My wife and I lived in our homeland of Germany, close to the Frankfurt airport, to fulfill my assignment to bring the gospel of

Jesus Christ to the people of the former Soviet Union and its satellite countries. I suffered a stroke during this time and was taken to a nearby hospital. As soon as I became conscious again, I became aware that I was in a room with another patient who was very grouchy. Anything a nurse or some of the many helpers or the doctors did to help him or to serve him did not satisfy him. Nothing was right. He always complained and expressed his dissatisfaction.

After having spent three days together with him, he suddenly approached me with a harsh and somewhat offensive voice, asking: "And you, you are here with me and the only thing you can do is to be happy and to smile. And you are much worse off than myself because you just had a stroke and you do not even know whether you are going to make it. What is it that makes you happy?"

I turned my head as far as I could and looked straight into his eyes and said, with a sudden impulse of great joy: "I believe in Jesus Christ, our Savior and Healer."

He reacted as though he had been struck with a whip. For a while he was in a state of shock. After a short time he spoke again, but with a very different tone in his voice: "I believe I am in terrible need to learn about Jesus Christ. Will you please help me?"

My voice was still a little bit feeble and weak, so he did most of the talking. I learned very quickly the reason for his previous irate behavior. His life had been a disaster of insensitivities, rudeness, cruelty, and of reaching only one goal in life—financial success. I could see once again that an individual might be able to gain all the material things of the world, but those things mean nothing when the soul has been damaged. I could also see that the pain and the suffering of one who is in darkness may cause him to develop a hunger and thirst for the blessings that come from a living God. As soon as I was out of the hospital, this man invited me to talk about Jesus Christ in front of a group of thirty of his friends. He was excited that he had found a man who believes in Jesus Christ. I could feel him thirsting after a knowledge of the living God. I have come to recognize that this thirsting is found in the vast majority of God's sons and daughters on Earth. At times, that thirst is simply hidden under a callous and selfish attitude or a heart that is surrounded by sadness.

During much of my youth, I could feel *myself* thirsting but did not know where to turn to quench my suffering. Through the gospel and a witness of the Restoration of the gospel of Jesus Christ, the reality of my world was changed. And so can it be changed for each who is suffering, longing, and thirsting after the peace that comes from a sure knowledge of a living God, who loves us and sent His Son to redeem and rescue us.

Appendix

Christianity and the Hope of the Future

Editor's Note: The following talk is representative of Elder F. Enzio Busche's desire to testify of the truth and light that comes from the Living God. It was originally published in The Prophet and His Work: Essays from General Authorities on Joseph Smith and the Restoration *(Salt Lake City: Deseret Book, 1996) 129–45.*

THE OTHER DAY I WAS WATCHING A news broadcast on local television. A Protestant minister stated bluntly that Mormons cannot be considered Christians. As I pondered this statement, my thoughts went back to the history of the Christian world and several age-old questions that always are new: What is truth? Who is qualified or authorized to make judgment? Who truly represents the Lord and the truth coming from him?

These questions obviously are most significant. The Lord, Jesus Christ, during His earthly ministry, made the statement, "I am the way, the truth, and the life: no man cometh unto the Father, but by me" (John 14:6). In His foreknowledge, Christ must have seen what would happen to coming generations before He would restore His kingdom on this earth. He gave His disciples a profound warning: "Beware of false prophets, which come to you in sheep's clothing, but inwardly they are ravening wolves" (Matthew 7:15). He then explained how to find and identify His disciples:

> Ye shall know them by their fruits. Do men gather grapes of thorns, or figs of thistles?
>
> Even so every good tree bringeth forth good fruit; but a corrupt tree bringeth forth evil fruit. . . .
>
> Every tree that bringeth not forth good fruit is hewn down, and cast into the fire.
>
> Wherefore by their fruits ye shall know them. (Matthew 7:16–20)

Because some ministers of traditional churches want to deny us the right to be called Christian, I feel that we should look into the history of Christianity for clues to identify the fruit we should be seeking. I invite you, therefore, to join me in a short review of Christian history. This review not only will help us identify the fruit we should be seeking, but perhaps also will help us find the roots of the misery that challenges the very existence of mankind in our day.

When we look into the roots of our Western culture, we cannot separate political history from the history of the Christian churches. The two histories are connected and interwoven inseparably. As we dare to look back and study the development of the Christian churches and nations over a period of two thousand years, we understand that the wonderful message of Christ, "Glory to God in the highest, and on earth peace, good will toward men" (Luke 2:14), has never been fulfilled.

In fact, this scripture appears to be further from being fulfilled now than ever before. Even though we are not engaged now in another full-scale war, a complete loss of the fabric of a peaceful society in nearly all nations overshadows mankind.

Looking at the roots of past wars and the civil unrest spreading through the nations in our day, the one reason for all of them is apparent: The people of the world, including the so-called Christian world, refuse to pursue or even accept the first and great commandment of Christ: to love the Lord our God with all our hearts, and with all our souls, and with all our minds, and to love our neighbors as ourselves (see Matthew 22:37–39).

The absence of this principle of love and the obvious refusal to believe in this divine commandment, even the perversion of it by giving it lip service, find roots in the very beginnings of Christian churches. Because of a flood of old documents that have been discovered in many places in our day, the roots of Christian churches are hidden no longer in dark clouds of mystery. These roots no longer are subject to the exclusive interpretation of rulers in power.

In pursuing our investigation, we can make certain statements that illustrate dramatically the dilemma in which the Christian world, finds itself today. For instance, I draw your attention to the fact that today's historians suggest that the early disciples of Christ believed He would return very soon. Therefore, they did not write in detail any reports of His life for a period of one generation.

According to Karl Maly, a Catholic historian, not until A.D. 70 was the first attempt made to write the words and deeds of Jesus as a testimony and as a reason for Christian belief.[1] Alfons Kemmer, another Catholic historian, wrote that in the second half of the first century, the first writings of the Savior's disciples, the apostles, appeared. He mentioned that the complete list of the twenty-seven books that now comprise the canonical New Testament can be found for the first time in a letter by Bishop Athanasius of Alexandria in A.D. 367.[2]

Historians of our time leave no question that in the very early days of the development of Christian churches, so-called Christians disputed without end about the validity and authenticity of manuscripts, words, and interpretations. It seems that because of this background, the lay member of the Catholic church was, for many centuries, not given personal access to the scriptures. It took the churches of the Reformation to give to the individual member access to the Bible with the accompanying understanding that the Bible was flawless as to doctrine and authority. As mentioned before, a mass of old and new manuscripts has been found in our day. They shed more light on the fact that, from the very beginning of the Christian church, many different movements existed that were heretical or were called heretical by the established groups. We now understand that even the so-called canonical scriptures were established only amidst bitter contention.[3]

The intense discussions and the number of new Bible translations by various translators and various churches in recent years finally convinced the Catholic church to reevaluate its position. According to Alfons Kemmer, at the second Vatican Council called in November 1962, the so-called "battle of the Bible" arose. A minority wanted to hold rigidly to the old teaching from St. Augustine that the Bible is flawless and all-inclusive. However, during the third and fourth periods of the Vatican Council in 1964 and 1965, and after extensive debate, the Catholic church reached a compromise in a synthesis of traditional Bible understanding and modern Bible science. As a result, the second Vatican Council authorized a totally new translation of the Bible for the Catholic church.[4]

Different opinions about the question "What is the established truth?" arose very early in Christian history. The followers of various

Gnostic groups, who were widespread in the Roman empire for many centuries, emphasized the need for spiritual knowledge of truth and emphasized that such knowledge is essential for salvation.[5] The followers of Marcion (who died in A.D. 160) stressed the necessity for humans to develop charity as the Lord's saving power.[6] The Montanists, at the end of the second century, stressed the need for self-discipline. Their women, for instance, were required to wear veils.[7]

Because I cannot attempt to mention all of the various groups and developments in this brief summary, I will concentrate on some of the more interesting ones.

The followers of Origenes (who died in A.D. 254) believed that to be a disciple of Christ, a person must be an example in deed, in language, and in daily behavior.[8]

Arius, who lived in the days of the Council of Nice and who converted multitudes to Christianity, believed the Father and the Son to be two different personages. This belief contrasted with the Nicene Creed.[9]

In A.D. 418 Pelagius, a Roman citizen of British origin, taught that the children of God have free agency. This teaching clashed with the prevailing predestination teaching of Augustine.[10]

Later, when Christianity had spread over the entire western European continent and the Catholic church was established as the dominant Christian church, many people and groups still claimed to be inspired. They were in open opposition to the established church. The Cathari, for instance, did not believe in worshiping the bones of early Christian martyrs. They tried to take the scriptures seriously.[11] This group became prominent in the tenth century. Peter Waldo, who lived in Lyons, France, led another group. He believed that a priest of the Lord should be righteous and should have high standards of morality.[12] In the fourteenth century, the Begins and the

Begards originated in Germany. They believed that a man can become perfect when he strives to receive the gifts of the Spirit.[13] Also originating in the fourteenth century in Germany were the Salpeterer, who believed that worldly power and church power should be separated.[14]

John Wycliffe from England and John Huss from Bohemia were immediate forerunners of the Reformation. Finally, Martin Luther, Huldreich Zwingli, and John Calvin led the Reformation. But the Reformation did not bring a united, new understanding of truth. On the contrary, it only opened many new interpretations, new understandings, and, of course, new disputes.

We have considered only a few developments in how Christian belief has been interpreted. However, I believe I can make my first statement without contradiction: *The message of Christ and His gospel became subject, soon after His resurrection, to extremely controversial interpretations. Also, the question "What is truth?" continues to be controversial to this day.*

When we investigate another aspect of the history of Christian churches, we see that modern historians have reached an astonishing conclusion. They have concluded that present-day Christianity is the result of gospel interpretations made by those who were strong enough to suppress differing opinions.

During the first centuries after the resurrection of the Savior, a conflict raged over which interpretations were right and over the true requirements for salvation. It was ended by force after the Council of Nice. The Roman Emperor Constantine called selected Christian bishops to the council in A.D. 325. Regarding this council, the Catholic historian Karl Kupisch wrote:

> Of the 4,000 bishops, only 250 came. From all of western Europe only four bishops were present. The bishop from

> Rome was not present. Constantine did not subject himself to be questioned. He was the master of the conference. His ideas and his concepts were accepted.[15]

According to this same author, the Nicene Creed became the law of the Roman empire. Orthodox Christianity became an essential qualification for Roman citizenship. The Roman emperor wanted unity among his various provinces. He used Christianity as the tool to establish this unity by force. The Christians, who had been persecuted during the first centuries after the resurrection of Christ, now became the oppressors, paired with the power of the Roman empire.

With the coronation of the Germanic Frankish King Charlemagne in A.D. 800 as the emperor of the Roman empire, the secular empire was declared identical with the state of God (*civitas dei*), and the emperor understood himself in theory and practice to be God's representative. From that time on, the empire was called the "Holy" Roman Empire. It may be permitted to mention that the German historian Rudolph Wahl wrote in a highly recognized book about Charlemagne that Charlemagne was convinced that the Frankish people were the "God-elect people" of the new age.[16] This idea was expanded to all the Germanic tribes and widely taught in the nineteenth century by highly recognized Lutheran teachers in Germany.[17] It is not difficult to see that some consider this to be an important background for Hitler's ideas of Germanic supremacy and the holocaust.

Constantine, Charlemagne, and a multitude of others give us reason to establish my second statement: *Over a period of centuries, the interpretations of the gospel that prevailed were those linked with the strongest political powers. These powers, which provided leadership and interpretation of Christianity, were not free from wickedness, injustice, and unrighteousness.*

As we continue to investigate the roots of history and understand the situation of our day, we cannot ignore one most tragic and fatal fact. Obviously, many righteous individuals tried, over the years, to establish a knowledge of Christ's teachings by righteous living and by emulating His example of sacrifice motivated by love. But the fact remains that Christianity has used brutal suppression to destroy opposition and to persecute and even kill those who believed in different interpretations of Christianity. Very few people today recall, for instance, that Theodosius, the Roman emperor who was called "the Great," helped make the Nicene Creed survive by having 30,000 Arian Christians killed during a single night in an amphitheater.[18]

Several hundred years after Theodosius, Charlemagne established Christianity very zealously as a unifying power in his kingdom. When the Saxons did not submit to the emperor's will and become Christians quickly enough, he invited, in A.D. 782, 4,500 noble sons of the Saxons to a meeting in Verden an der Aller. He had all of them killed.[19] This was how Christianity was introduced to my own ancestors.

The dominant Christian church of the Middle Ages established the Inquisition for the sole purpose of finding individuals or groups who were not in full obedience and harmony with the established beliefs. The Cathari, the Waldenses, the Begins and the Begards, the Salpeterer, and many others were persecuted and killed, some groups to the very last person. John Huss, the Bohemian theologian who established the motto, "Search the truth, listen to the truth, learn the truth, love the truth, remain true to the truth, defend the truth until death," was burned, and his ashes were scattered in the Rhine River.[20] William Tyndale, who was the first to translate *and* print the New Testament in English, because he believed people should read and study the scriptures themselves, was persecuted because of his translation. Finally church authorities brought him to his death.

The Reformation did not bring a change in attitude. As soon as Reformation churches became established in various places, the reformers and their followers began to identify and search for heretics. Heretics were those who were "different," and so easily called "devilish." As did the medieval church, the reformers and their followers did not hesitate to bring heretics to painful deaths.

Many wars have been fought in the name of Christ, with millions losing their lives.

It seems to be necessary, in light of the confrontations between the peoples of Islam and the West, to recall the eight arrogant, bloody Christian crusades to the Holy Land between A.D. 1095 and 1291. Gerhard Konzelmann, an expert on the Middle East and a best-selling author, described how the Christian crusaders behaved when they arrived in Jerusalem:

> The knights from Europe changed into the most brutal beasts that ever took lodging in Jerusalem. They surpassed in their cruelty all other conquerors of the past. In the houses and on the streets, they slaughtered the ones with weapons or the ones without, young or old, men or women and children. In the morning of their second day no Moslem and no Jew was still alive in Jerusalem.

Konzelmann finished his report about the "victorious" first crusade with the following statement:

> The horrible massacre of the 15th and 16th of July in 1099 A.D. provided the roots for the opinions of Moslems about Christians: The Moslems looked at the Europeans from that time on as lustful, murdering bandits without

> conscience. What happened in those two days burdened the relationship between the people of the Islam faith and the Christian crusaders in a dimension that left no room for reconciliation.[21]

The Mayas, Aztecs, and Incas on the American continent suffered the same fate as the people in Europe suffered at the hands of such leaders as Theodosius and Charlemagne, as the Spanish conquistadors Velazquez, Cortez, and Pizzaro were following their motto, "Brothers—comrades! Let us follow the sign of the Holy Cross in true faith towards victory!"[22]

The famous French explorer and author, Pierre Honore, wrote:

> The reason for the quick destruction of the Indian kingdoms was the deep-rooted, traditional expectation among these ancient people that a white god would return to them. In their humble expectation of the rulership of their god, they became victims and their kingdoms and civilizations were destroyed in blood and smoke.[23]

I can therefore make my third statement safely without being accused of exaggeration: *Christianity has a long history of intolerance toward those holding different opinions. They were persecuted brutally, defamed as devilish, and, in many cases, put to death.*

After all I have said, we can conclude that *we* humans must fail when *we* try to interpret what *we* consider to be gospel truth without relying on a living prophet and divine revelation. The Bible, which for centuries was regarded as the flawless word of God, has become, in the eyes of theologians, archaeologists, and historians, the subject of serious questions about its origin, validity, and authenticity. As the people of our day have become aware of the suppression of early

Christian developments and other "fruits" of historical Christianity, they have come to a shocking understanding.

As early as the late seventeenth century, Roger Williams, one of the founding fathers of modern-day Baptists, said, "The church of Christ is not on earth until Christ sends forth new apostles to plant churches anew." The same Roger Williams termed it "blasphemy" to call Europe "Christian."[24]

Even though humans cannot interpret divine truth without being divinely inspired, thousands of honest, righteous, and humble people created their own circles of prayer and authored hundreds of different Christian beliefs. With the establishment of the Constitution of the United States, oppressed and frustrated Europeans were given a place of dreams, a place of hope.

We should not be surprised to see that the restoration of the true gospel of Jesus Christ, following the humble prayer of a fourteen-year-old youth, has brought suspicion, envy, and fear to some leaders of traditional Christian churches. The early members of the restored Church, which the Lord himself called The Church of Jesus Christ of Latter-day Saints, had to suffer many of the same difficulties as those brave souls who preceded them throughout the history of Christianity. The early members were persecuted, oppressed, and driven from their homes. They were driven from Ohio to Missouri and to Illinois on the Mississippi River. When the first prophet of the Restoration, Joseph Smith, suffered a martyr's death, the disciples of the Lord in the restored Church showed the fruit of their faith. They left their homes again and crossed the plains, the wilderness, and the roadless mountains to settle in the desolation of the barren desert of the West.

To understand the Restoration, we need to be aware of the tragedy of Christian history—not to create ill-feelings or to pass judgment, but to understand that for the first time since shortly after the death of the early disciples of Christ, we have the gospel in its entire purity, undefiled by human ambition and without human interpretation.

The millions of members of the restored Church are spread today over all continents, having come from many races and cultures. They are living witnesses of the divine restoration of the power and dignity of the priesthood of God. The Lord has restored the keys to preach the gospel according to the plan of salvation. All mankind will eventually have an opportunity to hear this message and will be invited to make a covenant with the living God.

Men obviously have separated themselves from the clear waters of divine inspiration. They ignore the message of Christ or give it only lip service. They have made masterful progress in the technical, materialistic world. But without divine light, they succumb all too often to the carnal mind in its drive for expansion, extroversion, and greed. Now the children of God suddenly seem to awaken and panic as they realize that the last possibility of expansion can mean the destruction of mankind, and the whole planet on which we live.

In this situation, hope is raised that the message of the restored gospel of Jesus Christ and the radiation of its fruits will eventually help the children of God to find the memory of their true origin and change the direction of their lives. Hope is raised that men will learn to turn their hearts to the only power and strength through which salvation can come—to the Lord, Jesus Christ. Hope is raised that we all will eventually learn through this majestic influence of His spirit—learn to respect one another, to trust, and to love one another. Hope is raised that the ultimate goal of Jesus Christ will finally be established: "Glory to God in the highest, and on earth peace, good will toward men."

Notes

1. Karl Maly, *Wie enstand das Neue Testament,* 3rd ed. (Stuttgart: Verlag Katholisches Bibelwerk GmbH, 1981), 41–42.
2. Alfons Kemmer, *Das Neue Testament: Eine Einführung für Laien,* 3rd ed. (Freiburg in Breisgau: Verlag Herder, 1980), 16–17.
3. See *Encyclopaedia Britannica,* 1980 ed., 2:939–40, 973.
4. See Kemmer, *Das Neue Testament,* 22–23.
5. See Karl Kupisch, *Kirchengeschichte* (Stuttgart: Verlag W. Kohlhammer GmbH, 1978), 1:30, 38, 39.
6. See ibid., 30–31.
7. See ibid., 33.
8. See ibid., 38–39.
9. See ibid., 71.
10. See ibid., 114–16.
11. See Horst Herrmann, *Ketzer in Deutschland,* ed. no. 7185 (Munich, Germany: Verlag Wilhelm Heyne, 1982), 124–25.
12. See ibid., 126.
13. See ibid., 135.
14. See ibid., 273–75.
15. Kupisch, *Kirchengeschichte,* 1:72–73.
16. See Rudolph Wahl, *Karl der Grosse* (Munich: Verlag Bruckmann, 1978), 208, 288, 293.
17. See Ernest Weymar, *Das Selbstverständnis der Deutschen* (Stuttgart: Ernest Klett Verlag, 1961), 33.
18. See Herrmann, *Ketzer in Deutschland,* 66.
19. See Kupisch, *Kirchengeschichte,* 1:148.
20. See Herrmann, *Ketzer in Deutschland,* 32.
21. Gerhard Konzelmann, *Jerusalem* (Hoffmann und Campe, 1984), 373–74.
22. *Encyclopaedia Britannica,* 5:195.
23. Pierre Honore, *Ich fand den weissen Gott* (Verlag Heinrich Scheffler, 1961), 14–15.
24. Chase, *Christianity Through the Centuries,* 202–3.

A Note from the Editor and Compiler

In the spring of 2001, I was typing up the notes from my mission reunion the previous fall. I had been privileged to serve under Elder F. Enzio Busche in the Germany Munich Mission. Through the efforts of other returned missionaries in Utah, and through Elder and Sister Busche's generous gift of time, we were fortunate to have mission reunions every fall before general conference.

It was my habit to take careful notes of Elder and Sister Busche's talks and then to type them up and send them to other Busche missionaries. As I typed up his talk that year, I thought how wonderful it would be to have a book of Elder Busche's experiences—not just the few pages of notes, but a whole book of the wonderful experiences he had shared with us as missionaries.

As I sat there wanting such a book, the thought came to me that perhaps I could help him write one. I had recently finished helping an aunt compile and write her personal history. I had also assisted other family members with theirs. I enjoyed writing, and some of my essays had been published. On a small scale, I had experience with such a thing. Even as the thought came that perhaps I could help Elder Busche, I dismissed it as impossible. Yet it wouldn't leave—and an experience Elder Busche had told us about on my mission came to mind.

He had been with his family at the beach enjoying the day of sun and swimming when he heard someone cry out for help. A little girl was out in the water, beyond the surf, and was obviously in trouble. She kept calling for help, and Elder Busche wondered why no one was helping her. As he waited for someone to help her, it came to him forcefully that *he* was that someone. He was the person who needed to act and save the drowning child. As he started to run to the rescue, another man joined him, and both were able to pull the little girl to safety. He told us that story as missionaries to explain that if we are the ones to see the problem, we are also the ones to act.

As I continued to receive the prompting and think about the lesson he had taught us, I felt that I was the one to do this. I was the one who should help Elder Busche publish an account of his experiences, feelings, and testimony.

When I approached Elder Busche with the idea, he was hesitant and humble—as he is— and doubted that anyone would want to read about his life. Feeling the call strongly, I persisted with what may have felt to him like pestering, yet he and his wife invited me to his home to show me what he had. When I saw what there was, I realized much of the hard work had already been done. Several years before, while he was president of the Frankfurt Germany Temple, he had recorded his experiences, and his secretary, Sister Jo Ann Klundt, had transcribed them. It was a pleasant surprise to see that so much had already been done. The work then was to take the binder full of anecdotes and compile them into larger units and edit them for clarity.

In the binder, Elder Busche had written the following prologue, which seems to serve a valuable purpose in this work as well:

> This is the first of July 1988 and I am in the temple of The Church of Jesus Christ of Latter-day Saints in Friedrichsdorf, near Frankfurt.
>
> Over the years the Lord has blessed me with many experiences, insights, and actual happenings of a spiritual nature that have strengthened my testimony. Thus far, because I have not written them down, they exist only in my memory. I have been referring to these experiences in talks to stress a principle of the gospel, or to help give insight as to some of the methods the Lord uses to help His children gain control over their lives. Inasmuch as my memory may become weaker in the future, many things may be lost or left to second-hand descriptions, which are sometimes distorted and not correct. What I am trying to do now is record major experiences and happenings so they might be preserved on paper for my posterity. . . .
>
> Each experience is so complex and has so many different aspects—as it is with all spiritual experiences—that it is not wise to look just at the happenings and see them as a story. Instead, each experience needs to be viewed and felt from many aspects before it can be evaluated. Also, I am aware of my limited capability to express spiritual experiences, as we have this world of feelings which resist, often, to be explained by words. I am trying to be as accurate as possible, but I might exclude some things that have already slipped from my mind. . . . However, in what I say there will

> be no fiction—only what I have actually experienced which, in my understanding, is absolutely correct.
>
> . . . It seems that I am always remembering, quite suddenly, in a certain situation, something experienced earlier in my life that has either slipped from my mind or that I felt at the time was not worth remembering. . . . I also have to apologize for my less-than-perfect English. . . .

As I read his prologue, I realized that he had recorded his experiences with the thought that one of his descendants might one day make them into a book. Although I am not a descendant of Elder Busche, I felt strongly that I was the one to help him accomplish that, and so that is what I have done. It has been a great pleasure to immerse myself in the experiences he recorded. I had heard many of them before, but many I had not, and it was uplifting and inspiring to read about the workings of the Lord in his life.

As I told Elder Busche more than once, I felt called to do this. I hope I have fulfilled my calling adequately and that those who have read this will be moved to live their lives on a higher level and draw closer to the Lord.

—Tracie A. Lamb

Index

Photographs are designated by italic numerals.

Aalen, Germany, 242–43
Adler, Fritz, 30
African tribes, 29
Agency, 2, 275–76
Alder, President and Sister, *145*
American service woman seeking endowment, 213–16
Athlete, proud young, 108–*11*

Bad Kissingen, Germany, 5–6, 17–19
Bad Oeynhausen, Germany, 192–96
Bavaria, 21
Beesley, Horace P., *186*
Benson, Ezra Taft: example of, 43; issues challenge to complete Dortmund chapel construction in one year, promises to return for dedication, 123–24; returns to dedicate building, 131; calls FEB as temple president, 206
Benson, Waldo, 123
Berrett, Elder, 261–62
Bielefeld District, photograph of FEB with members of, *100*
Birkhahn, Br.: attributes of, 170; loses job, begins new career, 170–71; spiritual sensitivity of, 171
Buddhism, 19
Buildings, insignificance of, 99–100
Bulgarian mission president, 256–58
Burckhardt, Rudolph, *118*
Burton, Theodore M.: meets with FEB, tells him to repent, 85–86; approves proposed Dortmund chapel site, 115; challenges Dortmund members to do 100% home teaching, promises miraculous solution to problem of obtaining land, 115–16, 119
Busch, Wilhelm, 76
Busche, F. Enzio

Childhood and teen years:

birth, 1; early spiritual yearnings, 1; lives in Catholic sanitarium during World War II, 5–6; ponders meaning of eternity, receives spiritual assurance, 6; lack of early religious influence, 6–7; influence of Goethe, 7–8; member of Hitler Youth, 8; photograph at age 14, *9;* photograph as a young boy with bicycle, *13;* June 1945 passport photograph, *18;* becomes interested in Buddhism after war, 19; survives in ruins of house during post-war years, 19; survives spinal meningitis after war, experiences spiritual awakening, 19; pre-war German political/social situation and moral goals, 20–28; photograph collecting offerings at age 5, *26;* government teachings on the Germanic and other races, 27–29; burning of Jewish synagogue, 29; 1936 Olympic Games, 29; growing awareness of German atrocities, 29–31; shame of German people over betrayal by leaders, 31–32; named after father's wartime companion, 36; lives in rural area outside Dortmund, 36–*37;* future wife, Jutta, destroys wooden block cathedral, 88–89; travels to farm to trade coal for food, 192–93; vehicle breaks down, prays for divine assistance, 193; experiences peace, receives help from British soldier, 194–95; photograph at age 19, *195;* observes reunion of woman and husband believed killed in war, 274–75

Conversion and baptism:

early skepticism, 1–2; baptism, 2, 92; spiritual awakening, 2; father's reaction to decision to be baptized, 40–42; liver disease as precursor to, 58, 59; visits Evangelical church minister to begin search for Christ, 59–60; begins attending Evangelical church services, 60; listens to claims of different church groups, 60–61; accepts invitation to visit Evangelical church members, 61; visits Evangelical church members, agrees with their objections, 62; experiences disappointment in instruction received from Evangelical church members, 62–63; petitions Lord for assistance in becoming a disciple, 63–64; meets with first LDS missionaries, 64–65; experiences tumultuous meeting with Evangelical church ministers and LDS missionaries, 65–68; meets regularly with LDS missionaries, makes little progress, 68–69; missionaries taken from town, 69–70; visits LDS Church meeting in Dortmund, 70–72; receives second set of missionaries, 72–73; called to repentance by missionaries, 73–75; taught by missionaries, rejects anti-Mormon teachings, and embraces restored gospel, 75–76; experiences panic over becoming Church member, 78; dreams of airplane plunging to ground and skiing down mountain path, 78–80; overcomes smoking habit through divine assistance and reading Book of Mormon, 80–82; photograph of Dortmund Branch members, *83;* discusses gospel questions with university student Br. Kissler, 83–84; discusses gospel questions with fellow investigator Mr. Weber, 84; meets with mission president Theodore M. Burton, told to repent, 85–86; experiences temptation to smoke again, 86; warned in prayer of consequences of not making baptismal covenant, 87; agrees to baptism, conditional on wife's baptism, 87–88; missionary reflects on, 88; gains testimony of restoration and Joseph Smith, 89–91; agrees to baptism, conditional on not being called to serve or asked to speak, 91–92

Dortmund chapel construction:
scarcity of land and difficulty of obtaining building permit, 114; famous architect locates land, seeks building permit, 114–15; building permit denied at insistence of city's youth department, 115; Theodore M. Burton challenges Dortmund members to do 100% home teaching and promises miraculous solution to problem of obtaining land, 115–16, 119; land and building permit obtained through miraculous intervention of Kurt Kauper, 116–19; head of city's youth department dies, clearing way for building permit, 119; fund raising for chapel construction begins, 119–20; Dortmund members take on envelope-stuffing fundraiser, succeed with divine assistance, 120–22; photographs of chapel under construction, *121, 124;* missionary work flourishes during, 122; challenges of constructing building with member labor and Church building missionaries, 122–23, 125; Ezra Taft Benson issues challenge to complete building in one year, promises to return for dedication, 123–24; description of construction process, 124–27; construction of chimney completed with divine assistance, 126–27; learns of Protestant minister's plan to disrupt construction, attends protest meeting with other brethren, 128–29; teaches protesters about Atonement and adjourns meeting, 129–30; photograph of branch members and finished building, *130;* building completed on time, 130–31; Ezra Taft Benson returns to dedicate building, 131

Early Church membership:
first service opportunities, 2–3; following prayer, accepts first invitation to speak in Church, 92–94; speaks in Soest Branch, 94–95; personal reaction to conversion and baptism, 96–97; reaction to members of Dortmund Branch, 97–98; branch member predicts short-lived activity, 98–99; understands insignificance of buildings and surroundings, 99–100; photograph with members of Bielefeld District, *100;* called as youth leader, learns to adapt programs, 100–101; arranges outing for youth in countryside, 101–2; impact of outing on youth named Wolfgang, 102–5; photograph with youth at two-mission conference (1961), *103;* attends youth conference as counselor to mission president, unexpectedly receives assignment to reorganize conference, 106–7; seeks and receives inspiration on reorganization of youth conference, 107–8; challenges proud young athlete to swimming contests, wins with Lord's help, and befriends youth, 108–*11;* impact of youth conference on those attending, 111–12; photograph at foundation of Rhine Ruhr District (1965), *118;* experience with Sr. Maischt, 166–70; experience with Br. Birkhahn, 170–71; experience with Br. and Sr. Schumann, 173–76; photograph with Ezra Taft Benson while serving as Rhine Ruhr District president, *186;* counsels young woman to remain in challenging temple marriage, 230–32

Family experiences:
loses and later finds son on Holland beach, understands importance of being an eternal family, 132–34; photograph with wife Jutta and children (1963), *134;* closeness developed due to loss of contact with

family members following baptism, 134–35; change of perspective and spirit of partnership developed after baptism, 135–36; photograph with wife Jutta and children (1970), *136;* develops system for recognizing, evaluating, and punishing wrongdoing by children, 136–37; oldest son adheres to self-imposed punishment at grandmother's house, 137; responds to oldest son's habit of swearing and using foul language, 137–39; contrast between children's home and school experiences, 139; helps oldest son respond to teacher's requirement to view X-rated movie, 139–40; responds to oldest son's refusal to attend Church, 140; photograph of Dortmund family home (1959–78), *141;* oldest son breaks foot in Church soccer match, fails university entrance exam, learns new self-discipline and faith, 141–43, 145; oldest son's classmate Gerd is baptized, brings future daughter-in-law into Church, goes on mission, 143–44; photograph of oldest son with mission president and wife, *145;* oldest son helped in employment by FEB business contact impressed by missionary service, 145–47; responds to prompting to demonstrate love by accompanying second son to pick up disabled car, 147–49; assists second son in making decision to go on mission *vs.* marrying non-member young woman, 149–50; photograph with wife, Jutta, and children (1979), *151;* wife, Jutta, responds to negativism of youngest son's teacher, 151–52; parenting style, 152–53; photograph with wife, Jutta, and children (2000), *153;* photograph with wife, Jutta, and children soon after move to United States, *168;* goes sailing with sons, caught in storm, 200–201; seeks and receives divine assistance, sails safely into harbor, 201–2

General Authority:

call as, 3, *265;* receives emeritus status, 3; reflections on service as, 3; father foresees call as, 48; meets son of proud young swimmer befriended years earlier at youth conference, 112–13; hiring of competitor's sales manager facilitates acceptance of call issued by Spencer W. Kimball, 161–62; assists LeGrand Richards in selecting new stake president, 181–83; photograph with other General Authorities at Sacramento area conference, *182;* inactive brother reactivated by LeGrand Richards responding to prompting to change hymn at stake conference, 183–84; experience with Sr. Neuberg, 187–91; photograph at desk, *190;* hosts German Protestant ministers visiting Salt Lake City, responds to questions about Church members receiving pay for services, 216–19; photograph with other General Authorities at mission presidents' seminar (1997), *229;* meets sister previously counseled to remain in challenging temple marriage, observes impact of faithfulness, 232–33; photograph with Siberian Saints on handcart trek (1977), *233;* experience with Eastern European sister discussing angelic visitations, 233–34; attends sacrament meeting in East Germany, hears experience of army sharpshooter ordered to shoot badly in contest, 234–35; attends dedication of Freiberg Germany Temple, hears experience of Dresden Stake president's daughter's commitment to temple marriage, 235–37; Dresden Stake president apologizes for 89%

enrollment in seminary, 237–39; photograph with general Relief Society president Mary Ellen Smoot, *238;* visits Hawaiian stake, hears experience of stake presidency member's daughter being saved from death by father responding to prompting, 239–40; visits Los Angeles Spanish stake, hears experience of Nicaraguan woman visited by men dressed in white, 240–41; tours Ohio Columbus Mission, hears experience of mission president's wife's German grandfather, 243–46; photograph with mission president in Alaska, *244;* attends downtown Detroit branch sacrament meeting, hears woman describe fulfillment of dream about temple, 246–48; experience with conversion of Joseph Schultz, 249–55; photograph at April 1999 general conference, *250;* experience with brother called as first mission president in Bulgaria, 256–58; photograph with James E. Faust, *261;* experience with woman on airplane recognizing spirit in his countenance, 263–64; experience with Coalinga, California, earthquake, 264–66; experience with stolen van, 266–67; Arizona stake president shares experience of bishop calling Primary president, 267–68; experience casting evil spirit out of missionary, 268–73; experience telling grouchy man in hospital about Jesus Christ, 276–78. *See also* Busche, F. Enzio, Mission president; Busche, F. Enzio, Temple president

Liver disease:
severity of illness, 50; feels panic as death seems certain, 50–51; photograph in hospital bed on Christmas day, *51;* covenants to live a different life if spared from death, 51–52; discovers hope in Christ's Atonement, 52; experiences light and voice suggesting prayer, 52; prays "thy will be done," 53; experiences profound spiritual awakening and insights, 53–54; receives assurance of recovery, 54; contemplates love represented in linen bedspread, 54–55; covenants to testify of hospital experience and seek out its Author, 55; experiences miraculous healing, 55; reads entire Bible, learns basic gospel truths, 55–57; asks nun if Catholic Church is true church of Christ, 57–58; as a precursor to conversion, 58, 59

Mission president:
assists second son in making decision to go on mission *vs.* marrying non-member young woman, 149–50; experience with Ingrid Engel, 171–73; experience with Br. and Sr. Seiter, 176–79; experience with Nephi Nabrotzky, 179–81; develops deep-vein phlebitis, experiences great pain, 202–3; seeks divine intervention, pain relieved, 203–4; photograph with daughter, *204;* experience with Br. Lee assisting in teaching of Korean family living in Germany, 241–43; experience with woman wishing to thank missionaries and request prayers on behalf of missionary son, 259–60; experience with missionaries seeking apartment, 260–62; experience with shy missionary, 262

Photographs:
age 14, *9;* as a young boy, with bicycle, *13;* June 1945 passport, *18;* collecting offerings at age 5, *26;* with mother and sisters before World War II, *28;* with friend in front of Dortmund cathedral ruins, *33;* with father and

sisters (1938), *39;* with father (1955), *47;* in hospital bed on Christmas day, *51;* reading (1954), *56;* with wife, Jutta (1954), *63;* with wife, Jutta, and first two children (1958), *69;* with wife, Jutta, on wedding day, *90;* with members of Bielefeld District, *100;* with youth at two-mission conference in Hessen (1961), *103;* with wife, Jutta, at youth conference swimming competition, *111;* at foundation of Rhine Ruhr District (1965), *118;* with wife, Jutta, and children (1963), *134;* with wife, Jutta, and children (1970), *136;* with, wife, Jutta and children (1979), *151;* with, wife, Jutta and children (2000), *153;* with printing equipment, *155;* with wife, Jutta, and children soon after move to United States, *168;* with other General Authorities at Sacramento area conference, *182;* with Ezra Taft Benson while serving as Rhine Ruhr District president, *186;* at desk, as General Authority, *190;* at age 19, *195;* as printing business executive (1966), *199;* with daughter, during service as mission president, *204;* with wife, Jutta, and temple presidency counselors and wives, *223;* with other General Authorities at mission presidents' seminar (1997), *229;* with Siberian saints on handcart trek (1977), *233;* with wife, Jutta, and general Relief Society president Mary Ellen Smoot, *238;* with mission president in Alaska, *244;* at April 1999 general conference, *250;* with sisters, *257;* with James E. Faust, *261;* with Spencer W. Kimball (1977), *265;* walking with wife, Jutta (1990), *272*

Printing business executive:
father informs cigarette manufacturer customer about FEB's baptism, 42–43; father puts FEB in charge of printing business, 44, 154; father makes FEB printing operation foreman, 154; photograph with printing equipment, *155;* reliance on Lord, 155; introduces participatory management techniques, 155–56; blessed with large orders prior to departure for general conference, 156–57; challenges of meeting family, Church, and business obligations, 157; photograph of Busche Printing building (1960), *157;* blessed with ability to successfully compete with other printing companies, 158; faced with possible financial ruin, seeks inspiration and hears voice telling him to "work," 158–60; describes company handicaps and resulting difficulties, 160; restructures company, 160; hires competitor's sales manager, making it possible to later accept call as General Authority, 161–62; business associate shares wartime prayer experience, 164; explains call as General Authority to company finance manager, 164–65; photograph of Busche Publishing and Printing building (1990), *165;* competitiveness of printing business, 196; travels to Paris to meet with customer, 196–98; refuses to drink wine with customer, 198; customer asks for forgiveness, becomes protector, 198–200; photograph (1966), *199*

Regional Representative:
meets Dortmund Branch member who earlier predicted short-lived activity, 98–99; on eve of stake conference, spends night accompanying son to pick up disabled car, 147–49; blessed with large printing orders prior to departure for general conference, 156–57; experience with Walter Kindt, 185–87

Temple president:
reaction to call, 206; reaction to viewing nearly-finished temple, 206, 209; obtains book containing names of Friedrichsdorf founding families, has ordinance work performed, 209–11; impact of service as president, 212; experience with Joseph Gilbert, 212–13; experience with American service woman seeking endowment, 213–16; hosts German Protestant ministers at temple open house, 219–20; visiting minister proclaims LDS Church non-Christian, 220; attends funeral in Düsseldorf, discusses perfection and sin with journalist friend, 220–21; photograph with wife, Jutta, counselors, and wives, *223;* Br. and Sr. Vreeken called to temple presidency, 223–25; experience of brother from Holland coming to temple, 225–26; experience of sister in wheelchair receiving healing, 226–27; experience of Br. Prinzl with deceased parents, 227–29

World War II soldier:
drafted at age 14, 8–10; runs, hides, and begs food to survive, 10; attitude toward government and war changes, 10–11; observes power of American army, 11; leaves German army to return home, 11–12; captured by released French prisoners, taken to fire station, 12; befriended by American soldier, 12–14; held in barn, 14; held in house, begs for food from townspeople, 14–15; swears to never take up arms, released to return home, 15; learns importance of food, 15–16; journeys home, begging for food and shelter, 15–18; vows to own tent, 16–17; gets ride on American army truck, 17; reunited with mother and sisters, 17–19

Busche, Jutta (wife of FEB): baptism, 2, 92; photograph with FEB (1954), *63;* photograph with FEB and first two children (1958), *69;* accepts invitation to be taught by missionaries, 87; agrees to baptism, 87–88; FEB on, 88, 89, 151–52; visits FEB home as a child, destroys wooden block cathedral, 88–89; photograph at age 13, *89;* with FEB on wedding day (1955), *90;* photograph with FEB at youth conference swimming competition, *111;* photograph with FEB and children (1963), *134;* loss of contact with family members following baptism, 134–35; photograph with FEB and children (1970), *136;* photograph with FEB and children (1979), *151;* responds to youngest son's teacher's negativism, 151–52; photograph with FEB and children (2000), *153;* photograph with FEB and children soon after move to United States, *168;* photograph with FEB and counselors and wives in temple presidency, *223;* photograph with FEB and general Relief Society president Mary Ellen Smoot, *238;* photograph walking with FEB (1990), *272*

Busche family history, 38–40

Busche [father of FEB]: character and attributes of, 35–36, 37, 38; names FEB after wartime companion, 36; reaction to German wartime atrocities, 37–38; assists Jews in escaping Germany, 38; interest in family history, 38–40; photograph with FEB and sisters (1938), *39;* reaction to baptism of FEB, 40–42; informs cigarette manufacturer customer of FEB's baptism, 42–43; asks FEB questions about the Church, 43–44; puts FEB in charge of printing business, 44, 154; interest in

nineteenth-century German Romantic paintings, 44–45; asks FEB to be faithful to Church, discusses prayer, 46–48; photograph with FEB (1955), *47;* death of, 48; foresees FEB's call as General Authority, 48; appears to FEB in dream, requests that temple work be done, 49
Busche [parents and sisters of FEB]: family listens to political broadcasts on radio, 20–21; photograph of parents on silver wedding anniversary, *23;* photograph with mother and sisters before World War II, *28;* photograph with father and sisters (1938), *39;* photograph with father (1955), *47;* gospel message carried to sister by Joseph and Birgit Schultz, 255; photograph with sisters, *257*
Busche Printing building (1960), *157*
Busche Publishing and Printing building (1990), *165*

Calvin, John, 210
Catholic Church, 57–58
Charlemagne, 28
Circumstances, life, 274–75
Coalinga, California earthquake, 264–66
Cologne, Germany, 83–84
Conscience, 77
Conversion, 76
Cowley, Wyoming, 245–46

Detroit, Michigan, 246–48
Didier, Charles, *229*
Dortmund Branch: missionaries reluctant to have FEB meet members of, 83; photograph of members, *83;* reaction of members to FEB, 97–98. *See also* Busche, F. Enzio, Dortmund chapel construction
Dresden Germany Stake president, 236–39
Dresden Germany Stake president's daughter, 236–37
Drieschner, Walter, 120
Düsseldorf, Germany, 220–22

Eastern European woman telling of angelic visitations, 233–34
East German sharpshooter, 234–35
East Germany, 234–39
Edersee Lake youth conference, *103,* 106–12, *111*
Efficiency, 221–22
Eisenhower, Dwight D., 18
Engel, Ingrid: converted to gospel, seeks baptism, 171–72; husband refuses to give permission for baptism, 172; husband relents, allows baptism, 172; counseled by FEB to love husband unconditionally, 172–73; impact of faithfulness on husband and children, 173
Eternal families, 133–34
Eternity, 6
Evangelical church: FEB visits minister of, 59–60; FEB begins attending, 60; FEB accepts invitation to visit members of, 61; visiting committee instructs FEB in beliefs of, 62–63; minister attacks LDS Church in meeting with FEB and missionaries, 65–68

Families, eternal, 133–34
Faust (Goethe's literary figure), 7
Faust, James E., *261*
Fear, 270–73
Fetzer, President and Sister, 222
Food, importance of, 15–16
Frankfurt, Germany, 85–86, 244–45
Frankfurt Germany Temple: announcement of, 207; difficulty of obtaining site for, 207; location of, 207; city council members travel to Swiss temple, give approval for temple construction, 208; photographs of,

208, 216; expensive conditions placed on construction of, 209; photograph of villa on grounds of, *211;* photograph of FEB with wife Jutta, temple presidency counselors, and wives, *223.* *See also* Busche, F. Enzio, Temple president
Fredericton, New Brunswick, 253
Freiberg Germany Temple, 235–37
Friedrichsdorf, Germany, 207, 210–11
Fuchs, Mr., 65–68

Garenfeld, Germany, 30
Gerd, 143–44
Gilbert, Joseph: expresses appreciation for temple to FEB, 212; conversion of, 212–13; commitment to temple work, 213
Goethe, Johann Wolfgang von, 7–8
Grandfather of mission president's wife, 243–46
Grouchy man in hospital, 277–78

Haller, Theodor and Luise, 207, 211–12
Hawaiian child saved from death, 239–40
Heinsen, Germany, 39
Herne, Germany, 84
Hess, Rudolf, 30
Hesse, Herman, 19
Hill, Roy and Erma, 123, 130–31
Hitler, Adolph, 1, 8, 20
Hitler Youth, 8
HLT, 211–12
Hoell, Karl, 164–65
Holland, brother from, 225–26
Holy Ghost: importance of, 97; following the promptings of, 105–6; importance of being in harmony with, 171
Home (Dortmund), photograph of, *141*
Hotel Vier Jahreszeiten, 254–55
Houston Texas East Stake conference, 266–67
Huguenots, 210

International Jewish Federation, 29
Irrenea, Sister, 57–58
Islam, 29

Journalist friend at funeral, 220–21
Joy: experiencing, 8; life circumstances and, 274–75; agency and, 275–76

Kauper, Kurt, 116–19
Kimball, Spencer W.: calls FEB as General Authority, 161; announces Frankfurt Germany Temple, 207; photograph with FEB, *265*
Kindt, Walter: serves in East German Mission, 185–86; simple faith of, 186
Kissler, Br., 83–84
Kutschke, Br., 130–31

Lee, Br.: contacts FEB for information on Church services, 241; accompanies FEB to Aalen, Germany and teaches Korean family, 242–43; faithful service of, 243
Leifhelm, Mr., 38
Life, purpose of, 2
Light of Christ, influence of, 33–34
Lion House, 44
Long, Luz, 29
Los Angeles area Spanish stake conference, 240–41
Loving others, 99
Luther, Martin, 28

Maedel, Br., 130–31
Maischt, Sister: outward appearance of, 166; relentless enthusiasm of, 166; personal history of, 166–67; testifies of truthfulness of gospel to FEB, 167; refuses FEB's offer of ride to Church, 167–68; temple attendance of, 169; fast offering contributions of, 169–70; death of, 170
Mannheim, Germany, 245
McConkie, Bruce R., 189

Mediocrity, trap of, 238
Missing targets, 222
Missionaries seeking apartment, 260–62
Missionary with evil spirit, 268–73
Möhnesee (lake) youth outing, 101–2
Monson, Thomas S., *182*
Munk, Mr., 38

Nabrotzky, Nephi: serves in Munich mission, 179–80; informed of mother's death by FEB, comforts FEB, 180; mother dies in farm accident, 180; completes mission and returns home, 180–81
Nabrotzky, Walter, 179
National Socialistic Party of Workers, 20
Native Americans, 29
Nazi Germany: in the context of German history, 21; as an alternative to post-World War I chaos, 21–22; slogan of, 22; moral, social, and political values and goals, 22–28; teachings on Germanic and other races, 27–29; 1936 Olympic Games, 29; atrocities of, 29–31; naiveté of German people, 30–31; control of information in, 31; betrayal of German people by leaders, 31–32; lasting impact of, 32, 34
Nelson, Russell M., 223
Neo-Nazis, 32
Neuberg, Sr.: predicts Salt Lake City flood, death of Bruce R. McConkie, 188–89; gives money for Native American missionaries to FEB, 188–90; death of, 190; unique attributes of, 190–91
Nicaraguan woman visited by men dressed in white, 240–41
Night of St. Bartholomew, 210
Nitz, Wilhelm, *118*

Oberviechtag, Germany, 14–15
Ohio Columbus Mission tour, 243–46
Ostermeyer, Br., 130–31
"O Tannenbaum" (song), 244–46
Owens, Jesse, 29

Parenting, 152–53
Paris, France, 196–200
Perfection, 221
Perry, L. Tom, *182, 229*
Peterson, President, 253
Pittsburgh, Pennsylvania, 249–51
Poecker, Rudolph, 185–87
Porter, Bruce D., *229*
Prayer: power of, 196, 199, 201–2; importance of sincerity in, 204–5
Priesthood, male and female parts of, 214–15
Primary president called after frightening dream, 267–68
Prinzl, Br.: arrives at temple without escort, 227; sees deceased parents in dream, 228; sees deceased parents in temple, 228–29
Prussia, 21

Quebec Montreal Mission tour (1992), 112–13

Richards, LeGrand: on Church callings, 181; assisted by FEB in selecting new stake president, 181–83; responds to prompting to change hymn at stake conference, reactivates brother, 183–84; FEB on, 184–85
Richards, Stephen C., 106
Routine, danger of, 97
Ruhr District Conference, 84

Sacrifice, 92
Saint John, New Brunswick Stake conference, 253
Scheen, Br., 212–13
Schiller, Friedrich, 27
Schultz, Birgit, 253–55
Schultz, Joseph: meets FEB, 249–50;

attends Church in Pittsburgh with business associate, 250–51; FEB teaches and prays with, 251–52; attends stake conference in Canada with FEB, 252–53; returns to Germany to bring gospel message to wife, 253–54; baptism of, 254; sealed in temple, 255; visits FEB's sister, 255
Schumann, Br. and Sr.: FEB and Jutta fellowship, 173–74; attributes of, 174; baptism of, 174; Sr. Schumann leaves husband, follows younger man to America, 174; response of Br. Schumann to wife's unfaithfulness, 174–76; faithfulness of sons, 176; pitiful situation of Sr. Schumann, 176
Sebald, Ralph, *118,* 130–31
Seiter, Br. and Sr.: attributes of, 176–77; Sister Seiter diagnosed with inoperable cancer, 177; missionaries arrange for transportation to America, 177–78; FEB pronounces blessing of healing on Sr. Seiter, 178; Sr. Seiter experiences miraculous recovery, returns and completes mission, 178–79
Sense of humor, 271
Service, gift of, 218–19
Shy missionary, 262
Sin, 222
Smith, Joseph, testimony of, 90–91
Smoot, Mary Ellen, *238*
Soest Branch, 94–95
Spiritual plateaus, 92
Spiritual potential, achieving your true, 53–54
Spiritual truth, finding, 76
Spokane, Washington Stake conference, 88
Substance, caring for the true, 45–46
Surroundings, insignificance of, 99–100

Tacitus, 27
Thompson, Bob, 71–76, *74,* 89–92
Topeka, Kansas Stake conference, 263

Voge, Meeka, *238*
von Plauen, Graf Enzio, 36
Vreeken, Br. and Sr.: called to serve in temple presidency, 223; conversion and baptism of, 224–25

Waldmüller painting, 174, *175*
Walker, Glen, 66–68
Walton, President, 144
Warner, Susan, *238*
Weber, Br., 84, 116, 117
Westermann, Mr., 145–47
Wheelchair, sister in, 226–27
Wolfgang, 102–5
Woman counseled to remain in temple marriage, 230–33
Woman on airplane, 263–64
Woman wanting to thank missionaries, 259–60
Woman with dream about temple, 247–48
Woodruff, Wilford, 245
World War II. *See* Busche, F. Enzio, Childhood and teen years; Busche, F. Enzio, World War II soldier; Nazi Germany

Youth conference (Edersee Lake), *103,* 106–12, *111*

Zander, Rudy, 92–95
Zion, 33, 34
Zion Elders, 245